Y0-CAR-370

## Additional Praise for
### *The Champion Mindset*

"Finally, mental training methods for athletes are catching up to physical training methods. *The Champion Mindset* represents a big step forward in this exciting process."　　　—Matt Fitzgerald, author of *How Bad Do You Want It?* and coach for Team Iron Cowboy and BSX Athletics

"Getting an inside look into a champion's mind is rare and invaluable. Joanna has experienced high-level success and she gives readers the real view of what it takes. *The Champion Mindset* shows readers what it takes to win."
　　—Dr. Jason Selk, director of sports psychology at Enhanced Performance Inc., and bestselling author of *10-Minute Toughness*

"When it comes to world-class athletes, what separates the very good from the very best is how they think and process information, not only in training but in the heat of competition. Joanna Zeiger didn't become an Olympian and an Ironman 70.3 World Champion through raw talent alone. In *The Champion Mindset*, she shares her secrets to developing the mental toughness to be great at anything you do."　　　—Bob Babbitt, host of Babbittville Radio, Ironman Triathlon Hall of Fame inductee, and USA Triathlon Hall of Fame inductee

"Dr. Joanna Zeiger engages all of us in her new book, *The Champion Mindset*. She is a competitor, a well-trained athlete, and a winner. She brings the full spectrum of sport to all ages and all levels of athletes. She breaks down the mental game, the visual, kinesthetic components, and the true grit in her elegantly written book, a must-read for all who love athletics."
　　—Dr. Steven Ungerleider, psychologist, International Paralympic Committee member, and author of *Mental Training for Peak Performance*

"The mental side of sport is as, if not more, important than the physical side. . . . That's why every athlete, no matter what level, should invest time and energy in 'training the brain' as well as training the body. There's no better person to advise on this than Joanna Zeiger. . . . This insightful, informative, and inspiring book goes a very long way in sharing many of these and helping others to reach their potential."　　　—Chrissie Wellington, 4-time Ironman World Champion

# The
# Champion
# Mindset

## An Athlete's Guide to Mental Toughness

### Joanna Zeiger, Ph.D.

St. Martin's Griffin
New York

THE CHAMPION MINDSET. Copyright © 2017 by Joanna Zeiger. All rights reserved. Printed in the United States of America. For information, address St. Martin's Press, 175 Fifth Avenue, New York, N.Y. 10010.

www.stmartins.com

Designed by Patrice Sheridan

The Library of Congress Cataloging-in-Publication Data is available upon request.

ISBN 978-1-250-09671-5 (trade paperback)
ISBN 978-1-250-09672-2 (e-book)

Designed by Patrice Sheridan

Our books may be purchased in bulk for promotional, educational, or business use. Please contact your local bookseller or the Macmillan Corporate and Premium Sales Department at 1-800-221-7945, extension 5442, or by e-mail at MacmillanSpecialMarkets@macmillan.com.

First Edition: February 2017

10  9  8  7  6  5  4  3  2  1

To my husband, Mark,

my parents, Bob and Karen,

and my sister, Laurie,

for their unwavering support

# Contents

The Champion Mindset

To Jack—
Reach for the stars!
Joanna Zeiger

# 1

## The Mental Game Exposed

**Memorial Day weekend,** *2000. Dallas, Texas. It was the first ever U.S. Triathlon Olympic Trials. The triathlon was to debut in September at the Sydney Olympics. The distance was a 0.9 mile swim, 24.8 mile bike, and 6.2 mile run (1.5 km swim, 40 km bike, and 10 km run). Twenty-five women earned the right to race at the Trials based on their International Triathlon Union (ITU) ranking, where a top-125 ranking was needed. Two U.S. women would make the team in Dallas; one person had already been selected in April based off of a finish in a race of the same distance on the Olympic course. This was my one shot, since I did not receive an invite to the April race because my ITU rank was not high enough.*

*I was nervous, but not overly so. The pressure was on the other athletes who were ranked higher and had many more years of international racing experience. I was a veritable newbie with only a handful of international races under my belt. As a PhD student who'd turned professional just two years earlier, I didn't have the time or luxury of globe-trotting. None of that mattered, though, when the gun went off. My competitive instincts took over.*

*I knew what to do. I felt nothing but the desire to win. To push myself to whatever limits I had on the day.*

*I came out of the water in a group of thirteen women, sixty seconds behind the two lead women, Sheila Taormina and Barb Lindquist. The two in the front rode like they were in a perfectly practiced ballet. Their synchrony was in stark contrast to the pell-mell of our group of thirteen. We couldn't get organized; indeed, it almost seemed like there was an intentional slowing down of our group to provide the front-runners with more of an advantage. By the time we hit the transition to the run, we were almost four minutes in arrears to Sheila and Barb.*

*Four minutes! That is essentially an eternity in triathlon parlance. Over a 6.2 mile run, that equates to roughly forty seconds per mile. Making up that amount of time is virtually unheard of at that level. When my feet hit the ground, I scrambled through the transition with those numbers floating through my head. I was angry. Angry that our group of thirteen could be so complacent. Angry that I was now racing for an alternate spot. Angry that my favorite hat had flown off within the first two minutes of the run and now the sun was relentlessly beating down on my head. I tried to ignore the oppressive heat and humidity and the fact that two days before the race I'd had to sit down on a park bench in the middle of a short, easy run due to dizziness from the Texas swelter.*

*I settled into a rhythm. I ran hard. I ran off my anger. Within two miles, I started hearing that Barb was faltering in the heat and that I had a sizable gap to the women behind me. Suddenly, the impossible became possible, as halfway through the run I was in second place, in contention for a coveted Olympic spot. All I had to do now was stay hydrated, stay calm, and not succumb to the heat and the excitement.*

*The homestretch was long and crowded with spectators who cheered for me as I made my way across the line. I raised my arms in jubilation. Years of training, injuries, dealing with asthma, and the complexities of being a student-athlete all came into focus. None of it mattered anymore. I was an Olympian. Sheila was waiting at the line. We embraced. No longer competitors, we were teammates.*

## Using the mental game to augment physical fitness

I'm often asked how much of my athletic success can be credited to my physical abilities and how much can be attributed to my mental makeup. Champions, as the familiar adage preaches, are not born—they're made. And to a large degree that's true. Reaching the top of any sport, or anything in life for that matter, takes years upon years of dedication and proper preparation. But if there's a huge pool of individuals who have undertaken the same commitment to become the best at something, and each has undertaken similar steps toward that end, what truly separates the winners from everyone else?

There was a time when I used to believe that excellence was primarily based on putting in the work. Those who touched the wall first in a swimming race or broke the finish tape in a running or triathlon competition just trained harder than everyone else. There is no substitute, after all, for hard work. At least that's the lesson that was continually drilled into my head during my formative years. At some point, though, as I continued to achieve higher and higher levels of success, it occurred to me that the prevailing wisdom was just plain wrong. What truly distinguishes the champions is their mental edge.

*The Champion Mindset: An Athlete's Guide to Mental Toughness* is a much-needed and long-overdue look into how to program a competitor's mind to achieve optimal success. Changing behaviors and ways of thinking are never easy, but the chapters in this book aim to simplify this process to make it manageable and achievable. This book will appeal to a wide array of athletes—from the weekend warrior, who wants nothing more than to complete his or her first 5 km running race or marathon, to those seeking to improve their personal records in the swimming pool or on the triathlon course, to those who dream of one day qualifying for the Ironman World Championship, and to those who have aspirations of one day becoming Olympians and World Champions.

## Get with the program

The turning point, for me, came when I was fourteen. My fledgling athletic career, rocky from the start, had taken shape some seven years earlier in a San Diego swimming pool. My parents had joined a swim and racket club, and since they knew my baby sister and I would be spending a lot of time in and around the pool, they enrolled us in swim lessons so that we'd be water-safe. It wasn't love at first dip for me—and I certainly wasn't a natural, à la Missy Franklin, a multiple Olympic medalist. My initial efforts were clumsy: a bizarre collection of body contortions, uneven kicks, and desperate arm strokes. I was actually rejected on my first swim team tryout, relegated to further lessons. Gradually, though, I started to see improvement.

Anyway, that pivotal day when I was fourteen, our team traveled up to Mission Viejo to participate in one of the biggest meets of the summer. At some point in the seven years from the beginning of my swim career to that day in Mission Viejo, I'd become enamored with the adrenaline rush that comes from trying to do something as wondrously pure as racing across a swimming pool as quickly as possible. On this particular occasion, though, I seemed to be lugging around a dark cloud tethered to the shoulder straps on my swimsuit because my coach, Mr. Weckler, had taken it upon himself to sign me up for the 400 meter Individual Medley. I'd been moping about the development for days, because the 400 IM is one of those dreaded events that most levelheaded swimmers try to avoid. It's so intimidating and grueling, in fact, that even Michael Phelps, the greatest 400 IMer in history, has been adamant in his refusal to add it back into his schedule no matter how many times he makes a comeback.

I wish I could say that my race that day proved to be an epiphany for me because I passed the arduous eight-lap test with flying colors. It would be nice to report that my performance was so stellar that I not only won the race but I had everyone in attendance on their feet as I basked in their ovation. The truth of the matter, though, was that

I stunk up the joint. I swam poorly from the moment I hit the water and things only got worse from there. I finished the race in one piece, but just barely. Afterward, as I made my way up to Coach Weckler, my cheeks drenched with tears and my body racked in sobs, I blubbered that I hated the 400 IM and that I'd never swim it again for as long as I lived. My coach, never the warm and fuzzy type to begin with, went absolutely ballistic. I can still picture how his face flushed to a hue of red I'd never seen before and how a vein popped out of his forehead that resembled a grotesque worm. "I don't want to hear this crap from you, Joanna!" he bellowed in front of my teammates, parents, and anyone else who was within earshot. "You had a bad swim. So what?! You'd better get with the program because some day the 400 IM is going to be your best event!"

Needless to say, it wasn't quite the reaction I was looking for. I could feel myself shrinking to something smaller than that alien creature above his eyebrows as I furtively looked for somewhere, anywhere, to hide. I don't know how I found the wherewithal to slink away, but I did. And at first, once I was alone and had finally regained my composure—partially, no doubt, because I realized there was no one around to witness my theatrics—I was mad as hell. I wasn't angry because the coach had called me out like that. I was ticked off because I didn't *want* to be a good 400 IMer. I mean, why couldn't he have chewed me out for having swum a lousy 50 meter freestyle? Heck, I would have even toed the line over a crappy 100 meter butterfly!

As it turned out, of course, my coach was right—100 percent right. Four years later I qualified for my first of seven U.S. Olympic Team Trials in, you guessed it, the 400 IM—and that occasion marked the official launch of my elite athletic career.

## Are you psyched up?

Does the mental game matter? As someone who's been fortunate to have reached the very pinnacle of her sport, I can unequivocally say that proper mental preparation is usually the difference between success and failure. In hindsight, my 400 IM that day in Mission Viejo was doomed even before my family and I had arrived at the swim facility after our long commute. In swimmer lingo, I'd psyched myself out rather than getting psyched up. I'd sabotaged whatever chance I had for performing well because my head wasn't in it. Michael Jordan didn't become the greatest basketball player in history by accident. Soccer great Lionel Messi doesn't score goals because he's wishy-washy about his abilities. He excels because he's convinced that every time he takes a shot the ball will wind up in the back of the net.

It's one of those fundamental lessons that I find myself repeating to the athletes I coach, time and again as they approach their big competition. Stay positive. If you're not entirely convinced that you will perform well, odds are you won't. It's as simple as that, and this book will explain why. Before you begin your journey of improved mental toughness, you can take my mental toughness quiz, which I dubbed the Sisu Survey (*Sisu* is the Finnish word for grit). You can use this quiz to determine your level of mental toughness as measured by eight separate mental toughness traits. You can access the quiz at sisu.racereadycoaching.com.

As I look back over the course of my own career, that moment—where I felt embarrassed in front of friends and family—was life-changing. I didn't know it at the time, but I'd reached a crossroads of sorts. As I sat by myself licking my wounds, I realized I was either going to learn from my mistake or I wasn't. Essentially, I was being presented with the choice of either steering clear of the difficult challenges that lay ahead in my athletic career or of tackling them head-on.

But what exactly did Coach Weckler's "get with the program" speech mean? For starters, it meant trusting my coach, trusting my training, and above all, trusting my abilities. He had seen something in me that I myself had overlooked. He could see that I was adaptable, gifted in my stroke versatility, and that I possessed an uncanny knack for endurance. He was also savvy enough to realize that I was someone who needed to be tested, continually, because he could tell that I had the resolve to persevere in the face of adversity.

I'm certainly not advocating that athletes need to be humiliated in order to perform to the best of their abilities. I didn't know a thing about sports psychology at the time and, clearly, neither did my coach, whose tact and timing were about as dreadful as that 400 IM I'd swum. But had I not experienced that wake-up call when I was an insecure teenager—still trying to find her footing as a competitive athlete— nothing that transpired later in my career would have occurred. I never would have earned berths on Olympic and national teams. I never would have won a World Championship or set a world record. And I certainly never would have captured all those national and international wins.

## The endurance sports explosion

Ours is a nation of overachievers. How else can one explain the explosive growth in endurance sports? When the New York City Marathon debuted in 1970, just 127 competitors were interested in seeing if they could run 26.2 miles. Today, over fifty thousand runners make the annual pilgrimage on race day and tens of thousands more are turned away because of field size constraints. When the inaugural Ironman Triathlon was unveiled in Hawaii in 1977, a mere fifteen competitors attempted the quirky swim/bike/run test of stamina. Today, Ironman has become a true global phenomenon and hundreds of thousands of athletes clamor for spots in dozens of sold-out races staged around the world.

Participation in running, swimming, cycling, triathlon, Spartan racing, mountain climbing, and other gut-busting activities has never been higher. Americans seem to seek out bigger tests of endurance each and every year and the numbers reflect that. USA Swimming and U.S. Masters Swimming have a combined membership in excess of 400,000. An estimated 46.6 million cyclists participated in various organized cycling events in 2013. Last year there were over 19 million finishers in U.S. running events (with a whopping 500,000 of those finishes coming in marathons). And in the sport of triathlon, 550,000 active members of USA Triathlon generate roughly 2 million race finishes per year.

## Winning the mental game

There are countless books devoted to the physical side of endurance sports. Anyone Googling "How do I run a half marathon?" will be presented with dozens of strategies and training plans to get from the starting line to the finish line. Interested in triathlon? There are an equal number of books devoted to making your multisport adventure an enjoyable one.

This book's approach, however, is different. *The Champion Mindset: An Athlete's Guide to Mental Toughness* will not only be a compendium of my own personal journey from struggling novice swimmer to Olympian and World Champion, but it will offer a step-by-step guide to help athletes of all levels develop their own mental edge so they can achieve their athletic dreams. Among the topics that will be covered are proper goal setting, keeping it fun, building your team, intention in training, improving motivation, promoting self-confidence, mind/body cohesion, bringing it on race day, coping with setbacks, taking ownership of your career, and becoming a joyous athlete for life. These broad topics will be broken down and examined in detail, with tips and tricks to help athletes change their way of thinking so that when it's their turn to shine, they will be ready.

A great many athletes know how to train their bodies. Far too few, as I've seen from personal experience, know how to properly train their minds. Many years of helping athletes of all ages and abilities has proven to me that with proper education and a little nudge, athletes are able to transform not just their physical game, but their mental one as well.

## Endurance sports as a metaphor for life

Train the brain as well as the body. It may seem like a lot of bother for what is essentially a hobby. Perhaps. I have found, though, when my athletic life is harmonious, it spreads into all other facets of my life. Starting off the day with a good run allows me to focus better on my work, I am a more agreeable person to be around, and my sleep is sounder. And the rewards of a good workout are immediate, in the form of an endorphin high that can last all day.

Christian Taylor, an Olympic and World Champion gold medal–winning triple jumper from the U.S., explained his perspective on being a professional athlete and how it relates to life outside of athletics: "I recognize this life is not normal, but it is important to remember that one day this phase of my life will be over, so it is important to take away bits and pieces from the sport to take into the next chapter of my life. I treat track and field like my internship for my next life."[1] Taylor went even further by describing how sports readied him for life. "One day my track and field career will be over and I'll have no real work experience either. Fortunately, I am responsible with money. . . . I had to make sacrifices, but the process was a good life lesson for me."[2]

It is said that participation in endurance sports is a selfish endeavor. Athletes are often made to feel guilty for their training regimens and commitment to racing. Cat Morrison, a multiple duathlon World Champion, hit the nail on the head when she said, "Being an athlete, especially in an individual sport can be a selfish pursuit. However, it does not mean that you have to be personally selfish. In my own journey I have always believed that the help and support that I received and demanded of others by necessity required that I gave of my time and abilities towards others."[3]

With the obesity epidemic sweeping the globe, endurance sports is a healthier alternative to watching TV or playing on the computer. The key is balance and moderation by not allowing sports participation to overrule work and family. The benefits of endurance sports participation—goal setting, dedication, perseverance, pain management, focus, and improved well-being—mostly outweigh the potential selfishness. It is a fine line between turning your passion for endurance sports into an obsession that can become so all-encompassing it overtakes your life. But I would venture to say that the most successful athletes realize when they've taken their enthusiasm too far and back down before it causes ruination.

It turns out that individuals who participate in endurance sports are more successful than their non-athletic counterparts, manifested in an income almost double that of the general population; that works out to a hefty sum. The average U.S. household income in 2014 was $72,641. Compare that to the average household income of triathletes ($126,000) and participants in the NYC Marathon ($130,000).[4] Endurance athletes know how to achieve success because it is something they practice every day. The very traits that propel endurance athletes forward on the playing field transfer to all realms of life. It is not a coincidence that CEOs of major corporations participate in Ironman triathlons and marathons. *Forbes* magazine recognized this very notion and published an article that stated triathlon and executive leadership both require "three core key competencies: setting a vision, developing strategy, and managing accountability."[5]

## The endorphin fix

Among the long list of the benefits of sports and exercise are the opportunity to test oneself on a regular basis, improved health, a social outlet, a general sense of well-being, goal setting, and improvement in self-esteem. I would be remiss to omit endorphins from this inventory. Indeed, an endorphin surge might even top the list, at least for me.

Endorphins are endogenous neuropeptides produced by the central nervous system and pituitary gland.[6] Endogenous means they are produced naturally by the body. Naturally! You don't have to buy them or take them in a pill or make some kind of endorphin smoothie.

Apparently there are at least twenty types of endorphins, a fact that I just recently found out. I erroneously thought there was just a single type of endorphin. No wonder they are so awesome, there are a ton of different kinds. Well, that and the fact that endorphins interact with the opiate receptors in the brain, acting in a similar manner to narcotics such as morphine and codeine. This means that endorphins can reduce our perception of pain. The release of endorphins can also give athletes a feeling of euphoria (e.g., runner's high), decrease appetite, reduce anxiety, and increase the immune response.

Just writing this makes me want to go out and get some endorphins, don't you? That begs the question, since you can't buy them in a store, how does one even get endorphins? A 2015 study suggests that endorphins and the concomitant runner's high arise from leptin, a fat hormone, whereby a decrease in leptin levels increases motivation for physical activity and food.[7] Yet another study suggested that perhaps it is the presence of endocannabinoids that create the runner's high.[8] Whatever the actual substance is that makes us feel good after exercise is less important than the fact that exercise makes us feel good.

Lots of studies have tried to determine the intensity or duration with which one must exercise to get an endorphin release, but the results are inconsistent and conflicting. Adding to the complexity of this issue is that some people just naturally have more endorphins than others.

My take on the situation is that everybody has a personal threshold for where they get a release of endorphins *and* each person's subjective response to how the endorphins feel is different. Just like some people enjoy a good buzz from a few drinks of alcohol while others do not. I personally rather like a good endorphin surge, and that may be the route of my self-proclaimed exercise addiction. Simon Lessing, Olympian and multiple World Champion in triathlon pointed out the potential pitfall with endorphins: "Common sense should prevail, but unfortunately, with endorphins, common sense goes out the window for most people."[9]

With all of this in mind, I decided to create an endorphin scale, which I hereby dub the EFG (Exercise Feels Good) Scale. Each activity yields a different level of endorphin release that varies from person to person. I think the Visual Analog Scale (VAS), a measurement tool used to assess a characteristic or attitude across a continuum (think of the pain scale at the doctor's office), can determine how many endorphins a bout of exercise is worth.

Here is an example of how the EFG Scale would work:

1. What exercise did you do?
2. How long did the bout of exercise last?
3. How intense was the exercise (mild, moderate, hard)?
4. Rate on the scale: How good did the exercise make you feel?

With this method you can determine your personal EFG Quotient (i.e., the number of EFG points needed for you to feel good). The first three questions are really meant to set the stage for you to determine the intensity and duration along with the activity that gives you the most EFG points.

I came up with the scale after having surgery in 2015. At that time, I was relegated to mostly walking. I hate walking. For me, walking has a very low EFG Quotient. Like, really low.

Let's take a look at a typical post-surgical day:

1. What exercise did you do? *Walking*
2. How long did the bout of exercise last? *60 minutes*
3. How intense was the exercise (mild, moderate, hard)? *Mild*
4. Rate on the scale: How good did the exercise make you feel? 2

After surgery, I took two walks per day, which gave me four points on the EFG Scale each day. Normally, I run or swim at a moderate to high intensity, which can give me anywhere from five to ten EFG points, and I do one or two sessions each day. I don't ever complete two sessions of ten EFG points in a single day, so I would say that my normal daily total is roughly five to fifteen EFG points.

You can see, then, that recovery from surgery left me with a huge EFG point deficit. I tried very hard not to recoup these lost EFG points by doing crazy training once I was healed. And, since endorphins can have an analgesic effect and reduce depression and anxiety, it behooved me to get back to running to increase my endorphin load. But, I can unequivocally say that my daily four EFG points was better than zero EFG points, and those four meager points greatly facilitated my recovery.

As a matter of fact, as someone who has dealt with chronic pain for over six years, EFG points were my salvation. They enhanced my mood, even in the darkest of days, and decreased my need for narcotics.

You can use this handy tool to determine your daily EFG points. Track your points and see how they correlate with your mood, your desire to train, your productivity, your health, or how it augments your mental game in pursuit of your goals. Don't be surprised if there is a positive correlation between them. If you find yourself in a snit, or if you have a propensity for depression or anxiety, or if you have some pain, go out and generate some EFG points, as they are bound to make you feel better.

## Understand your potential

Not everyone can become a champion. I knew from a young age that I would not be the next Mary T. Meagher; Janet Evans procured that honor. It wasn't pessimism that led me to that realization, it was realism. I also knew that even with all of my triathlon wins, I would not be the next Paula Newby-Fraser. My potential took me further than I could have imagined, but it did not propel me to legendary status.

Each of us has a ceiling, a limit in our ability to improve, meaning our potential is as individualized as our fingerprint. The theory of deliberate practice indicates that specific forms of practice are necessary to attain expertise, and that a minimum of ten years is needed, and furthermore the deliberate practice supersedes innate talent.[10] This notion was made famous by Malcolm Gladwell in his book, *Outliers*, where he explains the concept that ten thousand hours of practice is the key to reaching ultimate success.

My doctorate is in genetic epidemiology, the study of the interplay of genes and environment in complex traits. My background in genetics leads me to believe that the ten thousand hours theory is missing a key component—the role of our genes. David Epstein reviews the role of genetics succinctly in his book, *The Sports Gene*.

Studies have identified the ACE gene, which plays a role in swimming, with one gene variant more common in long-distance swimmers and another variant of the gene more common in sprinters.[11] If you've ever been frustrated that you are not progressing in your sport as quickly as your peers, that too might be genetic. Epstein described the HERITAGE study, which found twenty-one gene variants that play a role in exercise genetics. These variants help determine whether a person will respond to a training program or not, meaning that even with a strict training regimen, some people just don't seem to improve their aerobic capacity.[12] Further studies have shown that response to exercise does vary among individuals, but *everyone* will respond eventually; it is a matter of training for a long enough period of time (the study lasted six months) and going hard enough.[13]

Without innate talent, ten thousand hours of practice will not get you to the top; and without hours and hours of practice, innate talent is generally not enough. It is the combination of your genes, the ability to work hard, and of course, a finely tuned mental game that will allow an athlete to realize their potential. Shalane Flanagan, Olympic bronze medalist in the 5,000 meter, 2-time Olympian in the marathon, and American record holder in the 3 km, 5 km, 10 km, and 15 km, hit the genetic jackpot. Her mother held the world record in the marathon, and her father was an accomplished runner. Shalane is also known for her relentless work ethic. She has that wondrous combination of stellar genes augmented by more than ten thousand hours of hard work; this duality helped propel her to a sixth-place finish in the marathon at the Rio Olympics.

I suppose, then, I should blame my parents that I never became the next Paula Newby-Fraser, eight-time Ironman World Champion, because I definitely put in my ten thousand hours. Truly, though, my athletic ceiling was dictated not by my ability to put in the work, but by many of my innate shortcomings: asthma, a finicky gut that always had me searching out bathrooms during long-distance races, and a ridiculous propensity for dizziness that caused me to pass out or required me to lie down on the race course to prevent passing out. It is up to you to determine your potential, through your training and racing, so you are not disappointed by reaching for something that is not physically possible. Do not fall into the trap of comparing yourself to others, as their potential just might be genetically extraordinary.

## Desire and perseverance

I think we can all agree that endorphins rock. But, are they enough? Probably not. Desire is another piece of the equation. Even with plenty of endorphins, if desire is low, you won't even seek out the endorphins. Desire is what put Julie Moss and Ironman on the map. In 1982, Julie was leading the grueling event in Kona, Hawaii, which consisted of a 1.2 mile swim, 112 mile bike, and 26.2 mile run. With less than one mile to go, Julie started staggering until she collapsed. She picked herself up, yet collapsed again. Only yards from the finish, she finally crawled her way to the line, eventually finishing second after getting passed while she was on the ground. Desire is what compelled Kim Smith, a three-time Olympian in running for New Zealand, to continue to run eighty miles a week with a ruptured tibialis posterior tendon, a very painful leg injury.[14] Desire is what caused me to race until I passed out at the Boulder 70.3 and the Hy-Vee triathlon and triggered my collapse at the finish line at 80 percent of the endurance events I've done over the years.

Most people do not have that type of desire. Ultimately, the type of desire that causes you to keep going until you can't isn't necessary, isn't safe, and probably cannot be taught anyway. Desire, it turns out, is partially innate, in our genes. In his book *The Sports Gene*, David Epstein describes the story of Lance Mackey and his Alaskan huskies and Mackey's quest to win the Iditarod, a sled-dog race from Anchorage to Nome. Financial constraints led Mackey to breed huskies that were not the fastest but had the most desire; his dogs would "trot until they bored a hole in the earth."[15] You are probably thinking to yourself, "Nice story, but how does this relate to humans?" Well, it turns out that twin studies, the classical way of examining complex behaviors in humans, have shown that exercise behavior is 60 percent attributed to our genes.[16] That's a lot.

The mere fact that you are reading this book indicates that you have desire—desire to develop your mental game in an effort to improve your performance. It is that desire that will get you out the door to train in inclement weather or darkness or when you just aren't in the mood. Desire will allow you to finish your race when your body starts to ache. Eschewing a late night out due to an early morning training session can also be chalked up to desire.

Milk and cookies. Peanut butter and jelly. Holmes and Watson. Desire and perseverance. What do these four combinations have in common? They fit together like puzzle pieces. Desire needs perseverance for success. Jan Frodeno, 2008 triathlon Olympic gold medalist and 2015 Ironman 70.3 World Champion, had this to say after winning the 2015 Ironman World Championships in Kona: "It's never actually fun out there. . . . it's all about perseverance. The race unfolded not at all how I thought it would."[17]

I have powerful desire, but my athletic career has been defined by perseverance. I have dealt with injuries, ostracism, juggling training with academics, and of course the innate physical shortcomings mentioned earlier.

Nothing, though, has characterized my ability to persevere more than the aftermath of the 2009 Ironman 70.3 World Championships in Clearwater, FL. In 2008, I won the Ironman 70.3 World Championships in world record time. I started the 2009 race fitter and with more confidence than the previous year. I felt that nothing could stop me. I was very wrong. At mile 45 of the 56 mile bike section, I had an impressive, life-altering, career-ending bike crash. It happened at an aid station when the volunteer did not let go of the water bottle I was grabbing. Rather than a traditionally smooth handoff, I was rudely yanked from my bike. I flipped over the front end of my bike and hit the pavement hard. The pavement won that battle. I instantly knew that I'd broken my collarbone and several ribs. The policeman standing there was no help at all; he kept saying to me, "You're okay, right?" I kept telling him no as I shouted about a hundred expletives; I might have even made up a few words. I somehow managed to get myself and my bike to the sidewalk and out of the way of the oncoming racers. In case you were wondering, my bike was unscathed and only needed new handlebar tape.

My collarbone was surgically repaired a couple of days later. My ribs, somehow, never healed. I raced throughout the 2010 season, albeit unsuccessfully. I dropped out of almost every race I started due to rib pain, eventually calling it a career in August of 2010. From that fateful moment in 2009 until 2016, I endured chronic pain. Over that period of time I required six surgeries performed by four different surgeons to repair the extensive damage to my rib cage. Finding answers to the problems was perplexing for two reasons, the first being that imaging such as MRI, diagnostic ultrasound, and X-ray did not disclose any abnormalities and the second being that prolonged rib pain is rare because most traumatic rib injuries heal on their own. The search for surgeons willing and able to perform these surgeries was arduous, and many turned me down as they did not want to perform exploratory surgery on an otherwise healthy person. In fact, I needed four surgeons because none of them were willing to do repeat operations (until the very end, when I had my fifth and sixth surgeries performed by surgeon number four).

My first surgery was in August of 2012 when part of my eleventh rib was removed due to a fracture that never healed and a neuroma (a thickening of tissue around a nerve) was excised. In 2014, two titanium plates were fixed to ribs seven through nine to stabilize a fracture on my eighth rib. At that time, they removed my xiphoid process (a piece of cartilage at the tip of the sternum), which was displaced and stuck in my abdominal muscle. Then, in May 2015, the titanium plates were taken out because they became a hindrance to my breathing. Thankfully the eighth rib healed up. My travail was not over, though.

The worst of the pain occurred in the summer of 2015 when I was incapacitated by something called intercostal neuralgia, pain stemming from the nerves that run between the ribs. I'd had this disorder since a few months after the accident, but in the summer of 2015 it took on a whole new life. It is pesky, hard to treat, and can render sufferers incapacitated. This type of neuralgia generally affects more than one intercostal nerve, and in my case I had five nerves involved (ribs eight through twelve).

The neuralgia hurt all day, every day, infiltrating every facet of my life. The ongoing pain affected my ability to sleep, work, and train. It was constant and unrelenting. I had pain that wrapped around my rib cage, like tentacles squeezing me tight. I had stabbing pain in my side, analogous to the worst side stitch ever. I had pain in my back that caused constant nausea and occasional vomiting. I had relentless spasms in my upper abdominal muscles. Some days I felt like my head might explode due to the pain. It was hard to reconcile that a body that was once so fit and willing to do my bidding now malfunctioned so unremittingly.

Unlike a muscle injury that resolves with rest or ultrasound or manual therapies, intercostal neuralgia does not respond to and is often made worse by such conventional treatments. Maintaining some modicum of physical activity alleviated my symptoms better than anything I tried. Perhaps it was the endorphins, or maybe just the distraction. Either way, some form of movement helped.

That summer I had over two dozen injections, including localized shots of cortisone, nerve blocks, and nerve ablations (under X-ray guidance large needles with an electrode are used to create an electrical current with the intent of interrupting nerve conduction) to try to alleviate the pain. None of it worked. Doctors wanted to put me on high doses of narcotics and nerve pain medications with noxious side effects. They became frustrated when I refused to poison my body with medications that were unlikely to help.

The unrelenting pain with no abatement in the foreseeable future was disheartening to say the least. My life was indescribably altered. I tried hard to focus on what I could do (such as having the time and ability to write this book) and not on those things that I love but had to forgo, such as triathlon, running races, and sleeping soundly. I allowed myself to cry on those occasions when the pain and frustration reached unimaginable levels. There were days that I contemplated ending it all, as I could not envision living another day with so much suffering. Ultimately, my absolute conviction that *something* was wrong and could possibly be fixed, along with my desire to find that solution and with the support of my family, kept me going.

The search for resolution culminated in what was my fourth surgery, in September 2015. I met with a new thoracic surgeon who, upon listening to my history and performing a thorough physical exam, agreed that a surgical intervention was the only answer. The surgeon found a hot mess. My twelfth rib was clicking, due to an unhealed fracture. He removed six centimeters from that rib. He found a neuroma, so he excised it. There was a ton of scar tissue around my eleventh rib with some nerves caught up in it. He removed about four centimeters from my eleventh rib to help him eliminate the scar tissue and free up the nerves, which he buried under muscle to prevent further damage to the nerves. Most important, he did not need to remove the entire ribs, preserving the attachment to the spine and sparing muscle damage in my back. My lung got nicked during the surgery, so I ended up with a chest tube.

You may be wondering why I ended up with so many fractures that never healed. Each fracture was in the cartilaginous part of the rib. Cartilage fractures of the ribs do not heal and are nearly impossible to visualize on standard imaging.

At this point, I will never be a torso model. I have so many scars on my abdomen it looks like medical students used me as their cadaver. But who cares, because each surgery fixed an anatomical abnormality that alleviated pain. I adopted a new philosophy. If I can't run fast, then run slowly. If I can't run slowly, then walk. No matter what, keep moving.

In the seven days after the September 2015 surgery I walked fifty-one miles, and then I began to slowly run. Incredibly, two weeks after that surgery, I did a tempo run workout with my group. It wasn't fast by any means, but I accomplished the run without the pain I'd experienced beforehand. My coach, Darren, said to me, "You are different from most people. You want it badly. Most people are content to sit on the couch." Yes, my desire runs deep and infiltrates every facet of my life, whether it is trying to qualify for the Olympics, excelling in my work, finding a solution to the pain, or coming back from surgery.

Even with all of the pain and dysfunction since the accident, I managed to maintain a successful running career as a masters runner (over forty). In 2011, I qualified for the 2012 Olympic Marathon Trials by running 2:43:09 at the California International Marathon, which was well under the standard of 2:46:00. I won a Cross Country National Championship in 2012. In 2014, I narrowly missed the 2016 Olympic

Marathon Trials standard en route to winning the Shamrock Marathon. Later that year, I broke the Colorado 40–44 age group record for the half marathon, and I placed second at the Masters Marathon National Championships in the Twin Cities Marathon, a mere two days before I had the second of my six rib surgeries.

I've listed some of the highlights of my racing during the period after triathlon, but I also had several disappointments. I dropped out of numerous races due to pain. I missed weeks of running and months of swimming and I stopped riding my bike altogether. Desire and perseverance kept me afloat during that tumultuous time; I applied the champion mindset that I used to win races all over the globe to dealing with chronic pain. I used my arsenal of tricks, many of which I am sharing with you in this book, to continue to compete both in life and on the proverbial playing field.

Rather than giving up on my athletic dreams, I continued to press on, setting goals for myself and training as hard as my body allowed, all the while understanding that there would be setbacks along the way, but realizing that misses are okay, because trying is always better than cowering in fear. Even with an abundance of desire and a propensity for perseverance, sometimes things just do not pan out, and comprehending this notion that success is not guaranteed no matter how hard we try is a big step in the right direction of winning the mental game.

## Unlocking the mind

You might find this crazy, but I wrote seventy-five percent of my doctoral dissertation while I was in Sydney preparing for the Olympics. Many of the ideas in this book were born during a run. When the cursor on my screen flashes incessantly and my fingers cannot type because my brain is unwilling to release an idea, I go for a run to reset. Racking up the EFG points just makes it easier to concentrate and sit for long periods of time.

Not only does exercise free up your mind for a more productive work life, it also can improve your brain health. Exercise decreases the cognitive decline and loss of functional brain health inherent in aging populations.[18] That's really good news if you are already exercising because you just need to maintain your desire and endorphin flow so you continue to exercise until you are like ninety-two-year-old Harriette Thompson who finished the Rock 'n' Roll San Diego Marathon in 2015 in a time of 7:24. If you aren't convinced about the benefits of exercise on brain health, a very promising study showed that treadmill running can reverse the cognitive declines seen from early and late stages of Alzheimer's disease.[19] Granted, this was a mouse study, but many of the great scientific breakthroughs in humans started with mouse models.

## Tips for a Mental Makeover

What is mental toughness? This concept is bandied about in the sports world, often used recklessly. Is it mentally tough to forge through a race injured, bleeding, or puking? Or, is it mentally tough to train while sick or when the weather is poor? Perhaps this is merely bad decision-making, something I have fallen prey to in the name of "mental toughness." I think that the construct of mental toughness is overused philosophically and underused in practice. Mostly this is because mental toughness is generally misinterpreted, rendering true mental toughness hard to find. Mental toughness is not any one thing. It is an amalgamation of so many different things, and that is why it is hard to truly define and achieve it. But mastering at least some of these aspects of mental toughness will undoubtedly make you a better athlete.

- Mental toughness is the ability to toe the line at a race, and no matter which athletes show up, not letting them affect you or ruin your game plan.
- Mental toughness is racing to your potential whether you are first, thirty-first, or last.

- Mental toughness is looking at your workouts for the week with a small amount of fear and a large amount of excitement at the challenge set forth.
- Mental toughness is putting aside the chaos of life for a designated amount of time each day to properly execute your training.
- Mental toughness is doing the little things that make a big difference.
- Mental toughness is finding that last ounce of energy to keep going until the finish line when your body wants to quit.
- Mental toughness is going back for more even if you've been disappointed or embarrassed.
- Mental toughness is taking adversity and turning it into an advantage.
- Mental toughness is not being a lemming and just doing whatever everyone else is doing.
- Mental toughness is having self-confidence and not self-doubt.
- Mental toughness is savoring the small victories and knowing they will lead to larger ones down the road.
- Mental toughness is having trust in yourself, your coach, and your advisors to lead you down the right path.
- Mental toughness is learning how to focus.
- Mental toughness is taking pride in your effort.
- Mental toughness is making smart decisions with your head and avoiding poor decisions made from your heart.
- Mental toughness is not giving up because it is too hard.
- Mental toughness is sharing with others what you have learned.
- Mental toughness is being gracious whether you win or lose.

# 2

# Proper Goal Setting

**A tweet by** Joe Friel, coach to Olympian Ryan Bolton and prolific author, encapsulated so much in so few words: *"A dream becomes a goal when you create a plan, and a reality only if you fully commit to it."*[1] In 1988, as a high school senior, I had a singular goal and that was to qualify for the USA Swimming Olympic Trials in my best events: the 200 meter breaststroke and the 400 meter individual medley (IM). Obtaining the qualifying standard for the Olympic Trials is a quadrennial rite of passage for many athletes, an opportunity to attain a preset time standard in any of the events on the Olympic swimming docket and race against the nation's best in their event at the Olympic Trials swim meet. Only the top two in each event make it to the Olympics, so the overwhelming majority of swimmers at the Olympic Trials swim meet do not actually go to the Olympics.

Up until that point, I had never had such a concrete mission, nor had I chased anything with the utter and absolute focus that I put forth in those ten months. I missed only a single swim practice, to take the SAT (school always had an uncanny way of disrupting my training).

In training, I swam twice a day five days a week, once on Saturday, with a much-needed respite on Sunday. I swam 400 IM repeats until my eyes watered and I was certain my arms would fall off. My hair perpetually smelled of chlorine and my fingers always had that puckered look from too much time in the water. I had no idea that the pursuit of a goal would be so difficult. Or so rewarding.

Qualifying for the Olympic Trials was not ludicrous, based on my times going into the Olympic year. It would involve shaving off a few precious seconds in each event, an entirely reasonable endeavor. I did not take this a step further, though, and reach for the stratosphere by making my goal qualifying for the 1988 Olympics in swimming. I knew to dream big but not dream crazy because even at the tender age of eighteen, I understood the difference between a realistic goal and a foolhardy goal; this was the era of Janet Evans and other superstars, so I was not anywhere near the top two in the country in my events.

I swam several meets that summer and had some close misses. Rather than wallow in disappointment and fret over the fact that time was ticking, I worked harder. I honed my stroke and my turn technique. I went to the gym to lift weights. I left no stone unturned in my pursuit of the Olympic Trials qualifying standards.

A few weeks before the Trials, I swam at a "last chance" meet in Clovis, CA, where temperatures topped out over a hundred degrees in the shade (it makes for a rather unpleasant time sitting around waiting to swim, but it certainly made the water feel like a nice and cool relief). My first event was the 200 meter breaststroke. When I glanced at the giant scoreboard after my swim and saw that I'd qualified, I was jubilant that the hard work had paid off. The confidence I gained in that event propelled me to meet the standard in the 400 IM as well. I had reached my goal.

What exactly is a goal? When it comes to sports, there are three agreed-upon types of goals: outcome, process, and performance.[2] Outcome goals are the type that most athletes focus on, those related to winning or placing in a certain way—this type of goal is often not within an athlete's control (just think about the races where a ringer shows up and steals the win). Process goals are those things the athlete needs to focus on while performing their sport, such as biomechanics or nutrition; these types of goals are under an athlete's control. Finally, performance goals are what you are trying to achieve, such as a best time or a qualifying standard.

I imagine that endurance athletes think they have a grasp on understanding goal setting since the achievement of *something* is their usual endgame. The problem is that as athletes, we often live in a fantasy world that is highly disconnected from reality (such as: it doesn't matter that I have a torn hamstring, I can still compete in the Hawaii Ironman), further complicating our mission. It is reasonable to dream big. Some of the biggest sports stories come from athletes who believed in themselves but defied the odds and the pundits by beating seemingly more qualified athletes. But all goals must be formulated with an eye on reality.

Why do I say athletes "think they have a grasp"? Because all too often endurance athletes struggle to set goals. Oftentimes, athletes under- or overestimate their abilities and innate potential, thereby setting goals that are too easy or too hard. Or, goals can be too general or too specific. Goals can be intrinsic or extrinsic. Goals can be long-term or short-term. As you can see, goal setting is much more complex than stating, "I want to qualify for the Olympics," a sentiment I have heard from athletes who have absolutely no grasp on their reality.

Simon Lessing, five-time ITU World Champion and a 2000 Olympian in triathlon who has been a coach since 2008, had this to say about his experience with athletes and their goals: "Goal setting has to be realistic. There is a total misconception about what people's dreams are and what they are trying to achieve and what they are realistically capable of doing, considering their work environment, their family environment. They are trying to do a time-consuming sport. You have to realistically take baby steps and not have these big huge aspirations and then be extremely disappointed when you don't achieve them."[3]

## Know your athletic circumstances

Prior to setting any goals or planning a race season or even figuring out what workouts to do in a given week, you must assess your athletic circumstances. By this I mean the interplay of five factors: family, health, work, ability, and desire. The assessment of one's athletic circumstances needs to occur on two levels.

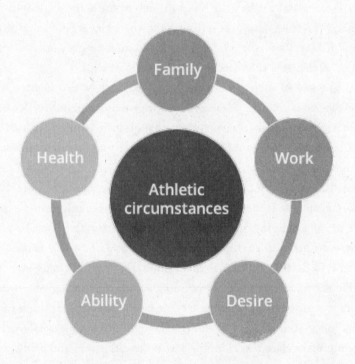

The first level is the yearly level. At the start of each season, it is important to honestly determine where you fall on the spectrum for each of these factors before setting any goals, because these factors are volatile and can change from one season to the next. Your desire can wax and wane, or family demands can be greater one year over another.

Qualifying for the Hawaii Ironman probably isn't immediately feasible if your ability right now has you finishing in the bottom half of your age group. The second level is the daily level. Even with a set schedule (which you should have), you still need to ensure that there is balance between the five factors. A last-minute work meeting or a child missing school due to illness can potentially change the daily training plan and alter your very-short-term goals.

The ability to reach a goal requires a happy balance between the five factors, and the balance will be different for every single individual. Goal setting must take into account where you are in your athletic circumstances and might be defined as not missing any workouts for a given week rather than setting a best time in a race.

The key to maintaining the happy balance, which in turn will increase your chances of achieving your goal, is adaptability. Because athletic circumstances are always changing, it is up to you to be malleable and re-create balance when something becomes off-kilter. Athletes are notoriously resistant to change, so adaptability is not easy. Learning to manage your athletic circumstances by becoming more adaptable is incredibly useful, because the application extends far beyond training and racing. Mastering adaptability to balance out your athletic circumstance will give you the tools needed to maintain balance in factors that comprise your life circumstances. Here are some examples of becoming adaptable: moving your workouts to a different day or time if there is a work conflict, taking some time off if your desire has waned, scheduling family vacations that are not race-related, or skipping a workout altogether and being okay with it.

## Goal setting the statistical way

Proper goal setting requires an honest assessment of ability and potential plus factoring in all of the miscellaneous missteps that inevitably occur along the way. I am a biostatistician who likes to geek out on modeling data. I believe that goals can be expressed as a regression equation (don't let this make your eyes roll back into your head). Regression equations are used to predict outcomes, such as "does height predict weight" or "does smoking predict lung cancer." In the box below, the equation is a standard regression model.

### Standard regression model:
*Y (outcome) = a (constant) + βX (predictor) + e (error term)*

You're wondering, how does this type of equation relate to setting goals? Let's see how such a model can help to predict the success of reaching a goal.

### Goal regression model:
**Goal = innate ability + (β)training + stuff that happens**

In the goal regression model, the goal is Y; innate ability is the constant (the ability to reach your goal with no training); the predictor is training, which is demarcated by a specific level (i.e., β); and the error term is everything that occurs in life that will attempt to derail your goal (e.g., stuff that happens).

The idea, then, is that achieving your goal will rely on the four factors above: a realistic but challenging goal, an understanding of your innate ability, a proper training regimen, and an ability to roll with the punches. This equation is merely speculative. But here is how it works in theory. Think about all of the athletic goals you've set, and then think about the hours of training that you put in. Then factor in the error: injuries, illness, and your athletic circumstances. Do you see a relationship between your training and goal achievement? Is there a certain number of hours that seems to be your sweet spot and anything more or less leads to not attaining your goal?

## The four outcomes: keeping it real(istic)

"You can achieve whatever you want if you try hard enough." This overused adage is the crux of the American Dream. We are told from a very young age that we can be or do anything we want. I believe that it is false and misleading. You cannot achieve whatever you want. There. I said it. It is true that often, when goals are set they are met, particularly if you try hard. But it is also true that one can devote months or years of time and energy to accomplishing a certain goal and that goal may never be met. Accomplishing a goal requires more than blood, sweat, and tears. There is also luck, timing, and savvy.

When you are trying to achieve a goal, there are four potential outcomes.

### The four goal outcomes

1. The road is smooth and the goal is successfully realized.
2. The road is rocky but the goal is achieved.
3. The road is smooth but the goal is not attained.
4. The road is rocky and the goal is missed.

To be clear, outcome #1 almost never happens. It just doesn't. And guess what? Outcome #3 happens a lot. You can train your hardest and reach new milestones in training, but for some reason you just cannot achieve your goal.

Shalane Flanagan is a perfect example. Her overarching goal at the 2015 Boston Marathon was to win. In 2014, she finished seventh, setting a huge personal best time, fueling her passion to climb higher in the results the following year. Her 2015 race did not pan out the way she anticipated. She finished ninth, five minutes *slower* than in 2014. Two days after the race she was still puzzling over her poor performance:

"In general, I felt mentally really prepared, physically prepared in terms of my workouts heading into the race—nothing would indicate a bad day. I'm just not used to going out and having bad performances. I may not reach my goals, but usually I run pretty solid."[4]

The fact is that you can train to the point where you are achieving best times in workouts and still have a terrible race. And, often, the reason for that terrible race on the heels of stellar training can remain a mystery. Sure, you can come up with theories as to why you delivered a poor performance, but ultimately sometimes you just cannot determine why you fell apart. Whether you are new to endurance sports or a decorated veteran, goal attainment is a vexing proposition.

The fact that smooth sailing does not equate to achieving a goal is not a dose of pessimism. It is realism. Goals do not care if you are deserving, nice, or hardworking. As mentioned above, achieving a goal is a complex equation. It is often only in retrospect, when all the factors are reviewed, that one can say why things went right or wrong. The goal regression model can help you predict whether you can accomplish your goal, but that pesky error term (you know, "stuff that happens") is what makes things unpredictable. But it is the unpredictability that keeps things interesting and allows us to sign up for races even after a catastrophic race experience; we just know it will be better next time, allowing us to achieve the goal.

Joe Maloy, who became the first American winner of the renowned Noosa Triathlon in Australia in 2015, understands this. "There really isn't such a thing as a 'high' or a 'low.' The highs and lows aren't part of the process, they are the process. There will be failures anytime you're challenging yourself, and those failures will suck. If you let them bring you down, though, you're missing the point. You can't let them beat you, because failing means you're on the right track. Failure means you're challenging yourself to grow, and that is the path to success."[5]

In 2010 I raced my last triathlon. As a person who thrives on goals, I needed a new endeavor, and I needed it quickly. A goal that was lofty, but not totally out of reach. A goal that would keep me going when things got tough in life or in training. A goal that would leave me with a feeling of accomplishment, whether or not the goal was met. I decided in February 2011 that I would dedicate my time and effort to running and try to qualify for the 2012 Olympic Trials marathon. Much like with the Olympic Trials in swimming, to qualify for the Olympics in the marathon one must meet a qualifying standard and then run in the Olympic Trials marathon; a top-three finish is required to make it to the Olympics. Here are the facts. The standard was 2:46.00. My previous best time was 2:47:06 set in the 2000 Olympic Trials marathon. I had not run an open marathon since 2001. It would be a challenge on many levels; I was eleven years older than when I set my previous best time and I was injured. Lest you think I was dreaming crazy, I did have enough good training sessions and races to let me know this endeavor was merely dreaming big, rather than unrealistic.

My first attempt at qualifying was the Los Angeles Marathon in March of 2011. The day was miserable, with a driving rain and cool temperatures. I missed the standard by two minutes. I considered this a worthy first attempt. I ran several half-marathons and 10k races over the ensuing months, building up to my next try at qualifying.

I chose the Twin Cities Marathon in Minneapolis because it served as the Masters Marathon Championships. My road to Minneapolis was a rocky one. I started the endeavor still dealing with the serious rib injury, and despite all of my best efforts, the injury lingered, to the point I stopped calling it an injury and referred to it as a situation. The situation dictated whether my races were a personal best or a DNF (did not finish). The situation allowed me to run a fast workout or walk home frustrated. Throughout the entire process I believed that I could run fast enough to attain the Olympic Trials time standard and that belief buoyed me when the situation flared up and could have left me prostrate on the couch.

I ended up not being able to finish that race in Minneapolis. I was having pain and trouble breathing due to the rib situation. Undeterred at two failed attempts, I bounced back from the pain and disappointment to run the California International Marathon a few months later. I knew from the second mile that my body was going to cooperate and the rib situation was not going to be a problem during the race. I stayed smart with my pacing in the early miles and tried not to get overly excited when I was under pace at mile twenty. I struggled mightily through the last 5 km; I stumbled along as my legs were starting to buckle from the fatigue. On that day, I ran 2:43.08 to qualify for the Trials.

My road was rocky, I failed on several attempts, but eventually I achieved the goal. Indeed, of the four goal outcomes, I rarely, if ever, met the criteria for outcome #1 in my entire athletic career. My road has never been smooth, which is ironic because I hate rocks; I seem to trip on them.

## Long-term vs. short-term goals vs. very-short-term goals

The goal regression equation is just one part of the goal setting endeavor. You can use this equation to set long-term goals (I want to win my age group in a race within the next three years) or short-term (I want to improve my running biomechanics over the next few months to become a more efficient runner to help me win my age group) or very-short-term (I want to nail my workout tomorrow in an ongoing training process that will allow me to win my age group).

How long is long-term and how long is short-term? There really is no specific time frame. A lot depends on the perspective of the athlete, as some are more patient than others. One athlete may view six months as long-term whereas Olympic hopefuls often break their long-term goals into quadrennials to align with the Olympic qualifying process. Regardless of your time frame, intermediary goals are an imperative part of reaching the long-term goals.

Long-term goals, by definition, take a certain amount of time to achieve. Long-term goals take dedication, perseverance, resiliency, and motivation. The realization of a long-term goal is in the more distant future (perhaps one or two years), and given that two of the four goal outcomes indicate not reaching the goal, short-term goals are an essential part of the process. Short-term (or very-short-term) goals can be set often, should be in alignment with your long-term goal, and do not have to be as extreme or difficult to attain as the long-term goal. Setting and achieving short-term goals will help keep you motivated and let you know you are on the right path to achieving your long-term goal. If you keep missing your short-term and very-short-term goals, this will let you know that you need to make some alterations to your training or to the goals themselves.

In 2000, my primary goal was to qualify for the Olympics in the triathlon. I did not have a lot of international short course racing experience at the time; my only forays into the international scene were a race in Mexico where I was unable to finish due to a bike crash from an unseen rain-filled pothole, and the 1999 World Championships where I finished fifteenth. Neither was a stellar outing. However, after the 1999 World Championships, one of the U.S.A. coaches pulled me aside and told me I was going to qualify for the Olympics. It seemed unlikely and a brash statement at the time. The Olympic Trials were in May, a mere nine months away. After he expressed his confidence in me, though, it changed my outlook on my Olympic prospects. I made that my long-term goal.

I developed very-short-term goals of achieving certain times on the track for my runs (my run was where I felt I needed the most improvement) and a short-term goal of proving myself in races to test whether my long-term goal was even possible. In the spring of 2000, I raced several international fields and finished third at the Kona World Cup, first at the St. Anthony's Triathlon, and first at the St. Croix International Triathlon. My short-term goals showed me that my training was going in the right direction and that while qualifying for the Olympics would be difficult, it would not be impossible. When I toed the line at the Olympic Trials in Dallas, I had the confidence that came from the achievement of the short-term goals, which helped propel me to accomplish my long-term goal of qualifying for the 2000 Olympics in the triathlon.

## Formulating a plan and breaking it into manageable sections

Once you've come up with your goal, the next step is to figure out how to actually accomplish the feat. The most important concept is buying in, meaning you believe that you can actually accomplish the goal you've set for yourself. This sounds obvious, since you are the one who set the goal. However, sometimes we overreach and the goal is too hard right from the start. If you've set the bar too high, you need to reassess your goal quickly and make modifications. A goal should be just hard enough to keep you motivated, but not so hard that you cannot even picture yourself accomplishing the goal.

After a successful outing in the swimming pool at the 2012 London Olympics, Missy Franklin, multiple Olympic medalist and World Record holder, had to make a choice: go pro or go to college. She compromised. She spent two years swimming at UC Berkeley and then turned pro to dedicate some time to training for the 2016 Olympics and to reap the benefits of sponsorship. She had a long-term plan—qualifying for the 2016 Olympics—which she broke into two-year segments of college and post-college.

Goals cannot be met by "winging it," yet that is exactly how a lot of athletes train. They wake up in the morning and decide what to do for the day. This type of haphazard training can lead to injury, burnout, and underperforming. A training plan is a necessary part of goal attainment. This plan can be developed by a coach, through your own past experience, or by educating yourself with available information.

As an aside, I personally believe everyone needs some type of coaching. Steve Magness, a running coach, eloquently stated: "I strongly believe in having a coach. It's not so much for the training, though that is important, it's for the outside observation. It's to prevent smart people from making dumb mistakes."[6] It is almost impossible to be objective when it comes to your pursuit of goals; athletes never think they are doing enough training or are fit enough. A coach can help guide you through the process and keep you sane.

Successful goal attainment requires consistency over time. Even though the weekly grind can get tedious, that is what will get you to your goals. Rather than looking at the big picture, use your weekly training to help you chart your progress. It makes the long-term goal less intimidating when you know you've been able to reach milestones along the way.

## Don't be a chaser

Here's a problem. Once a goal is achieved, most of us do not rest on our laurels. We set the bar higher, and then higher, and then even higher. We are somewhat like rats running on a wheel—constantly moving and chasing, an infinite cycle of running to nowhere.

I know I am a chaser in the pursuit of my goals. I chase my workout buddies during interval sessions and I will chase competitors in races. I chase goal times every week that tell me whether I am fit. I chase good health with massage and dry needling, and I chase strength and muscle balance by doing gym work. I chase the workout buzz that comes from the surge of endorphins after a stellar run. The pursuit of a singular goal requires a lot of chasing.

This is not a particularly negative thing, though. It only becomes harmful when the endless pursuit of goals starts generating destructive thoughts or behaviors. By this, I mean ignoring the warning signs that the chase has gone too far and the goal has become all-encompassing, causing poor decision-making or a loss of perspective.

As a coach and an athlete, I have a unique viewpoint on the pursuit of goals. I not only set my own goals, but I also help others set their goals, making me a goal chaser and the overseer of goal chasing. What it boils down to is that the constant chasing can cause us to forget some fundamentals. The endgame becomes so important that the chase becomes one-dimensional. Once this happens, the small things, like a missed workout or a bout of food poisoning, become an overblown crisis instilling thoughts that the goal is now unachievable. Even rats take a break from the wheel and so should we; it will make the chase easier in the long run and the achievement of the goal more probable.

## Goal setting 101

### Make your goals realistic

Meteoric improvements are rare and are reserved for those with a phenomenal athletic background. This is true both in the professional and amateur ranks. For most of us, reaching our potential, whether it is an eight-hour or seventeen-hour Ironman time, requires precision in training by learning the nuances of each sport. Your past results are the best determinant of future success. In this vein, when you are setting your goals, set more than one goal. You can have levels where your A goal will be incredibly difficult to accomplish but your B and C goals will be easier to complete.

### Extrinsic vs. intrinsic goals

Goals can be categorized as extrinsic or intrinsic. Extrinsic goals are those that are a means to an end, such as financial reward, fame, trophies, or impressing others. Intrinsic goals inherently satisfy psychological needs for autonomy, competence, and growth, such as community feeling, love of the sport, or physical fitness.[7] This distinction is an important one. The attainment of goals is a manner in which athletes satisfy their needs, and some goals will achieve this better than others. Studies have shown that focusing on intrinsic goals leads to higher well-being while the opposite is true for extrinsic goals.[8] There is no doubt that goal setting will probably involve some combination of both types of goals, since enjoyment of sport (intrinsic) is an imperative to continue the hard work and nobody is immune to the desire to win awards or beat their nemesis (both extrinsic). Those who are too intrinsically focused often lack the killer instinct to make the progress needed to achieve their goals, while those who are too extrinsically focused can end up with race anxiety or even lose interest in the goal pursuit.

When I was racing, I always had my best races when I was focused on having fun and performing at my best on a given day. If I started to think too much about prize money and sponsor bonuses, inevitably I had a poorer race because it made me more nervous. Indeed, Alexis Waddel-Smith, a former professional triathlete, studied this very topic for her master's thesis. She interviewed a group of female professional triathletes and she found that challenges, love of the sport, and togetherness (all intrinsic) kept the women motivated to continue competing. This is an important concept because motivation is one of the key elements needed to maintain interest and passion in achieving a goal.

## Setting non-outcome goals

Using performance as the only type of goal ultimately leads to disappointment. In addition, on any given day, reaching a PR (personal record, i.e., a best time), the podium, or the qualifying standard for a big race is extremely difficult. Earlier in the chapter I mentioned process and performance goals, and those are extremely important, too. Think about the factors that must come into play to have a sensational race: (1) The training needed to be consistent and excellent without disruption from injury, illness, and outside commitments, (2) You need to nail your taper, (3) Favorable weather conditions are important, (4) If you are looking for a podium, you need to be the outlier performer in your age group, (5) Your nutrition needs to be dialed in perfectly, and (6) You must have luck on your side.

The long list of factors needed to perform at your best is truly amazing. It is no wonder, then, that so often we fall short of the goals we set for ourselves. That is why I think it is vital to set non-outcome-related goals, things that can be accomplished even on the worst performance day.

1. *Nailing nutrition.* What works in training does not always pan out during a race. A half Ironman prior to an Ironman is a perfect opportunity to try out something nutritionally that has worked in training but has never been implemented in a race.

2. *Perfect pacing.* Usually go out conservatively? Maybe try a race where you go out a little harder and see if you can hold on to it. Usually go out like a bat out of Hell? Start a little easier in your next race and try to finish stronger.

3. *Just for fun.* Sometimes a destination race is just that—all about the destination.

4. *Test yourself.* Running races, bike time trials, and swim meets are excellent substitutes for a regularly scheduled training session. A race that is used as a training session keeps you in the racing mode, allows you to go harder than you would during training, and helps you boost your fitness and confidence going into your goal race.

5. *Implement your new mental game.* Every race is an opportunity to practice and make strides in upping the mental game. The ensuing chapters in this book can be applied to your races and will help you cope with days that fall short of expectations.

6. *Work on balancing family, work, and training.* Yes, keep the athletic circumstances in balance.

7. *Perfect biomechanics.* Every race is a chance to hone your skills by improving your fundamentals, such as gait, pedal stroke, and swim technique.

## Practice visualization

I first heard about using visualization (also known as mental imagery and mental rehearsal) to improve performance as a collegiate swimmer. We actually practiced as a group. It was a combination of meditation and Savasana (the corpse pose at the end of a yoga session), two things I generally do not enjoy. We were told to close our eyes and imagine the perfect race. Given my amped-up nature, I was not amenable to lying still while awake, so I didn't buy into the notion of visualization.

Visualization has long been known to improve sports performance and can be used for performance enhancement, cognitive modification, rehabilitation, and practicing complex sports tasks. Mental imagery, no matter how vivid, does not induce muscular fatigue; no need to worry that it will make you tired. If you are rehabilitating an injury, visualization can actually speed up the process.[9]

As I became a more mature athlete in a sport that was more complex than swimming, I revisited the art of visualization. I would lie quietly and picture myself racing. I would go through the whole race, including transitions. I would see myself executing a perfect race. Sometimes I would get so caught up in my visualization, I could actually feel my heart rate increase. If it was a familiar course, I could put myself on various parts of the course and see myself conquering a difficult hill or running smoothly.

Many professional triathletes have discussed their use of visualization, including Cameron Brown, a triathlete from New Zealand who won Ironman New Zealand twelve times. In an interview with *Triathlete* magazine he stated, "I use visualization in a positive and negative way. I think about how I'll feel winning the race. It gets me fired up if I'm having a hard training day. I also think of the negative things that can happen—a flat tire, a bad swim, a mechanical—so when it does happen I'm prepared and can feel that I've done this before. It's amazing when people get a puncture for the first time in a race how much time they lose, as they don't get their head around it and move on."[10]

Everyone should develop their own technique for visualization, but I am going to provide you with some steps to get started. Find a quiet spot, close your eyes, and imagine yourself executing the perfect race. If it is a course you are familiar with, place yourself on the course and picture yourself floating and feeling good. On an unfamiliar course, check out the course maps and elevation profiles so you have an understanding of how the course flows before your visualization session. Imagine yourself crossing the finish line exuberantly because you achieved your goal.

## Commitment

Attaining a goal requires a special focus, a commitment that will almost always mean sacrifice. Once you've decided on a training program or a coach with whom you plan to work, you need to commit to that program. Brett Sutton, coach of multiple Ironman, World, and Olympic champions had this to say in an interview: "People come to me in the first place for my coaching advice. Why should they ask for it and then not take it on board? It means they're in the wrong training group. I'm saving them time and money, as I know it won't be effective for that athlete in my environment."[11]

You must be ready to eschew activities that can potentially derail goal achievement. Late-night dinners, excessive alcohol consumption, and missing workouts on a regular basis are examples of habits that are not compatible with goal achievement. In 1988, the summer I qualified for the swimming Olympic Trials, I went ice-skating with my swim buddies, one of whom was also swimming in the Trials. My coach, John Weckler, found out and went ballistic. There are no words that can capture his temper tantrums. His face went red and he yelled a litany of reasons why ice-skating was a bad idea. One of his arguments was that doing any activity that could cause an injury showed a lack of commitment to the bigger goal. He was right. Athletes throughout time have injured themselves celebrating their victories or doing seemingly mundane tasks. Ryan Lochte, the American swimmer who is an eleven-time Olympic medalist and world record holder, famously tore his MCL when he fell catching an overzealous fan. In 2015, champion golfer Rory McIlroy ruptured his ankle playing soccer ten days before his British Open defense (I realize that golf is not an endurance sport, but to play as well as someone like Rory, one needs the mental fortitude of an endurance athlete).

## Accountability

When Simon and I chatted about accountability he had this to say: "Age groupers really struggle with the accountability aspect. In other words, they sign up for a race, then they really struggle with the consistency of the workouts. They're great for one week, two weeks, maybe a month or two months. But, in order to improve, it takes years. Literally, years. If they are going to achieve the goals that they've set for themselves, it's going to take years. And they really struggle with that commitment and what that represents. They are dumbfounded [when they hear what it takes] and they blindly lie to themselves they are doing enough, when in reality they are only doing a third of what it takes."

You must be ready to hunker down and train hard and train with purpose. Even though athletes realize that they need a special drive and determination to achieve a goal, many feel aimless in their training, especially if they do not have any oversight. As mentioned above, a coach can be influential in helping you maintain your focus, but even more important, a coach adds a level of accountability; just knowing that someone expects you to complete a workout is often enough motivation to get you out the door, particularly on days when you are tired or weather is not optimal. Regardless of your coaching situation, keep a training log. Nobody wants to see a zero (i.e., a missed workout) in their log.

A training log is also a way to fend off short-term memory loss. By that I mean that athletes only seem to remember their most recent workouts. Just today I got a call from an athlete incredibly frustrated over a dreadful swim. I reminded him that for the last few weeks he has been making progress with his swimming and that most of them had been quite good. "That's true. I kind of forgot about that," he responded. How easily we overlook the good workouts in the face of a bad one or two. Writing it all down not only keeps you accountable to your workouts, it is also a reminder of all of the hard work you've put in. Training partners or group training sessions are other ways to increase accountability and create a more enjoyable training environment.

## It's okay to "fail"

Sometimes, no matter how hard you try, you just cannot make your goal happen. That's okay. If you recall, two of the four goal outcomes dictate that you will not reach your goal. The process of achieving a goal is also important, and trying and failing is more purposeful than not trying at all. Unachieved goals still give you a boost in fitness and can help you grow both as an athlete and as a person. I have just as many "failed" goals as those I have accomplished. I have been unable to finish many races in my career, mostly due to physical ailments or mechanicals on the bike. In those cases, the majority of the time, "quitting" was not a conscious decision; the decision was made for me either by my body or equipment that could just no longer continue.

In 2010, I made a very conscious decision to abandon a goal. After crashing on the bike defending my 70.3 World Championship title in 2009, I made a declaration in the emergency room: I wanted to reclaim my title in 2010, becoming the first forty-year-old to win a triathlon world title. I spent 2010 pursuing this goal despite ongoing problems with my ribs. I was unable to finish most races I started due to the pain, and in August of that year I raced my last triathlon at the Lake Stevens 70.3. I "quit" my world title pursuit, knowing that continuing along that path was futile. While it was not an easy decision, it was the right one.

Even with a history littered with goals unmet, I cannot say I regret tackling any of them. It is because I love sport in and of itself and because the process is rewarding. I have been able to bounce back time and again when I have not achieved a specific goal.

Each and every goal I've set in my athletic life has pushed me physically and mentally and those experiences are just added to my arsenal for my next pursuit. Goals that are not realized help you understand your limitations, which provides a deeper understanding of how to determine your next set of goals.

In 2001, Peter Reid, winner of the Hawaii Ironman in 1998 and 2000, walked off the Hawaii Ironman course when he ran past his condo. He was in second place at the time, but he realized that he just didn't have the will to push himself to the limit. He had lost his ability to suffer and he knew he could not achieve his goal—winning—without that capability. On that day, he "failed," and began the start of a short hiatus from the sport. He was able to resurrect his career with another Hawaii Ironman win in 2003.

## 10 Tips for a Goal-Setting Mental Makeover

- Keep your goals realistic.
- Break up your goals into very-short-term (daily), short-term (e.g. monthly, quarterly), and long-term (e.g. yearly).
- Your goals should be in line with your athletic circumstances.
- Goal achievement depends on accountability, consistency, and a well-formulated plan.
- Not all goals should be related to performance. Create goals that can be achieved even under the worst of conditions.
- Visualization is an important part of the goal achievement process, but it must be practiced.
- Write down your goals.
- Commit yourself to goal achievement and train with purpose.
- Often the road to goal attainment is fraught with difficulty. Do not give up just because things are hard.
- Not every goal will be met, but that does not mean your goal pursuit was a failure.

# 3

# Building Your Team

> Surround yourself with good people, surround yourself with positivity and people who are going to challenge you to make you better. If you just kind of let yourself stay alone and be by yourself, the negative, it is just not going to help you.
>
> —Ali Krieger[1]

## Why you need a team

"It takes a whole village to raise a child" is an African proverb popularized by Hillary Clinton. The crux of this saying is that the responsibility for raising a child is shared with an extended family; it is a communal effort. Anyone who has participated in a team sport readily acknowledges that success is predicated on the squad, comprised of teammates, coaches, and support staff. After the big game, star players compliment their teammates, the fans are thanked, coaches are lauded, and teammates know that if they have an off day, someone else can pick up the slack.

Meanwhile, endurance athletes liken themselves to lone warriors, out on the battlefield fending for themselves. I like to joke that I am not a team player. My history involves competing only in individual sports. I don't even have experience playing in a youth soccer league.

What we consider "individual" sports is still a team effort; none of us exist in a vacuum. Training and competing in "individual" sports requires a litany of help and understanding from those around us, ranging from the support of family members to the volunteers on the race course.

Athletes competing in individual sports often seek out a coach or participate in group workouts to help them manage their training. Given that 37 to 55 percent of runners are injured annually[2] and crashes from bike riding are commonplace, I think it's fair to say that many athletes have at least one doctor and a physical therapist on their team roster. When I raced professionally, my sponsors were an integral part of my team, which is why I always made sure I aligned myself with companies I believed had the best products for my purposes. I also had various agents and consultants.

Simon Lessing's take is this: "I would honestly say that any athlete in any sport that has achieved success is typically pretty intelligent. In other words, they are able to take control of their destiny and they are able to put the right people around them. Even if they [athletes] are unable to make certain decisions or need to bounce ideas off of someone, they have the right people to do so. It's important to surround yourself with people who objectively say 'good idea' or 'bad idea.'"[3]

What about training partners? The person you call late at night for an early morning run is also part of your team. If you have a favorite shop that you rely on to purchase and tune your equipment, they, too, are part of your team. I happen to have an incredibly understanding and truly remarkable boss who never says no to time off (I am self-employed), but if your job situation requires you to confer with work staff to help accommodate your training/race schedule, they have become part of your team. Many athletes use massage and chiropractic care as recovery tools. The volunteers on the race course who provide you with nourishment and encouragement are also part of your team, albeit many of them are anonymous to you.

As you can see, athletes competing in individual sports actually have a large team around them. Without the power of "we," our athletic shelf life would be as long as that of a carton of milk.

## Your support team

I briefly mentioned above the people who are either naturally part of your support team (family and work) or those you need to enlist (everyone else). Athletes on the Olympic pathway often have the benefit of training at a specialized center that provides world-class coaching, physical therapy, nutritionists, strength and conditioning coaches, physicians, chiropractors, and other athletes who can serve as training partners. National governing bodies understand that reaching the pinnacle in any sport cannot be done without a team. The majority of athletes are not privy to this all-in-one type of team approach, which means building the team piecemeal, picking members with a careful selection process.

## Our parents

Many years ago, when I was interviewing for admission to a master's degree program, I was asked the following question: "How did it feel to have your parents force you to swim?" I was so taken aback by the question, particularly since nothing I had said would indicate my parents had "forced" me to swim (although they did force me to study), that I wasn't sure how to answer. I stammered through an explanation that I actually loved swimming and my parents were very supportive, and if anything, they tried to hold me back because I was too overzealous. I was offended by the notion that I had pushy sporting parents. My parents attended as many swim meets as possible, and once I transitioned to triathlon, they were there, too. In fact, my mother traveled with me hither and yon during my triathlon career. Aside from her loud snoring, which could wake a neighborhood, we had fun and created a treasure trove of memories. I have been lucky that throughout my career, through success and through injury, my parents have played an up-front and supportive role.

No matter our age, we want the support and approval of our parents, especially when it comes to our passions and dreams. As youngsters, we are beholden to our parents in our pursuit of sporting excellence; they pay the fees for clubs and equipment and provide the taxi service. Studies have shown that in young elite athletes, parental involvement is critical in making the transition to intensive training.[4] Parental support extends beyond childhood; decisions about whether to continue a sport later in life stems from their earlier support.

Stories abound about parents on the sidelines, many of whom exude alarming behavior that includes berating their kids and coaches, while other parents merely drop their kids off at practice and show no interest at all. The parental habits we see in childhood often spill into our adult years; many of my athletes have parents who have never seen them race, while other parents are intimately involved. It is a fine balance between showing too much interest and none at all.

Parents also have the ear and influence over other family members. If the parents do not approve of your athletic endeavors, this disdain will infiltrate the attitude of the rest of the family.

## The coach

Many endurance athletes employ a coach to help guide them through the training and racing quagmire. The advent of social media and training sharing sites such as Strava means that athletes are posting their workouts on a regular basis. Nothing breeds insecurity like seeing that other people are doing more than you. Distance runners continually push the upper limits of weekly mileage, with professional marathoners logging upwards of 120 miles per week. There is a trickle-down effect whereby amateur runners learn about this type of training regimen and want to emulate what their idols are doing. A coach or mentor can help bridge the gap between what you want to do and what you should do.

I have already written quite a bit about my high school swim coach, John Weckler. He was much like many of the swim coaches of his era:

unapologetically abrasive, short tempered, and out of shape, instilling fear in all of the swimmers who attended his workouts. He was a contentious fellow, prone to temper tantrums, but he managed to push us to our absolute limits. At the end of the day, despite his foibles, he squeezed the potential out of each and every swimmer.

John was not my first coach, but he was the first coach who helped me understand my athletic potential and then he pushed me hard to get there. I was a malleable but stubborn teenager, ready to soak up the knowledge he bestowed upon me. I learned from John all of the attributes necessary to become a champion: dedication, perseverance, dealing with the pain of training, and becoming a gracious winner and loser. I have lost touch with John, but to him I say a hearty thank you.

As a professional triathlete, I had the pleasure of working with all sorts of coaches, from Troy Jacobson to Dave Scott to Dr. Philip Skiba. They varied in their coaching philosophy and personality, but they all were generous in sharing their wisdom and providing encouragement and, most important, nurturing my potential. As I have developed my own coaching style over the years, I did so by combining the best characteristics of each coach and eliminating those I found counterproductive and then adding in my own brand of tough love.

Coaches can offer so much more than a training plan. Athletes are often their own worst enemy; a good coach can ameliorate this problem. After winning the one-million-dollar triathlon Triple Crown in 2015, Daniela Ryf, who also won the 2015 Ironman and Ironman 70.3 World Championships said, "The last six weeks after Kona, I put my head down toward this race, and I'm so happy I could finish strong and take this win. I'm so grateful for this opportunity. It's been a great journey and I'm also grateful for the support from my team . . . and of course, my coach. He supported me so much and the last weeks were not easy. I was really struggling to keep the focus."[5]

## The training partners

Part of what makes endurance sports the enjoyable endeavor it can become is the social aspect. Training partners are an integral part of success, both to push you, keep you accountable, and to keep you entertained. When I was a swimmer, I learned the value of being surrounded with motivated, like-minded people. In high school, my predominant social group were the very people with whom I suffered countless hours racing in the pool. The camaraderie of attending swim practice at 4:30 a.m. and then having to return for another swim in the afternoon led to mutual respect and the realization that most of my non-swimming peers did not want to hang out with a water-logged, chlorine-smelling, prune-fingered group of people who could barely pass algebra but were experts at figuring out the wall clock (six-time Hawaii Ironman champion Dave Scott likes to call it "jock math").

As I transitioned to triathlon, assembling a training group became even more important, what with three sports and all. Professional triathletes the world over often join training squads with a head coach and hand-picked athletes who train together and often travel the world searching for perpetual summer. Due to my academic circumstances, I was in graduate school and then a researcher for my entire professional career, and was not in a position to leave my hometown for extended periods for training.

Over the years, I have built small training groups with athletes who are well-matched on an athletic and friendship level. A compatible training partner will push you when you need it but not thrash you when you are down. Training partners should offer support in times of need, praise when it is deserved, and let you know when you are being a training pain. I have had epic meltdowns and achieved new levels of fitness all in front of training partners. Indeed, research has shown that a "task-cohesive group" is the most important aspect in sticking to an exercise program.[6]

Gwen Jorgensen, a 2012 and 2016 Olympian in triathlon and the 2014 and 2015 ITU World Champion, described what training in a team environment means: "Being in a daily training environment with other ITU athletes is beneficial. I have the unique opportunity to train with my peers (and competitors). We are usually on a similar race schedule, and trying to achieve the same goals. Jamie [her coach] has done an incredible job at creating an atmosphere where we are able to push each other to improve. My belief is this raises the bar for what it takes to be competitive on the world stage."[7]

Tim DeBoom, winner of the 2001 and 2002 Hawaii Ironman, told me that his tenure training with three-time Hawaii Ironman champion Peter Reid upped his game to a level that he never reached with any other training partner. His stalwart training partner was his brother Tony, a former professional triathlete. Tim explained that training with Peter lifted his game because he was pushed harder and he enjoyed the daily challenges that Peter presented.[8]

Just as training partners can improve your training and ultimately your racing, so too can they hinder your progress. Training with the wrong person or group can nullify any benefits. The first year I moved to Baltimore from Chicago, I chased a group of male cyclists up and down the hills of Baltimore county. I was spread thin with training and graduate school. My body was not prepared for this extreme effort, especially coming from an area where a bridge constituted a hill. The acute bout of overtraining suppressed my immune system and I ended up with mono and was out for an entire season.[9] I did not eschew that group, as they became good friends and supporters. I changed my tactics when training with them and begged off group rides when I knew I needed a recovery day.

This type of overtraining scenario is not uncommon. Three-time Ironman Hawaii champion Craig Alexander frequently spent his summers training in Boulder. Up-and-coming triathletes from all over the world clamored to train with him. Craig would go on to win in Kona while many of his training partners were laid to waste from overtraining and therefore never reached their potential. Craig's training was right for him, but clearly, not productive for many of his disciples.

In 2008, arguably one of my most successful triathlon seasons, I had a trio of male triathletes (Billy, Brandon, and Shane) with whom I trained nearly every day. Sometimes our schedules coincided and we all did a similar workout. On other days we merely started out together and dispersed to do our own thing. The guys were stronger riders, which meant oftentimes when we did race pace intervals they were far up the road in front of me and then we would reconvene for our rest period between intervals. If we went for a track session, we would adhere to our own paces. Some days one or more of us would get dropped big time, but there was an unspoken agreement that unless somebody was in real trouble, that was acceptable. None of us swam the same pace, but we met at the pool every Saturday to hammer out swim intervals.

Even though the trio of training partners was regularly late for our training sessions, to the point that we created a sign-in sheet and handed out demerits to the very tardy, the group dynamic elevated all of our performances, in particular my own; that was the year I won the Ironman 70.3 World Championships in world-record time.

## The health and wellness crew

Every endurance athlete needs a health and wellness crew; injury and rehab are as much a part of sports as is the training itself. Members of your health and wellness crew might include a massage therapist, physicians, a sports psychologist, a nutritionist, an alternative medicine specialist, and a chiropractor. Over the years, with a long history of injuries, I learned how to navigate the quagmire known as our medical system. You are your best advocate. If you are not getting the care you believe you require, move along and find a provider who better suits your needs. Indeed, I have had several doctors, upon not being able to diagnose the exact nature of my injury (e.g., I had a foot injury that made walking impossible, but nobody could determine why; and six years into my rib injuries, doctors still do not understand why I have continued pain), tell me that my issues were psychological only to be vindicated later when another specialist figured out my health conundrum.

Whether you are a newbie to the world of endurance sports or you are a seasoned veteran, a yearly physical should be on your docket to ensure that you are healthy enough to train and race. As part of your physical, get a blood draw to measure your complete blood count, iron levels, and vitamin D. Endurance athletes are notoriously iron and vitamin D deficient, which can affect not only your performance but also your general health. Be certain, though, that you work with a physician knowledgeable about the needs of an athlete, as the normal blood values for an athlete are different than for non-athletes.[10]

Physicians familiar with athletes' needs can provide proper guidance on iron supplementation, identify symptoms of chronic fatigue/overtraining syndrome (an imbalance in the hormonal, muscular, and nervous systems) early, and refer athletes to the proper specialists if there is an injury. Many endurance athletes manage chronic conditions, such as asthma or diabetes. Your medical team will be instrumental in supervising your care to optimize your performance without exacerbating your medical condition.

Your wellness crew is also an important part of your health and recovery. Massage and chiropractic care are not luxuries but an essential part of your training regimen. If you wait until your body is aching, it is almost too late. Schedule regular appointments to ensure your muscles are functioning properly and your body is in correct alignment.

## The furry friend

Sometimes an unconventional training partner can unexpectedly be your most coveted training partner. A four-legged friend who loves to log miles can provide companionship, security, and faithful reliability. In 2010, my husband and I rescued a puppy from the Boulder Humane Society. I was experiencing a bout of depression after my bike accident, and the wagging tail and happy face of a puppy was just the medicine I needed. Little did I know at the time that Diesel, an Australian cattle dog/retriever mix, would become such an effective running partner. His ability to run in any weather condition over any distance has made Diesel my most consistent training partner. I am not here to discuss the nuances of how and when you should run with your dog; those topics are better to discuss with your vet. I merely want to laud the many aspects of sharing your training with your furry friend.

My first run with Diesel was short, only a couple of miles. Over time, I built his mileage as I would with any athlete I coach—methodically, to ensure he didn't get injured and with an analytical eye to ensure he actually enjoyed it. Diesel always seemed to enjoy a run, but I was worried that maybe I was expecting too much from him. I asked a friend of mine who is a dog trainer about my concern and she explained to me, "Ask him if he wants to go for a run. He will let you know what he wants to do."

That seemed like a strange tactic, but I already talked to my dog anyway, so asking him questions and expecting answers didn't seem so far-fetched. Her idea seems to work. Before every run, I shout, "Diesel, want to go for a run?" He meanders to the mudroom and lies down and awaits my own readiness. In the five years I have been running with Diesel, he only turned me down once by walking away from me and lying down on his bed; to this day I have no idea why.

Running with Diesel gives me a sense of security when I am on isolated trails or in new cities. His gigantic smile when we are out together does not escape the glances from strangers who often remark on the sheer joy on his face. Diesel somehow pulled me home on days where I struggled. And, he never cares if I have to slow down or stop and walk home from a run gone wrong. I often envy his ability to "go" whenever he wants, because *every* runner at one time or another has frantically searched for a mid-run bathroom. My only gripe with Diesel is that he never looks like he is working hard, no matter how hard I am working. Oh, and he never laughs at my jokes.

When you are choosing your training partners, keep in mind that they can often turn up in the most unexpected places.

## Managing the team

Guess what? You are a player-manager. In baseball parlance, the player-manager was not only signed to play for the team, but also was tasked with managing it. In the modern era, this practice is moot, but it does pertain to endurance sports. In the history of Major League Baseball, there have only been 221 player-managers, indicating how difficult it is to both manage a team and to be an athlete oneself. Professional endurance athletes often have an agent or manager who oversees sponsors, but the role of coordinating training, the health and wellness team, and daily tasks are usually left to the athlete. When I raced as a professional, I had an agent who facilitated sponsorships, but it was ultimately up to me to cultivate relationships with those sponsors, direct my medical team, communicate with my coach, arrange my travel schedule, organize training partners, and oversee any minutia that arose.

The majority of endurance athletes do not have the luxury of a team manager. It is up to you to orchestrate and manage your team, which means settling differences of opinion, maintaining open discussion with team members, delegating activities, creating a healthy team culture, and coordinating the efforts of team members who have overlapping jobs.

## The 3 Cs for successful team management

*Communication* with your team is the foundation by which the team will help or impede your success. Explain to them what you need from them as part of your support crew and the reasons why. Family may become irritated with your need for quiet evenings at home or special nutritional requirements, but if they understand the reasons for such needs, they may be more prone to acquiescing.

*Conflict-avoidance* is imperative, as it is natural that some team members may not get along. Designate tasks to each team member. In circumstances where team members have overlapping tasks or complementary tasks, introduce the team members and open their lines of communication; for example, ask medical professionals to speak to each other to coordinate care or have your coach confer with your physical therapist.

If a conflict should arise, go back to the first C—communication— to resolve the issues. Most people are afraid of confrontation and avoid conversations they deem uncomfortable. In my view, when conflict arises, rather than viewing it as confronting the team member, think of it as a rational discussion. Keeping an even keel and presenting the issue in a non-accusatory tone will help keep the conversation equable.

*Compromise* will also be an important factor. Understanding that team members can only give a certain amount of support is crucial, particularly the family team.

## Team culture

In the corporate world, the phrase "company culture" is often bandied about. Company culture is the combination of values, attitudes, beliefs, and practices of a company's employees. A company's culture may be hard to define, almost intangible, or it can be very precise, handed down from generation to generation. Regardless of the culture, it is clear that some people will fit in and others will not. As the player-manager, it is your job to create a culture amenable to your personality and ensure that your team members fit that mold. Your success depends on developing a team built with positive energy, honesty, a goal-oriented emphasis, and enlisting team members who pay attention to detail. Discussions with potential team members should elucidate whether the person will fit into your team culture. Certainly, you do not want to fill your team with robots who cater to your every whim; however, you do want unity. If a team member is adding a toxic energy, even with repeated appeals to change their attitude, that team member should be dismissed. Lauren Fleshman, a multiple National Champion on the track, stated: "When you're partners with another athlete, pro or amateur, you are their cheering section every single day."[11]

Two of the most important facets of your team culture are leadership and honesty.

*Leadership by example.* Your team will take cues from your actions, words, and body language. The signals that you emanate project onto your team: Are you intense or lighthearted? Are you having fun or is it a drudgery? Do you bestow compliments? Are you high energy? Are you intimidating? Each one of these traits will affect your team culture and how your team members interact with you. Focus on conveying the atmosphere you want when interacting with your team members. Remember: positivity is infectious; if you exude a positive attitude, so too will your team. Conversely, negative energy breeds a negative team culture. For example, showing up to training sessions with a smile rather than a complaint will enhance the morale.

*Honesty.* A positive and supportive team culture is the objective; however, you still want your team members to bestow the truth. There is a delicate equilibrium between honesty, positivity, and negativity. Honest team members will gently let you know if you've set your goals too high or if you are making poor training decisions. Honest team members will provide advice that will lead you down the best path, even if it is something that you do not want to hear. Honest team members will nudge you in a direction that you may have shunned as untenable.

In my triathlon career, I did not always receive honest guidance from my team members, often due to my own optimism and ability to bargain with team members who advised me against things I wanted to do. I did not create a culture in which my team members felt comfortable telling me the word "no."

In 2005, I tore my hamstring five weeks before the Hawaii Ironman. My stubborn nature led to a refusal to acknowledge that I might not be able to race and this attitude rubbed off on my support team.

I conferred with my coach and medical support team and everyone agreed that I would be able to race, *even though I was still unable to run race week*. Had I been open to the possibility of not racing, my support team might have been more truthful with me about my situation.

When I gave this chapter to my father to read, he not-so-gently pointed out that he and my mother had emphatically told me not to race with my bad hamstring; but, really, who listens to their parents? His comment was, "You needed to get over fantasizing and not accepting reality due to your overpowering desire to compete and win." Hmm. Hindsight is amazing, I really should have listened to him. And, given that my father is a physician, his opinions on medical matters really should have counted!

On that fateful race day, I somehow made it through the swim, bike, and ten very slow and painful miles on the run before I dropped out. It took almost six months before I was able to run pain-free. That experience, as upsetting as it was, had a bright side: it shaped my own views on coaching and how I communicate. I provide my athletes with my honest assessment of a situation even if it is not what they want to hear.

## Get your family involved

Your family should be at the top of your team. Without familial support, the entire athletic endeavor becomes a difficult battle. Creating a harmonious family environment is essential to maintaining balance in your athletic circumstances (a concept I introduced in chapter 2). Since I started this chapter with somewhat of a cliché (the "It takes a village" parable), I offer you another one: "Families that play together stay together." I do not suggest that you train with your family, per se. But getting them involved in sports, either yours or some other sport, will increase the odds that they will remain your cheerleader and be more amenable to the hours you need for training and racing. The benefits of a sporting life are well-documented (e.g., increased well-being, better health). Additionally, when parents provide a positive influence with regards to sports participation in their children's early life, and extended into their adulthood, it instills a lifelong involvement in sports.[12]

More and more often, in professional and amateur ranks, families are connecting and building stronger relationships through sports. Keeping sports in the family creates a bond of shared goal pursuit. Ben True qualified for the 2015 Track and Field World Championships in the 5000 meters and his wife, Sarah True, is a 2012 and 2016 Olympian in triathlon. Katie Rainsberger, a teenage phenom in track and field who won the 2015 Nike Cross Nationals, is the daughter of Lisa Rainsberger, winner of the 1985 Boston Marathon. Siblings often compete together (brothers Alistair and Jonny Brownlee won gold and bronze in triathlon at the 2012 London Olympics and gold and silver at the 2016 Rio Olympics representing Great Britain) and against each other (Matt and Shane Reed competed at the 2008 Beijing Olympics in the sport of triathlon for separate countries, the U.S. and New Zealand, respectively). At triathlon and running events worldwide, two or three generations of family members race each other to the finish line.

## Do your research

There are two steps to assembling your team. The first step is figuring out what it is that you want from each team member and creating a list of the characteristics that are compatible with your needs. The second step is doing research to determine who fits your vision. Once you've set your parameters, interview your potential team members, and this includes medical professionals. Gone are the days of blindly being matched up with a provider and then accepting whatever he or she suggests; we are now in an era of empowerment, where you can make decisions based on your needs and wants.

For example, if you are looking for a coach, you need to decide whether you want a lot of communication or infrequent check-ins. Do you need a lot of encouragement or just a small amount? Does your coach require an impressive athletic résumé? Do you want a coach who sugarcoats the truth or just tells it like it is? Once you've created your list of needs, search online for potential coaches. Read about the athletes they've coached, and determine their coaching style and the types of events for which they normally coach their athletes. Set up interviews with potential candidates. Write down your questions so you do not forget to ask for pertinent information. Regardless of whether you decide to work with a potential coach, be mindful of their time and always send a thank-you note and let them know your ultimate decision, even if you decide to go in another direction. I have had dozens of athlete interviews, and only a fraction of the time do I receive any communication from those that select another coach, their silence speaking louder than an e-mail.

This process is no different if you are looking for a medical professional or a physical therapist; just because your good buddy had success with a particular person does not mean that person is right for you. Referrals are an excellent way to begin your search, but ultimately, your judgment and personal connection should prevail. Remember: create your list of requirements, do the research, and conduct an interview.

Once you've made your decision, give yourself a chance to get to know your team member. After a given amount of time, if the team member is not working out, do not be afraid to express your concerns through the first C (communication). If things cannot be reconciled, it is time to find a replacement.

## The anonymous team members

Most of your team is comprised of members you chose. Race volunteers are crucial to your success even though they are anonymous to you and have not been through your personal vetting process. I raced hundreds of triathlons before I actually volunteered at one, and the experience changed my whole perspective on the kind souls who dedicate their time so others can reach their goals.

I am by no means a volunteer expert, as the only job I have performed is working at run aid stations in Olympic, 70.3, and Ironman triathlon distances. My volunteering involvement does not extend beyond the Boulder city limits, my repertoire only includes races that have been incredibly hot and dry, and I have handed out aid to pros and age groupers. I have spent time conferring with all sorts of athletes in distress, offering up whatever advice seems to fit the circumstance.

I offer up my background as a preamble to the comments and observations that I am going to share. My perceptions of what happens on the race course are of course skewed by my own personal volunteering experiences, by my stint as an athlete (both at the professional and age group level), and by the keen and sometimes critical eye of a coach.

Just as in "real" life, on the race course there are those who are kind and those who are meanies. Kind athletes are genuinely thankful and express their gratitude verbally or through nonverbal expressions. Meanies get annoyed if they miss their drink of choice and they often shout unnecessary expletives or give dirty looks. When I crashed on my bike due to a water bottle handoff gone wrong, clearly the fault of the volunteer, I never even confronted the person. To this day, people tell me they would like to get even with him for the years of pain I endured from one moment gone wrong. I do not feel that way, though, as I know the person meant no malice and would feel terrible if he knew the mistake he made was so consequential. And truly, the fault lies with the lack of education on the proper water bottle handoff procedure by the race organizers, which means I have heard about many similar accidents since my own.

Volunteers genuinely want to help, otherwise they wouldn't be there. They stand outside for hours on end in the elements. They bake in the sun or freeze in the rain. Volunteering causes aching and blistered feet and a sunburned and dehydrated body. Clearly, it is not the goal to sabotage an athlete's race. On the contrary, volunteering at a race is altruistic. If you are handed the wrong drink, it was unintentional. If you are missed altogether, they just didn't see you. Rather than have a fit, just grab what you want at a different table or simply wait a mile until the next aid station. Do not lash out and do not let it spoil your race.

In order to better understand the incredibly intricate mechanisms of being a race volunteer, I highly suggest you sign up to work at a race at least once a year and help hardworking athletes build their anonymous team. Your racing success depends on volunteers, as does the success of other athletes.

## 10 Tips for a Team-Building Mental Makeover

- Success in endurance sports cannot be achieved alone. A team of family, friends, coaches, training partners, and health care professionals is imperative to achieve your goals.
- Do not be afraid to ask your team members for help.
- You are never too old to want or need the support of your parents.
- You are in charge of your team culture. Lead by example and establish the energy that you want surrounding you.
- Treat your team with respect and honesty.
- Communicate regularly with your team to avoid conflict.
- Allow your team to tell you things you do not necessarily want to hear, such as when it is time to take a break, or that you should miss an important race because you aren't truly ready.
- Plan family sporting outings.
- Make informed decisions about who to place on your team by doing research.
- Volunteer at a race to appreciate the magnitude of this service.

# 4

## Taking Ownership

### Doing it for yourself

Leading into the 2012 London Olympics, Lanni Marchant was the top Canadian marathoner. She met the Olympic time standard in the marathon by five minutes, which should have made her a shoo-in to be nominated to the Canadian Olympic team. However, she fell short of the overly ambitious Canadian Olympic standard by two minutes (Team Canada wanted to send only medal contenders). Lanni pled her case to Athletics Canada to no avail and she was left off the team.

It was difficult putting that devastating oversight behind her, especially because she was told that she was never going to be good enough and wasn't viewed as a potential standout in the sport. Lanni proved them wrong by setting the Canadian marathon record in 2013, and then qualifying for the Olympics in the Toronto Waterfront Marathon in 2015.

After that performance, Lanni spoke about her omission and what it meant to defy the odds and then to qualify for the Olympics:

"It's not that I'm doing it out of spite. I'm doing it for myself. I wanted to know that I'm good enough," she stated. "It's now four years later and they [Athletics Canada] have even made the standard five seconds faster [than 2012], and I crushed it."[1] Yes, Lanni, doing it for yourself will generally produce the best results.

In chapter 2, I discussed the role of intrinsic and extrinsic motivation in the pursuit of achieving goals. These two motivational profiles are important not just in goal setting specifically, but also in sports participation in general. Intrinsic and extrinsic motivation, along with their "wicked" stepsister amotivation (lack of motivation, can you imagine?), fall under the umbrella of self-determination theory.[2] "Self-determination theory argues that, throughout life, people strive to integrate and organize new ideas and interests both within themselves and with others."[3]

Let me refresh your memory about intrinsic and extrinsic motivation. Intrinsically motivated athletes participate in sports for the pleasure and satisfaction derived from it; these athletes are process-focused rather than concentrating on external rewards (extrinsic motivation) or avoidance of negative consequences from not participating at all (amotivation).[4] Moreover, intrinsically motivated athletes participate in sports for themselves, take a satisfaction in being achievement-oriented, and try to explore and understand new ways to achieve better performance.[5] Intrinsic motivation is the highest level of self-determination (the ways in which a person controls their life), since it generally yields the most positive outcomes including improved quality of life, increased exercise behavior, and achievement of exercise goals.[6]

Extrinsically motivated athletes are not process-oriented and look to reap rewards and to avoid negative consequences. Amotivated athletes find ways/excuses not to engage in an activity altogether. I think it is safe to say that we've all cycled through these different types of motivation. I call it the motivation pyramid, as pictured on the next page.

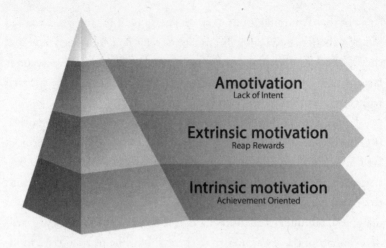

Throughout our athletic life, we oscillate between the three types of motivation, sometimes experiencing more than one at a time. Intrinsic motivation optimally should be the broad foundation of your motivational pyramid, accounting for most of your motivation.

Extrinsic motivation is inevitable, as most athletes are not immune to the delight from cool race T-shirts, giant medals, and accolades from friends and coworkers. Amotivation should only encompass a small part of your pyramid, if at all; if it starts taking up too much of your pyramid, it is probably time for a break.

Colleen De Reuck, a four-time Olympian in track and field and a multiple national and world record holder, has been a competitive athlete for decades. Colleen explained to me that when she was at the height of her running career, her primary motivation was personal bests and winning races, with making money a secondary goal, even though running was her livelihood. At the age of fifty, Colleen started doing triathlon, and over a two-year span won age group World Championship titles in both the 70.3 and Ironman distances. As a masters competitive triathlete, her motivations are to keep fit and healthy and to improve her swimming, biking, and running. Intrinsic motivation is clearly Colleen's foundation, but she also had extrinsic motivators in that she ran for a living, so earning prize money was important.

When amotivation crept into her athletic life, Colleen would take some time off and "when the desire returned, I would begin training again."[7] In addition, Colleen meets friends for training to boost her motivation levels when it wanes. Given Colleen's incredible longevity, and the fact that I have trained with her for five years, I can confirm that she rarely suffers from amotivation.

Simon Lessing's motivation for racing when he first started in the sport of triathlon was predicated on two things: making ends meet and winning a World Championship, extrinsic and intrinsic motivators. Yet, when you read Simon's account below, you will see that his primary motivation, the one that propelled him when things were incredibly tough, was to win, the ultimate intrinsic motivator.

I left an isolated South Africa as an eighteen-year-old. I never traveled internationally and ended up going overseas and ended up in France. I didn't have the support of anybody; no financial support. So, I was really racing from one race to the next. Catching trains, paying a campsite fee because I couldn't afford a hotel. Zipping myself up in my bike bag, sleeping in all of my clothes, and then waking up the next morning and racing. And knowing that I had to do well, because if I wasn't going to do well, I wasn't going to be able to survive. And that was the reality of the situation. What I am getting to is that this was a process of discovering who I was and how important what I was doing was to me. How much does this sport mean to me? I am doing all this. It sucks. But I am not going to really think about it. I am going to get on it with it. Do it. Because I want the ultimate goal. For me, from a very young age I wanted to be World Champion. And I'd set my mind on that. That was the goal. And, it didn't happen overnight, obviously. I had to go through a lot of adversity until I finally got to that point where I was able to win a World Championship. It didn't just happen automatically. I think a lot of people feel like they are just going to do the training and it is going to happen.[8]

Simon's early motivation was to win and make ends meet. Then he became a highly decorated athlete who rarely lost. Suddenly, there was a shift in his motivation pyramid whereby he no longer was primarily intrinsically motivated. Extrinsic motivation became more predominant, which caused him ambivalence. He explained: "You are not just doing this for yourself. The personal satisfaction that you get from what you accomplish is from the people around you. People that mean a lot to you. Close friends. Family. It's their reaction that is [the] reward. It is not just you coming across the line and putting your hands up. And, that is what I found difficult in the sport."

When Simon was winning regularly, he had the adulation of fans, sponsors, family, and friends. At some point, though, the wins became almost mundane to those around him because they began to expect it, and their enthusiasm waned with each win. Once the reaction from the outside was less exuberant, Simon felt dejected because each win was no less excruciating to him and still required copious amounts of hard work. In his mind, "it takes away the fun aspect of actually achieving a goal and winning races because people took it for granted."

The 2000 Sydney Olympics was a disappointment for Simon. His ninth-place finish was far below his goal. That race was a turning point, though, which led to some soul-searching. He asked himself some hard questions, regained new perspective with the birth of his first child, and ultimately rebalanced his motivational pyramid with intrinsic motivation at the bottom. Here is how it happened: "I had to get back to reality and ask myself, 'Am I really enjoying this? No. Why am I not enjoying this? Because I am not doing it for myself.' Basically, I made a decision after Sydney not to be so hard on myself. Because I would be mortified if I got beat. I set myself some new goals and new objectives, and that was refreshing. And to get back to racing for myself. Because that is the only thing that counts at the end of the day."[9]

## The no-excuse protocol

Imagine my surprise when I searched the scholarly literature for "excuses in endurance sports" and virtually nothing showed up. I was perplexed, because endurance athletes seemingly have a collection of excuses at the ready. My favorite is the one where a triathlete says before a run workout: "My legs are really tired from riding hard yesterday."

The reason I couldn't find any research on excuses in endurance athletes is partially because the phrase "excuses" is ostensibly too banal for researchers, and in the literature excuses are dubbed "self-handicapping." Once I learned that ditty of a phrase, a whole new world of fascinating research opened itself up to me.

Simply put, self-handicapping is a mechanism whereby individuals proactively place obstacles to successful performances to protect or bolster their self-esteem.[10] That is just a long-winded way of saying that sometimes (frequently in some) athletes make excuses before races or training in order to preserve their image, i.e., they are high self-handicappers.

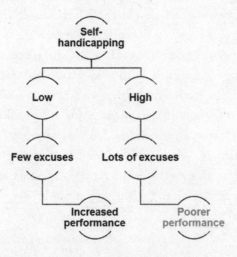

The notion of self-handicapping has been studied in a variety of settings to understand how this concept affects academic achievement, happiness, work, and social anxiety. Overwhelmingly, those who report high levels of self-handicapping, compared to those who are low self-handicappers, show negative consequences such as poorer performance in school, higher levels of anxiety and depression, lower levels of well-being, worse coping mechanisms, and reduced self-esteem.[11] Self-handicap enough and you can start a self-handicapping vicious cycle where self-handicapping results in poor adjustment, which in turn causes more self-handicapping.[12]

Self-handicapping is most commonly measured by the Self-handicapping Scale. The Self-handicapping Scale is a nifty tool that measures two types of self-handicapping, excuse making and effort expended.[13] In the sporting world, the excuse-making trait is quite strong while the effort-expended trait is not. Athletes seem to try, but then hedge their capability with a ready-made excuse.

Athletes engage in self-handicapping when they are confronted with a circumstance that could threaten their image of physical ability or their self-esteem, both in training and during competition.[14] The most commonly cited excuses include reports of exaggerated injury, school/work commitments, anxiety, or poor playing conditions. Compared to athletes who scored low on the Self-handicapping Scale, those athletes who scored high on the scale responded differently to a performance slump, using denial/avoidance and wishful thinking as their primary coping mechanisms, both of which are maladaptive because they delay finding effective ways to deal with the drop in performance.[15] In addition, athletes with a propensity for self-handicapping show high levels of pre-competition tension and anxiety.[16] All of this means that athletes who resort to self-handicapping tend to have difficulty with coping mechanisms, experience higher levels of anxiety, and turn to denial and wishful thinking to overcome dips in performance.

How many times have you heard athletes say that they are just training through a race or the race is just a low-level competition and doesn't matter? This may be the ultimate form of self-handicapping, because the less important an event is deemed, the more an athlete tends to self-handicap.[17]

Clearly, self-handicapping is not constructive. The test below can be used to measure your level of self-handicapping. Read the answers carefully; they are not all the same! In particular, statement #4 is different from the others.

## Self-Handicapping Scale[18]

1. *I tend to make excuses when I do something wrong.*
   1 = completely disagree, 2 = disagree very much, 3 = disagree a little, 4 = agree a little, 5 = agree pretty much, 6 = agree very much

2. *I tend to put things off until the last moment.*
   1 = completely disagree, 2 = disagree very much, 3 = disagree a little, 4 = agree a little, 5 = agree pretty much, 6 = agree very much

3. *I suppose I feel "under the weather" more often than most people.*
   1 = completely disagree, 2 = disagree very much, 3 = disagree a little, 4 = agree a little, 5 = agree pretty much, 6 = agree very much

4. *I always try to do my best, no matter what.*
   1 = agree very much, 2 = agree pretty much, 3 = agree a little, 4 = disagree a little, 5 = disagree very much, 6 = completely disagree

5. *I am easily distracted by noises or my own daydreaming when I try to read.*
   1=completely disagree, 2=disagree very much, 3=disagree a little, 4=agree a little, 5=agree pretty much, 6=agree very much

6. *I try not to get too intensely involved in competitive activities so it won't hurt too much if I lose or do poorly.*
   1=completely disagree, 2=disagree very much, 3=disagree a little, 4=agree a little, 5=agree pretty much, 6=agree very much

7. *I would do a lot better if I tried harder.*
   1=completely disagree, 2=disagree very much, 3=disagree a little, 4=agree a little, 5=agree pretty much, 6=agree very much

8. *I sometimes enjoy being mildly ill for a day or two.*
   1=completely disagree, 2=disagree very much, 3=disagree a little, 4=agree a little, 5=agree pretty much, 6=agree very much

9. *I tend to rationalize when I don't live up to others' expectations.*
   1=completely disagree, 2=disagree very much, 3=disagree a little, 4=agree a little, 5=agree pretty much, 6=agree very much

10. *I overindulge in food and drink more often than I should.*
    1=completely disagree, 2=disagree very much, 3=disagree a little, 4=agree a little, 5=agree pretty much, 6=agree very much

Higher scores indicate higher levels of self-handicapping, with a score of 30 or above indicating high self-handicapping and a score below 30 indicating low self-handicapping (maximum score is 60, minimum score is 10).

If you find that you are a self-handicapper, positive self-affirmations (i.e., reflecting on positive aspects of yourself) can reduce this behavior.[19] Self-affirmations potentially protect self-worth, which can increase expectations of success, reducing the need for self-handicapping. Self-affirmation may also reduce stress.[20] Here are some examples of positive words you can articulate: "I worked hard and deserve to do well"; "It is okay to struggle, I will get through it"; "Everyone goes through tough times, it will pass"; "It doesn't matter what other people think."

Do you remember Stuart Smalley, played marvelously by Al Franken, from *Saturday Night Live?* This skit involved a daily affirmation, with the main quote being "I'm good enough. I'm smart enough. And doggone it, people like me." Of course, the *SNL* skit and the quote itself were meant as a parody. All kidding aside, though, that message is important, especially for self-handicappers.

## Ego adjustment

Self-handicapping is an ego-protective mechanism. Setting aside one's ego is probably the most difficult aspect of racing, an attribute that many athletes never develop. You need to lose the E in ego. What is the E? Embarrassment. Once embarrassment is removed from the equation, it frees up the mind and body to race smart and to handle races that fall below expectation or ability. A wounded ego is the bane of athletes the world over. Imagine, then, if embarrassment was truly non-existent; a blight to the ego would take a lot more than a poor race, reducing the need for self-handicapping.

The age of the Internet has many obvious benefits. For endurance athletes, there is a major drawback—race results are immediately accessible for anyone to peruse, which can be a predicament if there is a result you would like to bury. And, therein lies the problem. Why should anyone want to hide their race results? Any finish, regardless of the time and place is an accomplishment. However, as a whole, endurance athletes are too afraid of what others think, and they race accordingly, with many people dropping out of races and preferring a DNF (did not finish) over a slow time.

Athletes are under a microscope. Performances are dissected by family members, friends, competitors, and coworkers. Less than stellar results are often met with words of derision rather than words of encouragement, wounding the ego and potentially creating ambivalence about racing in the future.

I learned to let go of what others think a long time ago. I had to. My racing career has been littered with DNFs due to asthma and injuries. I've been on the NBC Kona coverage not for my amazing performance but because I trudged to the finish line, wracked by dehydration. I have passed out in front of large crowds due to overexertion, and there are numerous occasions where I simply underperformed for no particular reason other than just having a bad day.

A successful athlete requires more than talent and hard work; a successful athlete requires a thick skin and a complete and utter willingness to fail publicly by letting the derogatory comments of the uninformed slide away like droplets of water.

## Perfectionism

People tend to think because I am highly type A that I am also a perfectionist. Nothing could be further from the truth. I make mistakes all the time, because I do not dwell on doing things impeccably, rather, I jam as much into a day as possible, leaving room for potentially correctable errors. Of course, I try to mitigate gaffes that have harmful consequences, but I don't become preoccupied with matters I deem inconsequential. I want to achieve my goals, but I do not strive to achieve them immaculately. Sometimes that means that I left something on the table, not quite achieving absolute success. In my mind, perfectionism just takes up too much time and is too stress generating.

In terms of sports, my attitude toward perfectionism leaned toward keeping a balanced existence that superseded perfectionism. I never fully committed to the professional athlete lifestyle; instead, I finished my doctorate, coached, and worked. I was not the kind of athlete who gave up caffeine before races or cut out junk food during tough training blocks. Perhaps my lack of perfectionism was a way of self-handicapping, but I doubt it, because I did not use my lack of perfectionism as an excuse, nor do I believe that it showed a lack of commitment. Instead, I always viewed my lack of perfectionism as my way of offsetting the extreme demands of being a professional athlete.

Perfectionism, like so many of the ideas I've already discussed, is not a simplistic concept. There are two types of perfectionism, personal standards perfectionism (self-oriented striving for perfection and setting high personal standards) and evaluative concerns perfectionism (concerns over mistakes, doubts about actions, and concern about how others view performance).[21]

From these descriptions, clearly I do not rate high on evaluative concerns perfectionism, but I am fairly high on personal standards perfectionism. I want to perform as well as possible, but I do not need to do it flawlessly.

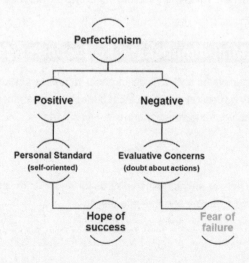

Personal standards perfectionism is associated with some awesome attributes, such as positivity, academic achievement, endurance, hope of success, competitive self-confidence, goal attainment, and lower levels of anxiety.[22] If you aren't high on the personal standards perfectionism scale, well, you need to be. Change your mindset by focusing on yourself and your ability to succeed and less on what people think of you and trying to live up to others' expectations.

In contrast, athletes who are perfectionists on the evaluative concerns dimension show maladaptive traits, such as poor coping, depression, and diminished well-being, that are harmful to success in sport performance.[23]

The distinction between the two types of perfection is so strong that personal standards perfection has been dubbed positive perfection and the other yucky type of perfection, evaluative concerns, is called negative perfection. In terms of attaining goals, positive perfection is linked to hope of success whereas negative perfection is correlated with fear of failure.[24]

Guess what? A group of researchers studied perfectionism in triathletes! They found that positive perfection was positively correlated with race performance and that athletes who were high on the positive perfectionist scale were more likely to report that their goal was to do better than others rather than avoiding doing worse than others.[25]

## Sport Multidimensional Perfections Scale-2[26]

Get out your pencil and a piece of paper to keep track of your answers. This is measuring two types of perfectionism, so there are two parts. Keep your answers separate for each part.

### Part 1

1. If I do not set the highest standards for myself in my sport, I am likely to end up a second-rate player.

1 = strongly disagree, 2 = disagree, 3 = neutral, 4 = agree, 5 = strongly agree

2.  I hate being less than the best at things in my sport.
    1 = strongly disagree, 2 = disagree, 3 = neutral, 4 = agree, 5 = strongly agree

3.  It is important to me that I be thoroughly competent in everything I do in my sport.
    1 = strongly disagree, 2 = disagree, 3 = neutral, 4 = agree, 5 = strongly agree

4.  I think I expect higher performance and greater results in my daily sport-training than most players.
    1 = strongly disagree, 2 = disagree, 3 = neutral, 4 = agree, 5 = strongly agree

5.  I feel that other players generally accept lower standards for themselves in sport than I do.
    1 = strongly disagree, 2 = disagree, 3 = neutral, 4 = agree, 5 = strongly agree

6.  I have extremely high goals for myself in my sport.
    1 = strongly disagree, 2 = disagree, 3 = neutral, 4 = agree, 5 = strongly agree

7.  I set higher achievement goals than most athletes who play my sport.
    1 = strongly disagree, 2 = disagree, 3 = neutral, 4 = agree, 5 = strongly agree

**Scoring:** PART 1 questions measure **Personal Standards perfectionism** (i.e., self-oriented striving for perfection). If you answered mostly 4 and 5 then you are high on this type of perfectionism.

# Part 2

1. Even if I fail slightly in competition, for me, it is as bad as being a complete failure.
   1 = strongly disagree, 2 = disagree, 3 = neutral, 4 = agree, 5 = strongly agree

2. If I fail in competition, I feel like a failure as a person.
   1 = strongly disagree, 2 = disagree, 3 = neutral, 4 = agree, 5 = strongly agree

3. The fewer mistakes I make in competition, the more people will like me.
   1 = strongly disagree, 2 = disagree, 3 = neutral, 4 = agree, 5 = strongly agree

4. I should be upset if I make a mistake in competition.
   1 = strongly disagree, 2 = disagree, 3 = neutral, 4 = agree, 5 = strongly agree

5. If an opponent performs better than me during competition, then I feel like I failed to some degree.
   1 = strongly disagree, 2 = disagree, 3 = neutral, 4 = agree, 5 = strongly agree

6. If I do not do well all the time in competition, I feel that people will not respect me as an athlete.
   1 = strongly disagree, 2 = disagree, 3 = neutral, 4 = agree, 5 = strongly agree

7. People will probably think less of me if I make mistakes in competition.
   1 = strongly disagree, 2 = disagree, 3 = neutral, 4 = agree, 5 = strongly agree

8. If I play well but only make one obvious mistake in the entire competition, I still feel disappointed with my performance.
   1 = strongly disagree, 2 = disagree, 3 = neutral, 4 = agree, 5 = strongly agree

**Scoring:** PART 2 questions measure **Competition Perfectionism** (i.e., concerns over mistakes, doubts about actions, and concern about how others view performance). If you mostly answered 4 and 5 you are high on this type of perfectionism.

**Putting it together**
1. High levels of **Competition Perfectionism** have been associated with high levels of competitive anxiety, worry, and disruption in concentration.
2. High levels of **Personal Standards Perfectionism** will help propel you toward your goals and actually decrease worry, anxiety, and concentration, but ONLY if it is in combination with lower scores on **Competition Perfectionism**.

# Integrity

Meb Keflezighi, an American distance runner who won a bronze medal in the marathon at the 2008 Olympics, winner of the 2014 Boston Marathon, and a qualifier for the 2016 Olympics in the marathon, is not only a celebrity in the running dominion, he is one of the few athletes who crossed over into popularity with the general public. His recognition is such that he goes by a one-name moniker, Meb, analogous to other sports greats such as Pelé and Serena. At a state dinner at the White House in 2014, former president Jimmy Carter moseyed up to Meb and said, "You are the most popular person here. You're the one they want to meet."[27]

You might think all of the popularity made Meb unapproachable.

Quite the contrary. Meb is known to lead pace groups at half marathons, connect with fans, and none other than Dave McGillivray, race director of the Boston Marathon, bestowed some heady accolades toward Meb: "His character, demeanor, and integrity are second to none."[28]

More important than achieving success is *how* success is achieved. In Meb's case, his success did not come at the price of his veracity. Meb described the honor he felt at taking the top spot in the *Runner's World*'s fifty most influential people in running: "They always write, 'Nice guys finish last.' But you can be nice and still be most influential."[29]

That statement is ever so true. Being nice and being successful are not mutually exclusive. Edging up to the starting line of a race or getting ready for that group training session can certainly bring out the lion in all of us, but it should not come at the price of being a full-time ninny.

Great athletes are not only measured by their successes, but the manner in which they handle success and failure. Showing enthusiasm at the finish line after a stellar performance is perfectly acceptable. Taking that success to malign your training buddies or boasting at work is not acceptable. A show of disappointment at the finish line of a poor race is perfectly acceptable. A full-blown temper tantrum and yelling/cursing at volunteers, spectators, or family members is not acceptable. Proper behavior is an essential part of the athlete package.

Performance enhancing drugs (PEDs). Drafting. Outside aid. Course cutting. The ways athletes cheat, often ingeniously and creatively, represent the scourge of sports. No level of sports is immune to the effects of cheating, not a first timer, not professionals, not age group winners. There are famous cheaters, such as Lance Armstrong and Marion Jones, and more obscure cheaters such as Nina Kraft, a professional triathlete who had her 2004 Ironman World Championship title revoked due to a failed drug test. Eventually these dopers admitted their wrongdoing with varying amounts of remorse.

Course cutting is another form of cheating that has been brought into the limelight by sleuths who scour race results looking for anomalies, such as missed timing mats, lack of course photos, on-course splits that appear unrealistic (e.g. an athlete who runs a nine-minute-mile pace for the first half of a race and a five-minute-mile pace for the second half ), and finishing times that are seemingly too fast compared to past race results. One such detective is Jonathan Cane. He relentlessly searches race results for anomalies and claims to have discovered over five hundred cheaters in his eight-year search.[30] The big city races usually rely on algorithms that scan race results to pick up cheating; but, much to the chagrin of athletes who have seen their place drop in the overall standings, not every cheater is caught or brought to justice with disqualification.

The rationale for course cutting is unclear, but psychologists postulate that it comes from a high level of extrinsic motivation, that the finisher's medal or the adulation from others is reason enough to put their reputation at risk.[31] As well, course cutting has allegedly propelled athletes to Boston Marathon qualifying times and podium places in Ironman races, indicating that the "glory" is also justification for some wayward athletes. Whatever the motivation, it is clear that lack of integrity shows up in many unexpected places.

The notion of cheating is not new; cyclists in the Tour de France were using performance enhancing drugs since the inception of the race. Ask athletes to complete a Herculean task that is seemingly physiologically impossible, throw them a lot of money and fame to accomplish the task, and they will find ways to get the job done, even if it means circumventing the rules. Cheating and sports are seemingly natural bedfellows, and all too many athletes are ready to make a Faustian bargain to attain their end goal.

Cheating occurs at *every* level of sport—your local turkey trot may just as likely have competitors supplementing with testosterone as the Olympic track and field 100 meter final. In 2015, the Drug Enforcement Agency busted sixteen underground drug labs seizing a mind-boggling 134,000 steroid pills and other materials from which steroids can be made, indicating the prolific market for these drugs. The 2015 Independent Commission for Reform in Cycling concluded: "Doping in amateur cycling is becoming endemic. This was confirmed by riders, professionals, managers, and anti-doping personnel."[32]

A 2013 survey showed that 11 percent of high school students reported using synthetic human growth hormone and 7 percent admitted to steroid use, both of which are banned substances.[33] These are kids! Imagine what is happening on the adult scene. Good thing there is information about that—13 percent of triathletes in a 2013 survey admitted to doping.[34] In 2015, a leaked report revealed that one-third of all medals from Olympic and World Championship track and field events between 2001 and 2012 were won by athletes who had suspicious doping tests, and none of them were stripped of medals.[35] Gran Fondo cycling events have had a rash of doping positives amongst their amateurs.[36]

Clean athlete Alysia Montaño knows firsthand the dismay of losing out to drug cheats. In November 2015, an independent commission determined that doping occurred at the highest level in Russia, causing Alysia to miss out on five medals from the Olympics and World Championships. Her reaction was: "I never lost hope that I'd one day get these medals. I definitely tried not to hang onto it because it would make it impossible for me to move forward. She added: "When you're cheated out of a medal and you know it, it eats at you internally and you're going after it again. It's hard. The Olympics are huge and you think that's your shot and then you miss. You blame yourself and think, 'What can I do differently?' You realize how human you are and that these others don't feel those effects because they're cheating."[37]

Caster Semenya stands to benefit from the disqualification of the Russians, too. Semenya raced in that same event as Montaño in the 2012 Olympics and placed second, and could be upgraded to a gold medal. Her reaction was quite different from Montaño's: "There was someone that finished first in the Olympics; whether she doped or not, I came second and that will never change."[38]

Those are very different perspectives on the same situation. There is no right reaction, though. Since cheating is an inevitable situation in sports, what can you do? You can start by not cheating yourself. After that, nothing. Nothing at all. You cannot worry about cheaters. Ultimately, all any of us have is our integrity. Our race results do not matter at all if they were achieved in a fallacious manner. In my career, I witnessed all manner of cheating: athletes taking PEDs, drafters, course cutters, accepting illegal outside assistance, tampering with equipment, blatant blocking of forward progress, and purposeful aggressiveness to cause bodily harm (in one race in 1998, a competitor repeatedly made contact with me on the bike with the intent of knocking me over). My race placings were altered, thereby affecting my ability to gain sponsors; however, I did my absolute best to ensure that my psyche was never shaken. I understood that I was not able to control the actions of my competitors, and that no matter what, I could look at myself in the mirror without shame.

The message I want to convey is that cheating amongst your competitors will occur and it will at some point directly influence your race results. A cheater might cost you a Kona qualifying spot, or a place on the podium, or just rankle you, such as watching a group pass you during the bike portion of a triathlon while they are riding illegally close together. Rather than let the cheaters distress you, accept the notion that cheaters are out there and that your honesty and integrity will pay dividends in life, where it counts most.

## Learn to focus on the things you can control

Meb Keflezighi epitomizes the quintessential American hero. Or does he? Many cynics claim that because Meb was born in Eritrea he is not truly an American. What hogwash.

The public backlash to whether Meb is truly American could have been vexing to him, but it wasn't. Meb elucidated that after his Boston Marathon win: "I'm as proud of being an American as I was before. None of that changes who I am, but hopefully it changes other people and gives them perspective. I can't control it. It's funny. My daughters see the flag and say, 'That's Daddy's flag.' That's what they call it. They've seen it at the Olympic Games, or they've seen me carry it. That's the country that gave us opportunity. That's the United States flag."[39]

Participation in endurance sports is a finicky endeavor. Athletes want to control their destiny, control the words others may say about them, control the races of the people around them, and control just about everything. But so much of endurance sports is not truly within our control.

Take the weather. Running a marathon in eighty degrees is deemed too hot, as evidenced by the cessation of the 2007 Chicago Marathon four hours into the race due to extreme heat. The 2011 Los Angeles Marathon was marred by torrential rain and the mercury barely hit fifty; I was there, so I can attest to the fact that it was much too cold. The margin for success, when it comes to temperature, is actually fairly narrow. The problem is that we cannot control the weather. Sure, we can opt out of races that historically have conditions not amenable to our personal temperature window, but oftentimes, Mother Nature does not cooperate, letting loose a maelstrom that can undo anybody's day.

Since there is so much that is not under our control, the best way to cope is to seize control of the things you can regulate, thereby limiting your ability to use the excuse that something was out of your control as a means of self-handicapping.

## Training

You cannot control how your races will turn out, but you can control your level of fitness at the starting line. Train with purpose and consistency to enhance the odds that your race will turn out favorably. A well-laid-out schedule will better prepare you than a day-by-day decision-making process.

## Weather

Be prepared. If you are planning to race in a warmer climate, keep in mind how long it takes you to acclimate to the heat. Sometimes, it can take a few races or hard training workouts in the heat in order to race well when it's hot. Give yourself enough time to get used to the hotter conditions, whether it's early or late season. This same premise goes for the cold: don't plan to use a historically cold race as your Ironman qualifying event if you don't race well with the shivers. Always have a multitude of clothing options when going to a race to accommodate drastic changes in temperature.

## Other competitors

It is always a good idea to peruse the results of races to size up your competition. However, predicating your race on how someone else fares is a disappointment waiting to happen. There are no easy age groups, and at almost every race there is an age group outlier, that one person who just smashes the rest of the field. If you had your best day possible, yet you were still beat, there just isn't anything you can do about it. In addition, if your competitors are cheating in some manner, this, too, is not within your control; let it go.

## Equipment

If your equipment fails, or you forget to bring an important item to a race, you are doomed. Certainly, flat tires are an unavoidable byproduct of riding on debris-filled roads, but there are many things that are controllable.

+ Get your bike tuned and replace any old, creaky, rusty parts.
+ Make a list for your transition/race bag and make sure you have everything you need for it.
+ Check that your power meter has enough battery life.
+ Test out your race kit and wetsuit.
+ Ensure that your racing shoes are in good condition.
+ Make sure your goggles don't leak and you have the proper lens shade for the light conditions.

The two things that you have the most control over? Your ability to race hard and have fun.

## Get off the bandwagon

Are you doing races because you want to or because you think you should be doing them? I ask this because year after year, in spite of the time commitments, financial burden, and physical and emotional toll, athletes clamor to sign up for Ironman races or ultra-marathons or other ultra-endurance events that seemingly do not really fit into their athletic circumstances.

A recent conversation with an athlete I coach centered on this very issue. She raced Ironman every year for five years. Suddenly, work obligations would not allow her the time to train the same number of hours and so she questioned her ability to appropriately train for Ironman. I offered her a very radical suggestion: take a year off from Ironman and focus on the other distances. She was incredulous at the very notion, as she had not thought about not doing Ironman. When we talked it through, though, she became excited at the prospect of doing shorter races and honing her speed.

My last Ironman was in 2008. My gut shut down yet again, rendering me dizzy, depleted, and unable to finish the race. I decided that it would be my last Ironman. It seemed silly to continually damage my body doing a distance it seemingly rejected, especially with so many other racing options.

Triathlon is very Ironman-centric and I, too, was heavily on the bandwagon. I could not imagine planning an Ironman-less season. I anticipated that my training and racing would be unfulfilling in some way, that I would be less of a triathlete. I could not have been more wrong.

My training evolved to fit my racing goals. I substituted much of the long-distance training for shorter and more intense workouts. I began to really enjoy the new training format. I did not miss Ironman after all. I originally thought I could not be satisfied without that "smug" feeling of contented exhaustion from training all day. But I was.

I raced my last triathlon in August of 2010 and I have not ridden my bike for almost as long. I have again been surprised that after the initial feeling of loss, I am not discontented. Just as the transition out of the Ironman realm was relatively seamless, so has been my transition to running.

I realized that I don't need to log the endless training hours to quell my athletic "fix." I need to have concrete training and racing goals, and if those are met (or almost met), I am satisfied. I am still able to push myself in training and see the fruits of my labor on the race course.

I believe that endurance athletes have trouble moving away from the "crazy" event of their sport, even if their bodies are shattered or their personal lives are unable to handle the strain. This is because there is a belief that the high from training for that insanity and the accolades from those around them cannot be replicated by training for other, shorter events. Or, there is a fear that training fewer hours will result in being less fit. Perhaps there is a sense that anything less than something crazy is unsatisfactory, since there is a certain pride in telling others that you have finished a gazillion Ironman races.

Get off the bandwagon. Recharge your batteries. Get faster. Experiment with other races. Change up your training. Work on your weaknesses. Crazy events will still be there when you are ready to revisit the distance, only this time you will be renewed, faster, and raring to go.

## Blame and honesty

Oftentimes, when an athlete fails to reach his or her goals, the first line of defense is to blame the coach. "My coach overtrained me." "My coach did not properly prepare me." "My coach never communicated with me." "My coach forgot to give me workouts on a regular basis." "My coach never took into account my work commitments." "I got injured because my coach pushed me too hard." "My coach doesn't really like me." I have heard every single one of those statements uttered at one time or another by disgruntled athletes. My reply to them: "Why didn't you let your coach know you were unhappy with your interactions and the training situation?"

I am a huge advocate of formal coaching for athletes. This advocacy arises from fifteen years of coaching athletes and nearly forty years of being coached. Athletes are highly subjective when it comes to themselves and far too critical of their shortcomings. Even extremely motivated athletes need accountability. But athletes cannot put their entire fate into the hands of another person. Hiring a coach does not give an athlete license to shut off their brain and blindly follow instructions. Coaching should be a dialogue based on trust and openness. A coach does not and cannot know what is happening inside their athlete's mind and body unless the athlete tells them. Athletes need to take responsibility for their athletic well-being rather than blaming someone else, such as their coach, for lack of enjoyment in training, failure to meet goals, or injuries.

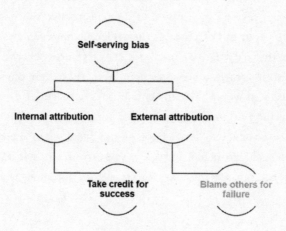

The tendency for an athlete to blame others for failure is called the self-serving bias. The self-serving bias is an interesting dichotomy whereby an athlete has a tendency to take responsibility for desirable outcomes (internal attribution), such as boasting about all the hard work that went into a personal best time in a race, and externalizing responsibility (external attribution) for undesirable outcomes, such as attributing a mediocre performance to poor coaching.[40]

Much like self-handicapping, the self-serving bias is a means of deflecting responsibility for lack of success. In essence, self-handicapping (i.e., making excuses) and self-serving bias (i.e., placing blame) are intertwined; the Siamese twins of bad behavior, because blaming others for failure is essentially providing an excuse.

Self-serving bias attributions change among athletes, and even within an individual athlete, depending on the level of success. Elite runners were queried about their causal attributions for the most successful and least successful races of their competitive career. The results showed that the same athletes rated their best performance as due to their own volition (themselves) and their worst performance due to some circumstance outside of their control (others).[41]

The self-serving bias operates as a protective mechanism for an athlete's ego, and oftentimes the athlete is not even aware of the behavior. In particular, when an athlete attributes success to internal causes, it creates a sense of control in that their physical and mental prowess were the main contributors to success.[42] In contrast, not accepting responsibility for a poor performance and putting the onus on a coach, bad luck, poor advice from team members, or other external factors helps preserve self-esteem and self-image.[43] In addition, the self-serving bias can arise from outcomes that do not meet expectations; another reason why creating realistic goals is important.

Simon Lessing expressed his thoughts on the subject: "[Athletes] are very quick to blame the people around them. And they're not prepared to take the responsibility and look at potentially the mistakes that they have made."[44] Athletes need to find ways to give others credit for success and accept responsibility for failure by honestly assessing each situation. Nobody is successful without the support of others and it is unfair to place the burden of failure on the shoulders of the very people who are trying to be helpful.

Next time you fail to reach your goal, ask yourself this: "What could I have done better?" and not "Who can I blame?"

## Nurturing the flame

You never thought this day would come. You couldn't wait to train. You promised yourself you wouldn't miss any workouts. You would race to your capacity. This would be the breakthrough year. Then, one day, you woke up dreading your morning workout. It filtered into the next workout and the next, and soon, you realized you were burnt out. You lost your love for the sport; amotivation has become the foundation of your motivation pyramid.

How did this occur? Is it just a midseason lull? Will it last the rest of the year? Will it creep into next year?

Endurance athletes are creatures of habit. Our weekly schedules rarely vary. Our training routes are always the same. Our training partners seldom change. We stick with the same coach. It is not surprising that boredom or burnout can occur. We race until we cannot race anymore.

Caroline Steffen, a two-time triathlon World Champion, switched coaches during the height of her career. Usually it takes a slump to make such a drastic change to a training regimen. Caroline switched because she was no longer finding enjoyment in the sport. "First of all, he [her new coach] gave me that joy back, doing what I am doing. I lost that a little bit back in the day...I needed change, I needed something new...He gave me that love for the triathlon sport back. That was a really important part to me. Just to enjoy myself again, training and racing...I love it...I like to win, that's why I am doing the sport."[45] This coaching change bolstered her motivation and rejuvenated her triathlon career.

In addition to the characteristic mechanisms that cause burnout, there has been a shift whereby there is no real off-season, with a plethora of races available all year long. When I first started racing triathlons, for example, the U.S. season kicked off with the St. Anthony's Triathlon in late April and concluded with the Hawaii Ironman in October.

Then I started racing ITU, and the season started a little earlier. I would often travel to Central America to get a jump start on fitness. Suddenly, races started dotting the calendar very early in the year— new races beckoning with Kona slots and midwinter respites from the cold. Races were then slotted into the calendar post-Kona, a chance to milk a season of training and perhaps qualify for Kona almost a year in advance. One could race virtually all twelve months without leaving the northern hemisphere, something unheard of only a few years ago. Add in other endurance events, such as running races, Gran Fondo endurance bike events, and open water swims, and one can race virtually every weekend.

In the past, the shorter racing season lent itself to a natural off-season: a time to rest and restore, embark on other activities, rectify weaknesses, spend time with family, or catch up at work. The winter was meant for base training, sitting on the couch, or snow sports. Without the lure of races in February, there was no need to get in shape quickly.

Now, athletes are signing up for races in what was once considered the off-season, requiring a healthy dose of training early or late in the year (much of it, perhaps, indoors).

I am not saying I am opposed to a longer season. I am not. The multitude of racing options available are astounding and showcase the incredible growth of endurance sports, a somewhat paradoxical notion when taking into consideration the simultaneous proliferation of obesity. I fear, however, that without careful planning, the risk of burnout (or illness or injury) is increased significantly. I am not just talking about seasonal afflictions. I am also referring to career-ending setbacks.

The continued cycle of racing almost year-round, in combination with the typical features of burnout, will eventually take a mental and physical toll and may even cause overtraining syndrome or chronic fatigue. With the next race on the horizon, there will be less time to take care of muscle imbalances and nagging pre-injuries. A year-round dose of extremely early mornings of training will eventually render an athlete weary and ready to toss out the alarm clock. The patterns of routine can become tortuous. Here are ways to nurture the flame:

*Plan your season(s) carefully.* If you are racing early in the season and have a key race late in the season, take some downtime in the middle of the season. This will keep you fresh and rejuvenated. Likewise, it is unwise to race a long schedule year after year. Alternate a long racing season with a shorter racing season. This will allow you to race happy and healthy for a longer period of time and prevent feelings of burnout. Go ahead. Allow yourself some time to be lazy. You deserve it.

*Make your training and racing social.* Plan a meal to coincide with your workout. Endurance athletes are notorious eaters, so use it to your advantage! Meet for your weekly ride at a local coffee shop or breakfast joint and stay for a few minutes afterward to catch up with your buddies. Call a friend you haven't seen in a while and plan a run or ride. With busy schedules it is often difficult to coordinate workout times. It will keep you fresh and the conversation will make the workout flow more quickly. Travel to races with friends. Whether it is a long trip in the car or a flight across the country, traveling with a buddy is always more fun.

*Find new routes.* When I train on the same roads too often, monotony settles in. Doing a familiar route backward sheds a new perspective onto the surroundings. You will be surprised at how different a road looks from the opposite direction. You will notice houses, different trees, and new potholes to avoid. Drive somewhere to ride or run. Grab a map, compass, or GPS and play Magellan. Starting a workout in a new location adds variety to your training, and gives you the opportunity to explore your city. Or, you can use sites like Strava and Mapmyride to find a new route.

*Run or ride on trails.* Running on the softer surface helps prevent injuries and training in the woods can be very peaceful. As an added bonus, you don't have to worry about road rage.

*Attend camps.* Camps are a great way to meet new people with comparable goals, polish up on techniques, pick up new tips, and train in a different environment.

*Enter a single-sport event.* If you are a multisport athlete, try your hand at a single-sport event. Running races are cheaper and logistically easier than triathlons. They are fun, too! Swim in a masters meet or open-water swim. These events are the perfect way to gauge your swimming improvement. Complete an organized bike ride, such as a 100 miler. This is a golden opportunity to test your endurance. It does not have to be competitive, especially if this is your first time. This is also great for Ironman preparation.

*Leave your gadgets at home.* We are often transfixed on our power and pace. Quit staring at the computer and enjoy your surroundings. Ride, run, and swim without any objective other than enjoying the workouts. Not every session has to be monitored carefully.

*Make time for non-athletic activities* (even if it means taking some time off). It is really easy to get caught up in the training/racing cycle and neglect other pastimes. Some suggestions: go see a movie, read the book that has been collecting dust on your shelf, rent a video, learn to cook, or go to a tourist attraction in your town. Engaging in other activities will keep you fresh and eager to start another day.

*Work on your technique.* Your endurance endeavors will feel so much better if you execute your activities with proper and efficient technique. Pain with activity oftentimes occurs due to poor biomechanics. I have reviewed hundreds of swim, run, and bike videos from athletes complaining of pain, achiness, or lack of power. Upon analyzing the videos, much of the time the athlete's complaint results from poor technique caused by muscle imbalance and/or tightness. Taking some time to rectify the problems will make you enjoy your sport even more.

*Get unfit to get fit.* I am offering you a key piece of wisdom. Get a pencil and paper and write this down: *You cannot be in top fitness all year.* Should I repeat that? *You cannot be in top fitness all year.* It's true. The fitter you are, the harder it is to maintain that fitness. You must allow yourself, not only between seasons but within a season, a period of time to rest.

## 10 Tips for an Ownership Mental Makeover

- Be an intrinsically motivated athlete—focus on satisfaction and pleasure derived from endurance sports rather than external rewards.
- Maintain low levels of self-handicapping. Fewer excuses can lead to better performances.
- Positive self-affirmations can help assuage self-handicapping. Repeat nice things about yourself to yourself.
- Personal standards perfectionism is a self-oriented striving for perfection and can be positively related to performance.
- Keep evaluative concerns perfectionism—the type of perfectionism where you are worried about how others view your performance—at bay because it can be harmful to success.
- Integrity is more important than performance. Act with dignity and honor, and do not cheat.
- Learn to focus on the things you can control and not to ruminate on those things beyond your control.
- Pick and choose your training and racing based on what makes you happy and will lead to success and not because "everyone else is doing it."

- Be introspective about your success and failure. Blaming others is generally not the answer, nor is it purposeful in making modifications to increase the chance for success in the future.
- If your motivation is starting to wane, it is time to make some changes to rekindle the fire.

# 5

# Intention

**After winning my** age group and placing in the top ten overall at the 1997 Hawaii Ironman, I made the decision to turn my passion into a profession. I turned pro. In hindsight, the decision was a no-brainer, but at the time, I vacillated because of my commitment to graduate school. Once I made the choice to race professionally, it was my intention to focus on Ironman racing rather than the shorter Olympic distance. My heart was with the longer distance. When I was putting together my race schedule in 1998, there was a problem with that plan, though: at that time, there were only a few long-distance events in North America (my travel time was limited by my graduate school obligations), but there was a prolific short-course racing scene. Even with the obvious shortcoming in the number of long-distance races, I stubbornly refused to change my focus. I wanted to become a long-course specialist.

I made my professional debut at the St. Anthony's Triathlon, an Olympic distance non-drafting race, where I placed fifth. I amassed a few other top-five results in the Olympic distance over the summer, but

I hit the big-time when I won the Mrs. T's Chicago Triathlon in late August. My intention changed mostly due to both circumstances and a realization of the big picture. I decided that I had the prowess for success in short-course racing, so I switched my focus to qualifying for the Olympics. Even though I did not give up on Ironman altogether, my new intention of Olympic qualification dictated my training and racing for the next several years.

## Intention-behavior relationship

The Theory of Planned Behavior states that the determinant of behavior is a person's intention to perform the behavior.[1] That theory is almost so simplistic it is hard to believe it is even a theory. Intention is comprised of three constructs: (1) attitude toward the behavior, (2) perception of the amount of control over the behavior, and (3) perception of the wishes of important others. A high positive association exists between these three dimensions and exercise intention.[2] Furthermore, when it comes to exercise, it has been proposed that there is a two-step approach to intention: action planning (formulation of the plan) and action control (actual behavior).[3] This applies to many of the topics covered in this book, with goal setting, racing, and team building, for example, falling under the auspices of action planning and action control. Such is the importance of intentions, Olympian and World Champion Gwen Jorgensen uses the very word as a motivator: "Intent and focus are always two words I write down before a race. They're highlighted and circled."[4] Gwen's focus led her to the top step of the podium at the 2016 Rio Olympics when she fulfilled her athletic potential by winning the first gold medal in triathlon for the U.S.

Interestingly, there is an intention-behavior gap whereby intenders fail to act on their intentions.[5] Think about all of the people with New Year's resolutions who crowd your gym for six weeks and then never come back. I hear athletes bemoan that their intention to do strength training was shelved by lack of time or desire. Even on race day, athletes fail to adhere to their intended race plan, only to miss their goal due to their foolhardiness.

Most of the studies on the intention-behavior relationship in exercise are about developing exercise habits; that is, do people who intend to exercise *actually* do it? Those of you reading this book are beyond the notion of creating exercise habits; however, we can take these theories and apply them to endurance sports and the pursuit of excellence. For example, it turns out intention is not enough when it comes to exercise behavior, and that there are goal intentions ("I intend to train for an Ironman") and implementation intentions ("I am going to ride long this weekend in preparation for an Ironman").[6] Every single day, endurance athletes are confronted with the intention-behavior duality, making decisions based on life circumstances.

As you can see, intention and behavior are intricately enmeshed, and that intention alone is not enough for success.

## Purpose

Do you train to race? Or, do you race to train? These are very different approaches to training and racing and there is no right or wrong answer, but it all comes down to intention. At the outset, the motivations for each seem similar, but I believe there is an inherent difference, and making the distinction will dictate your training and racing schedule.

### Training to race

I have been a competitive athlete for almost four decades. That is a really long time. My early life revolved around achieving time standards for various swim meets such as junior nationals, senior nationals, and the Olympic Trials. My coaches produced teams whose sole focus was to race, and all of our training was centered on accomplishing whatever goals we set out for ourselves. Certainly, we swam until our arms were ready to fall off, but the ultimate prize was time improvements at the swim meets.

It is tough to break habits, and as I morphed into a triathlete and now a runner, my training is still centered on achieving racing goals. Don't get me wrong, I love to train. Remember those EFG points from chapter 1? I rack them up on a daily basis with my training. But ultimately, I love racing more and my intention is to set personal records in races, thus the majority of my training is geared toward that end. My training is systematic and well thought out months in advance with an eye on whatever races are on the horizon. I am extremely competitive and I like to throw down on the race course. Even after so many years, I am disappointed when I don't meet my goals and I go back to the training to do better the next time.

## Racing to train

In 2012, I was at a running race in Denver. At the finish line, I spoke with a competitor. This was our conversation:

> RUNNER GUY: I have not missed a day of running since November of 2009!
>
> JZ: Really? I am not impressed. In fact, I think that is stupid.
>
> RUNNER GUY: Well, I have run three half marathons and two marathons this year and I even PR'ed the marathon.
>
> JZ: Maybe you would have gone even faster had you taken a day off. I really do not understand this whole business of streaking.
>
> RUNNER GUY: I have it all worked out. Have you heard about the one-day-hard, three-day-easy plan? That's what I do.

I later apologized to Runner guy for my unabashed candor (sometimes words just pop out of my mouth and I have no control). Clearly, though, this person races to train. After I thought about our brief exchange, I realized that his intention, while not congruent with my own, is really just fine. Training is his passion and racing is really secondary.

Over the years, I have encountered athletes who race to train. Their training strategy is very different from those who train to race. The workouts tend to be more haphazard without clear goals. Often, the workouts are more social or tend to be more racelike. Easy rides turn into long rides. Days off turn into a smash-fest with the group. It is true that sometimes race goals are achieved. However, race goals are also missed, very often because the training was not tailored to the racing.

Each athlete has their own intentions, but if it is done with enthusiasm and enjoyment that is what truly matters.

## Patience (or lack of it)

As a coach, I am privy to the diverse outlooks of my athletes, imparting a perspective on training and racing very different from my own. Despite their varying ages, abilities, goals, and time in the sport, they all have two things in common: lack of patience and short-term memory loss.

### Impatience

There are two parts to the impatience. The first is a question I get asked a lot during the winter months: "Why can't I do more?" I gently explain that in January and February one cannot and should not train as much as during the summer. Most of the important races are later in the year and it is hard to stay fresh for those races if the training load is too high too early. Winter offers a natural break in the training cycle with unpredictable weather and less daylight. A progression needs to occur so the body adapts, does not break down, and absorbs the training load. If the intention is to be fast in August, then the season should be built around that goal, and hammering out long rides in January is not wise.

The second part to the impatience is this statement: "I want to get faster. Now." Athletes should have the intention of getting faster; indeed, that is the main objective for so many of us. However, getting faster requires time and patience. Our desire for success and improvement is what compels us to keep training year after year. We set goals for ourselves, giving us a very good idea of where we would like to be. But, it does not, should not, and cannot happen overnight.

Making improvements in sports must be approached systematically. Running and swimming training paces or the proper number of watts to generate on the bike must be advanced in a manner that keeps an athlete from getting injured or overtrained. Pushing the limits week after week and setting PRs in training on a regular basis is not necessarily ideal and is not always compatible with the intentions we set for ourselves. I know when a top athlete may be headed for destruction when I hear them say, "I just put in the best training of my life." Not infrequently, they are injured the next day.

Those who make slow and steady improvements in training are generally the athletes that are able to show up on race day. It is not about crushing it, hammering, or flogging oneself on a daily basis. You should always have a little left because it is never about any single workout; it is about consistency over the long haul. Getting greedy in training is a recipe for disaster.

Now, I am not saying that athletes shouldn't push themselves or try to find their limits. I regularly test my athletes by giving them workouts that are on the edge of what they are capable of handling. I share their enthusiasm when they accomplish that workout. What I am saying is that those types of workouts cannot occur all the time. Getting faster is not something that happens "now."

I had a very interesting conversation with an athlete. He made an astute observation, a concept that I try to impress upon my mentees, but often is ignored or forgotten. He said, "It seems that triathlon rewards those that wait. A lot of guys I know have made really big gains over the last five years. What are your thoughts?" I thought: *Okay, he gets it.*

Athletes want to take shortcuts. There is the faulty notion that training more or harder will get one to their goal more quickly. This is true until an injury surfaces or symptoms of overtraining crop up. How about the training monsters who kill it during workouts yet fail to produce on race day? Why does this happen? Because the body only has a finite ability to produce and to suffer. Trying to bypass the laws of triathlon and endurance sports, in general, will not work.

Sarah True pointed this out in an interview after her third-place finish at the 2015 ITU World Championships: "You have to realize [that] for most people, it takes putting in hard, consistent work to see payoff. And that's the beauty of endurance sport. You can't look at the outliers. . . . But take a page from my book—I'm in my thirties and it's taken me a long time to be a consistent performer. I had some really bad years. Really bad years! And that's whether you're an amateur or aspiring Olympian—endurance sport is great in that way. You just have to do that work, stay healthy, and put the time in and you will improve."[7]

## Flexibility

Are you flexible? I don't mean in the bendy, Cirque du Soleil way. I refer to flexibility with your training. As an age-group swimmer, my coach was about as flexible as titanium wrapped in tungsten. If any of us had to miss a workout, to take the SAT, for example, our coach's face would turn red and the vein in his forehead would get all big and scary. His rigidity stayed with me decades after I left his tutelage and rendered me a slave to whatever workout I had on my schedule. My intention was to do whatever was planned for the week, no matter what.

Being beholden to a schedule can be a difficult proposition. On the one hand, having a plan makes training more effective. On the other hand, life frequently gets in the way of training and a lack of flexibility makes dealing with unalterable situations even more frustrating. Shuffling around workouts is often necessary and a missed workout is commonly unavoidable. A younger me would fret endlessly about missed or altered workouts. I would go into a shame and guilt spiral, certain that my goals would vanish into thin air, my intention ruined. Yes, my tyrannical swim coach instilled a phenomenal work ethic, but with that came some serious baggage.

One of the benefits of being a "mature" (okay, older) athlete is that I have learned how to be more flexible with my training. Don't laugh. It's true. My rigidity was thrown out the window once I had my bike accident. I was no longer beholden to a schedule, I couldn't be, as my body did not care what was planned training-wise. Pain was my guide on all workouts, dictating whether an interval session turned into an easy run or an easy run turned into a walk. Even though I still had a weekly schedule provided by my running coach, Darren De Reuck, I knew that I wouldn't really know what my body would allow until I woke up in the morning.

On one particular evening, I had a conversation with my father. I had just gone through a pain flare-up that was almost incapacitating, and I told him that the next morning I would be running on the track. He was aghast at that notion. I explained to him, "I reserve the right to be optimistic." That outlook propelled me to some astonishing work-outs when the previous day I could barely walk. Part of flexibility is knowing that things can change as quickly as the weather.

Flexibility in training takes on many forms. It may be a matter of deciding that a twenty-minute run is better than nothing at all or picking just one of the two proscribed workouts on a busy day. Sometimes it is realizing that if you cut the warm-up and warm-down short you will have just enough time to get in the intervals. Some days it may mean missing training altogether. Learning to be flexible does not equate to weakness. On the contrary, a flexible athlete will be happier and better adjusted.

## Picking and choosing your moments

In 2011, I ran the Los Angeles marathon seeking an Olympic Trials qualifying time of 2:46:00. Race day was chilly at fifty degrees, made worse by the torrential rain that soaked us all day and caused shin-deep puddles on the race course. It was my first open marathon in a decade, but I still remembered how to push the limits. Even though the weather was rotten, I ran hard until my legs just got so cold and tight they slowed down no matter how much I cajoled them. I crossed the finish line, shivering and bright red from windburn. I missed the time standard by two minutes, but I was still pleased with the effort.

Ten days after the Los Angeles marathon, I was still sore and tired. That was abnormal since I usually shed that type of soreness within a few days. Before you jump to the conclusion that age wore me down, hear me out on another explanation. I believe my post-race torpor stemmed from my actions on the race course: I went to the well.

Going to the well, entering the pain cave, giving it your all. These expressions represent the single notion of leaving a part of yourself on the playing field. It means that, regardless of the outcome, an athlete pushed through pain and self-doubt to cross the finish line, usually hobbled and incoherent. Of course, our intention is always to finish the races we start, but sometimes getting to the finish line requires a higher level of effort than others.

One can go to the well under any number of circumstances: bonking (that dreaded feeling of running out of energy from too few calories), too hot, too cold, undertrained, overtrained, started too hard, cramping, pushing for a PR, trying for the win, aiming for a Kona slot. You know you have been there if you started bargaining with God or whatever deity you believe in and you promise yourself that this is the last time you will ever do this (the irony, of course is that time heals all wounds and we all head right back for the starting line just knowing it will be different next time). Yes, this is the miserable feeling of pushing through when your body just wants to collapse.

In my own career, I have been back and forth to the well, withdrawing a piece of my soul each time. Thank goodness, my well seems deep and it has been spread out over many years. I have been to the well during Ironman on plenty of occasions, but I have also visited it on short races when the intensity and the weather have been steaming hot.

One never forgets their first trip to the well. Mine occurred during my first half Ironman race in 1994, the Muncie Endurathon. A combination of factors led to my demise on the race course. I was a newbie trying out a trick usually reserved for veterans, by doing a "double"; I'd raced an Olympic distance race the weekend before the half Ironman. I subsequently contracted a sinus infection from the nasty water. Additionally, I was grossly underprepared for such a long race. Race day was hot enough to melt the pavement and the soles of my shoes. I was so tired entering T2, I wanted to nap underneath the tree outside transition rather than run 13.1 miles. I forced myself out onto the course and trudged through the sauna, walking and running until I finally finished. I was bonked, dehydrated, and miserable. When my name was called at the awards ceremony to claim a Kona slot I ran hard in the other direction and let someone else suffer in Hawaii.

Going to the well is usually unplanned. Of course, we all believe that we can "go there" at any race. But most races do not necessitate such drastic measures. Most of the time, you can race hard and achieve your goals with some discomfort, but without extreme suffering. Going to the well takes a physical and mental toll. Use your trips to the well wisely, under circumstances that really count. One cannot make multiple trips to the well in a season.

And that brings me back to the Los Angeles marathon. The driving rain and cold temperatures affected me badly. I became disoriented during the race and my quads were burning. Yet, I pushed through. I went to the well. Interestingly, I did not even realize I was going to the well while I was racing. My brain had shut off and I was running on autopilot. It wasn't until hours later, when the shivering finally subsided, that I realized I'd used up a trip to the well.

Next time you approach the well, ask yourself, "Is it worth it today?"

## Consistency over time

Even though the weekly grind can get tedious, that is what will get you to your goals. The one-off amazing workout is just that—a one-off. It is the good workouts day in and day out that will take you to the next level. I see workout heroes all the time—they try to PR their runs, hit new wattage highs every week. These are the athletes that always fall short of their racing goals. It is not physically possible to PR in training all the time and then go to a race and PR. I know that seems counterintuitive. How can that be, you ask? During training, you need to work hard, and occasionally you will have a breakthrough workout. Most of the time, though, during training you will see small incremental changes, or maybe even none at all. But if you have nailed your times or watts day after day, week after week, you will build confidence, fitness, resiliency, and an ability to push yourself to the next level on race day. Don't be a workout hero, be a race hero! Unless, of course, you race to train, and then being a workout hero is really the endgame.

Your intention should be to maintain consistency over time. It sounds obvious and simple. But I still see people ignoring this simple principle all the time. There are the "weekend warriors" that train HARD all weekend and spend the rest of the week recovering. There are the "cyclers" who train HARD for a few weeks and then limp into a rest week or two.

Improvements come from training day in and day out, week after week. No single workout can make you, but it can break you. It is the conglomeration of workouts over time that will propel you to success.

## Quantity or quality?

This is not a book about training, but I would be remiss to skip over one of the big training debates: quantity vs. quality. Is it more beneficial to log lots of hours or to do less and go harder? I don't think that this is a case of either-or. The best training methodology is one that, first and foremost, is fun for you and, secondly, provides a good mix of fast and slow, long and short.

Studies have shown that short bouts of high intensity can increase your $VO_2$ max quickly and efficiently. What is $VO_2$ max, you ask? It is the maximum volume of oxygen that an athlete can use, and it is a predictor of performance, whereby athletes with a higher $VO_2$ max tend to be faster. It turns out that the highest recorded $VO_2$ max values come from cyclists and cross-country skiers, with little-known Norwegian Oskar Svendsen topping the list at 97.5. Greg LeMond, winner of the Tour de France, registered 92.5; Killian Jornet, a top ultramarathoner measured 89.5. Women have a lower $VO_2$ max than men, with Joan Benoit, winner of the 1984 Olympic marathon, recording 78.6.[8] Comparatively, the average $VO_2$ max for a sedentary female is 33 and 42 for men. Those of us who exercise regularly probably fall somewhere in between the sedentary and the elite.

Athletes tend to neglect doing very high-intensity intervals, the manner in which $VO_2$ max is trained. This is a mistake, since $VO_2$ max decreases about 10 percent for each decade past thirty and 15 percent by decade after age seventy.[9] This is significant because $VO_2$ max has been shown as the best predictor of age-related changes in performance in masters athletes.[10] And, interestingly, this drop in $VO_2$ max is even higher in well-trained individuals compared to sedentary individuals, probably due to their higher baseline level.[11] The cause for the reduction in $VO_2$ max in older athletes is not completely understood. Some have suggested that it is due to decreased exercise training stimulus (i.e., the duration, intensity, and frequency of training are reduced over time). Another benefit to increasing (or maintaining) your $VO_2$ max that is completely unrelated to improvement in sport, is that it also bestows cognitive gains.[12] That's right: the exercise you are probably doing right now is not only helping you stay fit and fast, but also smart.

Since there are decreases in $VO_2$ max over time, it would seem that lactate threshold (LT) would follow a similar pattern. Lactate threshold is the exercise intensity at which lactate starts to accumulate in the bloodstream, or simply, it is what you can hold for about an hour. LT does not change in the same manner as $VO_2$ max, and may in fact, increase in some older athletes. Paradoxically, even though there are increases in LT in older athletes, these increases did not predict performance. This differs from younger athletes whose LT is a very good indicator of performance.[13]

Over the years of coaching, I developed the notion that in order to achieve success, whether it is a 5 km or a marathon or an Olympic distance triathlon or an Ironman, an athlete must train both their aerobic and anaerobic energy systems as well as race-specific paces. This notion has become the philosophy of my coaching company Race Ready Coaching.

It's physiological; if you don't train it, you lose it. If you stop training your top end altogether, it will diminish, which in turn will have an effect on your lactate threshold and aerobic system. Even in an Ironman, athletes push their top end from 2 to 6 percent of their race, but since many don't train it, their power drops late in the bike and their run ultimately suffers. If you don't do sprints in the pool, you will not be prepared for the first 400 meters of your triathlon.

In addition, if you always train at a relatively strong intensity, you will not be able to call upon your top end when you need it because training too hard can leave you flat and perpetually tired. Think about how hard you have to push when you make a pass on the bike during a race, or how much your quads burn coming out of a corner; if you never train for those circumstances, your legs will rebel during the race.

If your intention is to become a well-trained athlete, train all of your energy systems, no matter your distance.

## Active recovery vs. passive recovery—and how they're both instrumental to the champion athlete's success

Remember those EFG points from chapter 1? A day off means no EFG points. No EFG points means I get cranky. Even though I am not a fan of days off, I realize their importance in a training cycle. Recovering properly permits all of the training to take hold, allowing the body to absorb the physiological effects of the hard work and alleviate the psychological toll of the extreme focus. But, which is better, a complete day off (passive recovery) or light exercise (active recovery)? Neither. Both types of recovery are necessary in a training schedule and augment your intention for health and fitness.

The notion of recovery is complex. Athletes differ in their response to training stress and fatigue levels, as well as dehydration levels, glycogen synthesis, and inflammatory response; additionally, the cellular and systemic demands of training affect muscle function and the rate at which these occur varies greatly between individuals.[14] I am sure most of you have experienced delayed onset muscle soreness (DOMS), that horrible heavy and sore leg feeling after a very hard race, a lot of downhill running, or a tough workout. Coming back too soon from DOMS can delay recovery for many weeks. Restoring muscle glycogen through carbohydrate intake is imperative; ingesting 1.2–1.5 grams of carbohydrate per kilogram (2.2 pounds) of body weight within two hours after exercise can aid in restoring muscle glycogen within twenty-four hours.[15] A banana, smoothie, energy bar, or performance drink are excellent ways to refuel quickly.

One underlying commonality is clear, though: all athletes need some form of recovery in order to perform their best. Recovery enables athletes to mitigate the effects of muscular damage and fatigue, central fatigue (fatigue caused by changes in the central nervous system), and neural fatigue (diminished firing of motor neurons).[16] Left unchecked, these types of fatigue can lead to the overtraining syndrome. Overtraining syndrome, while not entirely understood, does require a bunch of time off, which is much worse than the time off needed for regular ol' recovery.

**Active recovery.** A nice, easy spin on your bike, a slow jog, easy swimming, a walk, and yoga are all forms of active recovery. You are still moving your body, but at a low intensity and for a short duration. There is no evidence to show that active recovery is better or worse than a complete day off.[17] Engaging in active recovery is a personal choice based on how your body handles continuous training and your discipline to really go easy.

In the summertime, Boulder is a popular training ground for the Japanese national running team. The runners stay in my neighborhood, so I see them on a regular basis. I've witnessed their interval sessions, where they run in a tight pack, and I can see the effort on their faces and the sheer speed at which they are able to run. I've also observed their easy runs—they run alone, and they run slow. Really slow. Slower than you can imagine. Women who run a sub-2:30 marathon often do their easy runs at a pace that looks barely more than a walk. They take their active recovery seriously.

Triathletes, on the other hand, are notorious for doing their recovery too hard. The outlook, perhaps, is one where the number of hours spent on each individual sport is much lower than their single-sport counterparts, giving a sense of urgency to every workout. This is a detrimental mindset, because the number of overall hours is much higher than for single-sport athletes. Active recovery must be executed correctly, and if you cannot hold yourself back, then you are better off just taking the day off.

**Passive recovery.** *"Why stand when you can sit; why sit when you can lie down?"* This saying is a mainstay in the world of professional cycling. They take passive recovery to the next level. Even for athletes who prefer some movement to none, a complete day off is necessary. Passive recovery has several benefits, including allowing more time for sleep, a chance to efficiently replenish glycogen stores, and it leaves time for massage or other therapeutic modalities. A complete day off can also restore focus, and getting a little antsy will make the next training day feel even better.

In my family we call those days where you are so tired you cannot get out of bed "dead body syndrome." Preemptive avoidance of dead body syndrome by strategically adding days off to your training schedule is more effective than damage-control mode whereby a single day off may not even ameliorate the situation. Endurance athletes fear that a day off will somehow cause a loss of fitness. This couldn't be further from the truth, though. A day off enhances fitness and rebuilds vitality.

## Beyond training: Doing the little things

Your intention should be to maintain health throughout the year. As the season progresses, it is easy to get caught up in the training and not do the right things for recovery. Active and passive recovery are just a small part of the recovery equation. Other means of recovery exist that work harmoniously with active or passive recovery.

Myriad recovery modalities exist: massage, chiropractic care, stretching, ice baths and other cold therapies, compression gear, foam rollers, and electrostimulation, to name a few.[18] Find the one(s) that work for you with some experimentation. Certainly, research has not always backed up the efficacy of some of these modalities, but if they work for you, who cares? Science is not perfect and cannot always measure individual differences.

Compression garments, for example, have shown mixed results in alleviating muscle soreness as measured by blood lactate levels, during and after exercise.[19] My personal experience, though, is that compression socks rock; I wear them during hard runs, long runs, and for recovery due to perpetual soreness in my calves from my forefoot strike. The difference in my perceived soreness with the compression socks compared to without the socks is undeniable.

I detest ice baths, mostly because I detest being cold. In Boulder, it is customary during the summer months, when the training level is usually the highest, to soak in the ice-cold Boulder Creek. Even on a hot summer day when the thermometer topped out at ninety-five degrees, I would shiver uncontrollably during my soak and hate every minute of it. Imagine my utter glee when I found out that ice baths do not enhance recovery and can actually impede healing and make you weaker by suppressing inflammation and delaying the regeneration of muscle fibers.[20] What great news. I never soaked in the creek again. The studies that investigated the efficacy of ice baths showed that movement (i.e., active recovery) is preferable to ice baths. I just love studies that are consistent with my way of thinking. That doesn't mean you should avoid ice baths altogether if they make you feel good, though. Just use them sparingly and in combination with other modalities.

I know you are wondering about massage. Similar to the other types of recovery, studies regarding whether massage is effective for expediting recovery have been mixed. Massage may or may not reduce delayed-onset muscle soreness.[21] I find massage helpful in reducing muscle soreness and it rejuvenates me during particularly hard training blocks or after a race.

## Training insanity

It's a chicken-and-egg thing: Does training make us crazy, or are we crazy and that is why we train? Regardless of the origin, I call it *training insanity*. Let me explain. I had an interesting e-mail exchange with an athlete that encapsulates the whole notion of training insanity.

> ATHLETE: I tried doing my bike intervals today. I did the first one and it wasn't very good, and in the middle of the second one I realized it wasn't my day so I stopped.
>
> JZ: I am so happy you stopped and didn't push through. Take a rest.

One hour later I got another e-mail from the athlete.

> ATHLETE: I decided to try again. I am on the bike now.
>
> JZ: STEP AWAY FROM YOUR BIKE! You need a rest.

Now, I am not being judgmental here, because I have done the same thing. I have crawled off my bike too tired to continue, only to try again later in the day with no better results. And, don't lie, you've done something similar. Yes, indeed. We are all privy to training insanity. It is this very mindset that makes us run circles around the parking lot to round up the run to the nearest mile, it compels us to go out for a workout in the most extreme conditions, and it pushes us out the door when we are sick or injured. Training insanity makes us better athletes, but it can also make us worse because training insanity causes reckless and ill-thought-out decisions that can potentially cause harm. It is a precarious balance that can be the difference between a personal best and a personal worst. Most of the time, training insanity belies intention.

Here are a few tips to keep the training insanity in check and maintain intention.

*If it seems like a bad idea, it probably is.* You desperately want to do a workout, but your gut tells you to stay home. For example, the roads are icy or you are running a fever. Listen to your gut!

*Just because everyone else is doing it doesn't mean you should too.* All of your buddies are heading out for a century ride in the middle of your taper and you want to go with them. Don't do it.

*Bonus miles do not equate to bonus performances.* It is not necessary to add in extra workouts or throw in a few extra miles here and there. Come up with a plan and stick to it.

*One bad/missed workout does not mean you are out of shape.* I get e-mails all the time from athletes who think their next race is blown because they bombed on a key workout. They seemed to forget about all of the good ones before it.

*Multiple poor workouts in a row = time for rest.* All too often, athletes get discouraged with poor workouts and end up going harder thinking they can break the rut. Usually, several days in a row of poor training are a symptom of overtraining and the indication that it is time for a rest.

*Write down your intentions.* Stave off the intention-behavior gap by writing down your intentions. Refer back to your notes when you are ready to do something antithetical to your intentions.

*Plan ahead.* Your recovery is important so don't wait until the last minute to schedule a massage. Factor in your active and passive recovery days well ahead of time. It will give you something to look forward to during a hard training block.

*Listen to your coach.* If you are working with a coach, follow their instructions. You hired a coach for a reason and they should be looking out for your best interests. It is impossible to be objective about our own training, and a coach can help minimize training insanity and keep you in check with your intentions.

*If you feel overly tired, you are.* It turns out that the most sensitive measure of well-being and fatigue is purely how you feel, superseding blood markers, heart rate variability, and oxygen consumption.[22] Furthermore, studies have shown that subjective feelings of well-being worsen with acute training loads.[23] If you are harboring negative thoughts, feeling down, or noticing mood swings, it is time for some recovery.

*Naysayers be gone.* Even the best intentions will be met with criticism. Block out the negativity and maintain your positive mental attitude.

## 10 Tips for an Intention Mental Makeover

- Intention is a combination of attitude, perception, planning, and control. Define these parameters carefully before you pursue your goals.
- Determine your purpose, as it will dictate your training and racing regimen.
- Avoid the intention-behavior gap by developing good habits, creating a sustainable plan, and obtaining accountability through a coach and/or training partners.
- Take a patient approach to improvement, as this will help stave off injury, overtraining, and burnout.
- Be flexible. Once your intention is defined and your plan is in place, allow some room for changes as circumstances arise that dictate such alterations.
- Go to the well sparingly. Races that require such a Herculean effort require a longer physical and mental recovery.
- Consistency over time will yield the best results.
- The best training program mixes quality and quantity.
- Implement a recovery plan that includes both active and passive recovery.

- Stave off training insanity by sticking to your plan, resting when you feel tired, and staying away from training that you know is not smart.

# 6

# Developing Confidence

## The confidence cycle

Do you exude confidence? Do you have a firm handshake? Do you walk with a swagger? Do you march down to the starting line of a race with your head up high? Can you shake off a bad workout? Do you respect your fitness level and your ability to reach your goals? Do your friends call you cocky?

Confidence propagates confidence. I call it the confidence cycle, which can be measured with my convenient confidence meter, pictured on the next page.

At the low end of the confidence meter are the anxious athletes who, no matter what they've done to prepare, never feel like they are ready. They are scared and nervous before training and races. You've seen them, their faces are white as a ghost and they look like they are going off to war, not embarking on a physical event they are supposed to be doing for fun. On the opposite end of the confidence meter are the athletes who are cocky, who trash talk their opponents, and never question their own ability. You've seen them, they walk around gloating and telling their buddies how they are going to crush them. Most athletes fall somewhere in between, not overcome by worry but also not overly confident.

The confidence cycle indicates that in general you will perpetuate where you are on the confidence meter. Allowing yourself to shake off that bad workout increases the chances that the next one will be successful, instilling confidence, which then increases the chances that the next workout will also be successful. If you are a nervous wreck, chances are you will perform poorly, reinforcing the negativity, keeping you at the bottom end of the confidence meter. Suppose your run falls apart at every long distance event you do—at some point you will expect that to happen. Climbing out from the bottom of the confidence meter and moving up to a higher level takes a total mindset change, which is what this chapter is all about.

At the 2008 Ironman 70.3 World Championships, half a mile into the 13.1 mile run I *knew* I was going to win the race. I'd started the run with four other women, all highly decorated triathletes. It was audacious of me to even think I could win so early in the run. But, how could I not? I appreciated that my running sessions leading up to the race were fast yet accomplished with relative ease. My race record that year included three wins and a second-place finish at the 70.3 distance against competitive fields. I overflowed with confidence. I was not quite at the cocky level, that's just not my style, but I was as close as I'd ever come to that degree of confidence. The confidence I felt throughout the run propelled me to the finish line with nary a glitch; photos from the day show me grinning widely, reveling in my win.

In contrast, in 2010 I had no confidence. I started racing four months after my bike accident. Medical specialists insisted I was healed, or should have been healed, and I had the green light from them and my coach to resume training and racing. My first race was a 70.3 distance in Galveston, TX. I was so nervous before the race I actually cried thirty minutes before the gun sounded. I knew, deep down, that I was injured and the likelihood of performing well was nil. I lingered at the very bottom of the confidence meter, but I kept those feelings far back in my mind, repressed, hidden. I was in denial. I wanted to race so I let my heart rule my better judgment.

That day in Galveston ended after the bike leg. My ribs hurt mightily and I struggled to breathe. I raced several more times that year, my confidence waning each time I toed the line. And with good reason. My body was unable to perform due to multiple rib injuries that would require another six years and six chest wall surgeries to resolve. I never clambered out of the scared and nervous end of the confidence meter in 2010, prolonging my negative confidence cycle. I finally broke the negative confidence cycle when I hung up my bike and retired from tri-athlon altogether and started doing running races. My success in the running races enabled me to slowly rebuild my confidence and restored a positive confidence cycle.

An overriding theory in the world of self-confidence is that of self-efficacy: "beliefs in one's capabilities to organize and execute the courses of action required to produce given attainment."[1] That is very clinical. This theory has been adapted to better align with the confi-dence needed by athletes, and was aptly dubbed the sport-confidence theory. Sport-confidence theory asserts that confidence is "the belief or degree of certainty individuals possess about their ability to be success-ful in sport."[2]

Within the sport-confidence theory framework, there are nine ways an athlete can attain confidence: demonstrating their ability, physically and mentally preparing, mastering the sport, coaching leadership, situ-ational favorableness, environmental comfort, vicarious experience, and having social support.[3] Indeed, demonstration of ability was ranked as the highest means of developing self-confidence among a group of elite individual athletes from a variety of sports.[4] That means, get out there and train.

My confidence meter fits well with the sport-confidence theory. Any of the nine dimensions can be measured with the confidence meter. If it is cold and rainy and you like hot and dry, your confidence will go down. If your coach bestowed accolades upon you leading into a race, your confidence will go up. It then becomes an amalgamation of the various aspects of sports confidence that will contribute to your overall confidence.

## Humility vs. arrogance

Growing up, my mother once told me: "If you're good at something, you don't need to tell anyone. People will find out." What great advice. Those words instilled in me a level of humility that I still carry around today.

Balance is a theme that I've discussed in previous chapters relating to balancing training with work and family and balancing your training to ensure that you do not do too much or too little. Balance also plays a role in self-confidence. In order for success in sports, you need to balance humility and arrogance, you need to find that sweet spot on the confidence meter, whereby you need to be self-assured, but not so much so that you become complacent or annoying.

I presented two concepts of confidence: self-efficacy and the sport-confidence theory. Then there is the Martial/Commercial Model of competitive sports in which competition is perceived as a battle: the opponent is the enemy, and fame, wealth, and celebrity are key components to sports participation. In this model, winning is the sole goal and humility is disdained.[5] Athletes who fall into this category clog up my social media feeds with self-promoting photos in their race gear, touting their sponsors shamelessly. I am not a fan of this model, because I believe a dose of humility goes a long way, especially for the most fervently arrogant athletes.

Extreme endurance sports, such as BASE jumping (parachuting or wingsuit flying from a cliff or fixed structure) and mountaineering, demand humility. A small mistake can result in dire outcomes, including death. The unforgiving elements and inherent danger of extreme sports instill humbleness in the athletes who participate in such endeavors. Interviews with extreme athletes revealed introspective observations: "I can only compare myself now with what I used to be when I was not an adventurer and was a more closed, arrogant, limited, unbalanced person and you know the worst part was I didn't even know I was unbalanced."[6] Other athletes mentioned that their participation in extreme sports made them more forgiving and patient, vulnerable, appreciative of their surroundings, and adaptable.[7]

It shouldn't take a brush with death, or even the fear of such a consequence, for athletes to practice humility. Humility and competitiveness are not mutually exclusive. Philosopher Michael Austin explains: "Humility is not opposed to a competitive display of athletic skill engaged in for (in part) the purpose of victory. It is, however, opposed to a prideful, egoistic display of such skill."[8] Austin further points out that humility is a sporting virtue, providing numerous benefits because it "deters egoism, fuels athletic aspiration and risk taking, fosters athletic forms of self-knowledge, decreases the likelihood of an athlete seeking to strongly humiliate opponents or be weakly humiliated by them, and can motivate an athlete to achieve [a] greater level of excellence."[9]

It turns out my mother was right: you can be accomplished at sports, you just shouldn't brag about it.

## Training doesn't lie

I was foolish in 2010. I dropped out of several races due to incredible pain. In the midst of all the terrible races, I somehow managed to win one race, which was actually a double-edged sword since it gave me false hope. I never made it to the starting line of another race, when I decided race morning I was in too much pain. And then I eked out one final race, the Lake Stevens 70.3. I walked and cried most of the run knowing that it was my last triathlon.

The race dropouts and pain should not have come as a surprise, though. My training was less than stellar. There were days that let me know things were amiss. Like when my husband fetched me forty-five miles from home because my ribs hurt too much to ride back. Or the countless runs that turned into walks due to pain. I had just enough successful training sessions to give me the confidence to try.

You see, training doesn't lie. Your training lets you know whether you should walk with a swagger and march to the starting line with your head held high, or if you should panic a little before the gun goes off. Or even if you should sit out a planned race because you just aren't ready.

Most of the time, there really is no mystery when it comes to racing. The whole story is at your disposal, written into your training log, embedded in your memory. It is a matter of taking a hard, objective look at what you have done over the last several months. When deciding race goals and strategies, look to your training. What wattage did you hold on your long rides? What pace did you run your intervals? Were you consistent in your workouts over a long period of time, or were you hampered by injury or illness? This falls right in line with a survey of elite athletes whose confidence was predicated on their demonstration of ability.[10]

All of these parameters will guide you toward making the right decisions in race execution and will let you know where you stand on the confidence meter. Your training is the key to determining your race plan and whether you will be able to achieve your goals. Here's an example: suppose you want to run a 3:30 marathon. That is a solid 8:08 pace. Suppose during training, when you've run marathon-paced intervals, you generally held an 8:30 pace and during your long runs you fell apart every time over the last four or five miles. It is not likely you will reach your target of 3:30 based on your training.

Even seasoned veterans like Meb Keflezighi use training to build confidence. At forty years old, Meb spoke about his training prior to the 2015 New York City Marathon: "I have run over a hundred thousand miles [in my life]. I can't imagine doing the workout that I did in 2004, but if I get close to it, confidence should be high."[11]

Simon Lessing said: "I used to pride myself on [the adage] 'hard work pays off' and I would feel confident on the start line knowing that there was no one else on that start line who was training as hard as

I was. So, there was an element of confidence that I would bring to the race."[12]

Leading into the 2008 Ironman 70.3 World Championships, I nailed every swim, bike, and run workout. I often left the track thinking, *I can go faster.* I was hitting best times in training, but never felt overextended with the workouts. My training told me that I was ready to unleash some damage, and I did so by winning the race in world record time.

## Train for confidence: maximize your weaknesses and optimize your strengths

Training is the breeding ground for confidence. It becomes, then, a matter of determining how to allocate your precious time. Is it better to spend time capitalizing on the disciplines at which you already have a high level of proficiency? Or, is it more beneficial to focus on the aspects at which you are the weakest? If you are a triathlete who is a poor swimmer but an accomplished runner, is it more valuable to hone the swim or capitalize on the run?

One of the biggest issues in this debate is that as a whole, we tend to enjoy things more if we are good at them and we avoid those things that we are not so good at doing. I have a fairly long list of pastimes I avoid because I suck at them, including (but not limited to): golf (both regular and mini), darts, pool, and bowling. I would rather do just about anything than watch a ball I tried hard to center on the lane roll down the gutter. Certainly, this is a very specific example, but it does scale up to endurance sports, where the stakes are much higher.

There are many ways to handle a weakness. The easiest way is to simply ignore your weakness and move on. I am not an advocate of this approach. Sure, it is difficult to turn a weakness into a full-fledged strength. But that really shouldn't be the intention; ideally, your intention should be turning your weakness into less of a liability. Improving your weakness will make you more confident, pushing the arrow on the confidence meter in a more positive direction.

I raced the St. Croix triathlon for the first time in 1999. I started the run neck and neck with the legendary Karen Smyers, 1995 Ironman World Champion. She ran the first downhill effortlessly while I was tentative; she pulled away from me and I was never able to bridge that gap and lost the race by thirty-five seconds. It wasn't until after the 2000 Olympic Marathon Trials, though, that I took downhill running seriously. A masochist designed that painful course, with undulating hills comprising the last sixteen miles leading to a downhill finish. My quads quivered, protesting with every step, until at last I crossed the finish line and lay down on a cot, unable to move for an hour. The soreness lasted for days and I decided, with the St. Croix triathlon looming just two months away, to make downhill running part of my training. The extra effort I put into mastering downhill running paid off. At the 2000 St. Croix triathlon, I was brimming with confidence because I knew I'd mastered my weakness. I took that confidence to the run and beat Karen and the famously speedy Carol Montgomery.

One of the biggest problems with a weakness is that it can create undue amounts of anxiety and lessen your confidence. In my opinion, this is a more important reason to overcome a weakness than the effect a weakness can have on speed or overall placement. This is particularly true, for example, for poor swimmers who can experience panic attacks during the swim portion of a triathlon because they are uncomfortable in open water or those who are afraid of descending on the bike as it starts to rain or the wind picks up. In these circumstances, the weakness has now become a safety issue.

Overcoming a weakness does not necessarily mean becoming faster. Efficiency is also an important part of the equation. And, the longer the race, the more efficiency plays a role. You need to train your weakness, even if it means spending less time on your strength. A 2015 study showed that eight minutes of vigorous arm-cycling before a cycling test decreased time to fatigue by 38 percent![13] Blood lactate levels and heart rate were increased, but the leg muscles were perfectly fresh. If you are a multisport athlete, you can see how each of the previous sports can affect the subsequent sports; a lack of efficiency (and fitness) in a weaker sport will overly hamper your ability to perform to your ability in the other sports due to central fatigue and intolerable levels of sensory perception.[14]

Here are three examples of how you can work your weakness:

1.  A slow swimmer may not ever become a "fast" swimmer, but a slow swimmer can become a more efficient swimmer thereby limiting the damages to the swim and not taking the poor swim to the bike. If a person struggles mightily through a swim, it will take many miles of the bike to recover from the swim. As noted in the above study, arm fatigue plays a role in cycling fatigue.

    **The fix:** Swim more. Get instruction. Then, swim more. One of the biggest issues is that too many triathletes just don't spend enough time swimming. Swimming is a very technique-centric sport; thus, spending time improving your swim stroke is an imperative piece of the equation to improve your efficiency. A swim coach can be an excellent resource when it comes to technique development. A swim-specific training block of six to eight weeks where you swim four or five days per week can go a long way into turning this weakness around. Throughout the season, incorporate drills, race pace efforts, and wetsuit swimming into your regimen.

2.  An inefficient runner who overstrides and has excess body movement will lose time on the run and will slow down at a quicker rate than a person who runs with a more fluid stride. Just take a look at how beautifully Mirinda Carfrae, three-time Ironman World Champion, runs at the end of an

Ironman; it is no wonder she slows down the least among her peers.

**The fix**: Run drills are an excellent way to improve run efficiency. Practice running at a higher cadence (above 180 foot strikes per minute), particularly if you are a triathlete doing runs off the bike. A run-focused block where you increase your volume will also help you build your aerobic base. How much should you run? That really depends on your race distance and background. You can start by adding in one easier run per week for a couple of weeks, and then add in another interval run after that.

3. Hills are the kryptonite for so many people.

**The fix**: Practice running or riding hills with short repeats of twenty to forty seconds or a longer, sustained hill (if you are lucky enough to live in an area where this is possible) of twenty to thirty minutes (this can be done on the treadmill or a big gear on the trainer).

## What did the professionals say?

Let's take a look at what professional athletes had to say before their big day and compare that to how they performed. A lot can be gleaned from the words spoken by those in contention to win. We can view their pre-race sentiments as a gauge of where they fall on the confidence meter. The notions expressed by professionals are no different than those articulated by newbies or seasoned veterans—the main difference is that professionals are vying for media attention, money, and sponsorship. Yes, the material stakes are higher, but the mindset of the professionals who excel can be used by anyone trying to succeed in sports.

There was a lot of press leading into the 2015 Hawaii Ironman, so this was a natural place to look for juicy quotes from athletes. The

Ironman Twitter feed did not disappoint, and I was able to pick out a few gems.

Here is what Jan Frodeno, eventual 2015 Hawaii Ironman World Champion, said before the race: "Some guys need to play mind games, but I don't. I like to have confidence and focus, and I race best when I'm happy. It works for me."[15] In the pre-race press conference, Jan further said "Once the gun goes off I know what I'm doing, I know what I have to do."[16] Jan exuded confidence without being cocky. His confidence empowered him to *walk* many of the aid stations on the run, even though his competitors were breathing down his neck, to ensure he got enough ice and liquids. A win at the Ironman 70.3 World Championships six weeks earlier assuredly put him high on the confidence meter, creating a positive confidence cycle prior to the Hawaii Ironman.

Female winner of the 2015 Hawaii Ironman World Championships, uber-biker Daniela Ryf spoke about her main rival, fleet-footed Mirinda "Rinny" Carfrae, who outran her in 2014 by fourteen minutes for the win (Daniela placed second in 2014). She said, "I had some funny dreams lately. . . . I dreamt that Rinny ran 2:24 this year. . . . I think I can run fast, too. To be honest, my confidence has been sometimes almost better on the run than on the bike"[17] Daniela did not let the thought of Mirinda running an astonishing time diminish her confidence. It showed on race day, because Daniela won by a whopping thirteen minutes. Akin to Jan Frodeno, Daniela also started the 2015 Hawaii Ironman on the heels of a win at the Ironman 70.3 World Championships. No doubt, confidence instills more confidence.

Caroline Steffen tweeted this before the 2015 Hawaii Ironman: "*I'm fresh & strong . . . in a happy place. I want to be the best . . . the fastest and the first.*"[18] The goal of being first leaves absolutely no room for error. She was overconfident and this attitude led to her demise. In order to accomplish her goal, she pushed the pace early in the bike, leading for much of the first half, eventually faltering and falling back to ninth.

Here are the pre-race tweets by two former winners, Leanda Cave

(2012) and Frederik Van Lierde (2013). Leanda Cave: *"I'm prepared for the worst, it comes with years of experience; my training is better than '12."*[19] Was this statement a harbinger of something horrible? Was it self-doubt? Preparing for the worst indicates worry.[20] While Leanda could not have anticipated what ultimately occurred, she must have been harboring some concern about something. Leanda crashed during the early stages of the bike portion and ended up dropping out of the race.

Compare this to Leanda's pre-race interview in 2012 when she won the race: "This is my twentieth year doing triathlon. I'm racing better than I've ever raced. . . . I was never the best runner or the best swimmer or the best biker but I feel that over the years, compounding that training and the racing that I've done, I feel that now I am one of those athletes who has the talent."[21] This statement shows her confidence about her ability and this composure showed on race day when she won.

Frederik Van Lierde knows how hard it is to win: *"It's like a big puzzle, and you need to get all the pieces right."*[22] He did not get the pieces right in 2015, he finished twenty-fifth. Expressing his chagrin at the difficulty of the race is telling; his confidence was probably on the lower end of the confidence meter after finishing eighth in 2014, a reasonable letdown after winning in 2013. Fredrik's confident comments prior to his win in 2013 do not hearken any mystery about the race: "I know I had a good altitude training camp in the French Pyrenees . . . no big changes from last year. . . . [To win in Kona] would be special for me. If it would happen it would be great for me, especially for triathlon in Belgium."[23]

Three athletes expressed their expectations of themselves. The second-place finisher in the 2014 edition of the Hawaii Ironman, Ben Hoffman said in a pre-race interview, "I expect more of myself on race day. It's about my self-belief, which is high right now."[24] He had a rough day in 2015, walking much of the run, eventually finishing in twenty-seventh. Luke McKenzie, who placed second in 2013 said: "I *expect big things from myself, I am in the prime of my career.*"[25] He ended up dropping out. Finally, Julia Gajer, who placed sixth in 2014, expressed her goals for 2015: "My expectations are bigger than last year. I want to push for top 5."[26] She, too, did not finish the race.

It is interesting that the athletes who mentioned their expectations did poorly and did not reach their goals. This is assuredly a small sample size, rendering my speculations merely a hypothesis. Perhaps an "expectation" is simply too much pressure. Expectations do not connote poise or that things are alright, and the athletes who convey such haughty ambitions are seemingly paradoxically at the lower end of the confidence meter. Expectations leave no room for a middle ground; it is either success or failure, which means if expectations are waning during a race, the confidence cycle will become negative, opening the door for an undesirable result.

The Chicago Marathon was the same weekend as the 2015 Hawaii Ironman. Deena Kastor made a very public assault on the masters (over forty years old) American record in the marathon at that race, needing to run faster than 2:28:40. As an Olympic bronze medalist in the marathon, Deena knows what it takes to perform on the big stage. A few days prior to the race, Deena said, "This year feels like the perfect time to pursue the masters record. I love the pursuit of progress. . . . I like to go out hard and challenge myself mentally to overcome discomfort or signs of defeat. My physical progress has peaked but I still gain an edge from this sport every day I am out there training. I'm not ready to give up on progress, so I keep running."[27] Nary an expectation mentioned, just maintaining her place in a sport she loves.

Deena's confidence cycle must have been high leading into the Chicago Marathon. She broke the Half Marathon Masters world record in 2014, running 1:09:36, and a month prior to Chicago she tied the masters American record in the 5 km, clocking a swift 15:48. No wonder Deena ran 2:27:47 to break the American masters marathon record. What an inspiration.

It is only fair that I subject myself to the same scrutiny I placed on the other athletes whose quotes I included in this chapter. I dug deep into the archives and found an interview from a few days before I won the 2008 Ironman 70.3 World Championships. I looked poised, not nervous, and I integrated some humor into the interview, further demonstrating my calm demeanor. Here are a few snippets: "I try not to race with fear. I know that my training has been good. I've had some good races this year; it certainly makes you feel a little more confident coming into the race. You have to go out there on the day and have at it."[28] At the beginning of the chapter I discussed my confidence cycle leading into the race, and the words I uttered in the interview exemplify this composure.

## Implement a confident mindset

*Train with security.* I put this one first because I believe this is the biggest impediment to improvement—too many athletes are insecure with their training. Athletes who lack confidence in their training make detrimental mistakes, such as logging too many miles, going too hard, and deviating from their plan. It is the gateway to all of the other things that prevent athletes from success.

*Keep a training log.* Earlier in the chapter I wrote about the notion that training never lies. A training log helps with that honesty. At the 2000 Olympics, Joe Friel coached Ryan Bolton, one of the male triathletes competing. Joe was on the forefront of science in sport and had Ryan training with power on the bike, something that was unusual at that time. Everything that Joe did with Ryan was very calculated. Everything that I did with my coach was not calculated.

Joe and I spoke quite a bit about training methodology in the week leading up to the Olympic race. At one point, Joe said to me, "Well, if you don't keep a log, how do you communicate with your coach?" My answer: "I walk into his office and I say, I felt good today." Such a haphazard approach to tracking training is not a way to instill confidence because it is hard to recall workouts without writing them down.

Nowadays, I meticulously track my training and all of the athletes I coach track theirs as well. A training log, or an online training system, are highly beneficial for keeping tabs on what you've done and helps you "remember" the excellent training you've put in prior to your race. Conversely, your training log can also be a reminder that your training has not gone smoothly and you might need to adjust your goals accordingly.

*Take a rest day.* Look, I hate taking a zero (a day with no training) as much as anyone. However, rest days are imperative for mental and physical restoration. And sometimes you just need to get other stuff done. Coming back after a rest day should make you feel fresh, put a bounce back into your step, leading to improved performance, resetting your confidence cycle.

*Keep up with yourself and not the "Joneses."* Social media has given everyone the opportunity to post their workouts; pros and amateurs bombard Twitter, Facebook, and blog sites with intricate tales of miles logged and meters swum. It is very intimidating realizing your competition is training fifty hours a week with a full-time job and a family. My advice: cut it all in half and then lop off a few more hours and you'll get the real truth as to how many hours people are really logging. It doesn't matter what anyone else is doing, anyway. Stick to your own plan.

*Train within your means.* If your goal running pace is a seven-minute mile, do you really think you should be on the track hammering out mile repeats at 5:45? Enough said.

*Realistic expectations.* In chapter 1 I covered understanding your potential, and that every athlete has their own ceiling. It bears repeating that your confidence will wane if you reach for goals that are not representative of your capability. I would love to run a sub 2:30 marathon. How cool would that be? Alas, even if I was fifteen years younger and didn't run like a duck, a 5:43 pace for twenty-six miles is not something I am capable of running.

One of the biggest mistakes athletes make is that their expectations exceed their ability. Before you lambast me on this, let me explain. I am all about setting goals and reaching for the stars; it is, to me, the cornerstone of training and racing. But we all have our limitations and those need to be recognized. Setting goals that cannot be achieved will only create a negative confidence cycle. And, as we saw with the three Ironman Hawaii professionals mentioned above, rigid and aggressive expectations can potentially create undue pressure, resulting in a poor performance.

*Change it up.* It is easy to get stuck in a training rut. Long sessions on the weekend. Group rides on certain evenings. Long, steady distance. Intervals all the time. Going too hard. Going too easy. Training that worked for you a few years ago may not work anymore. Plateaus happen. Take a close look at how you are training. There are probably ways to change things up that will boost you to the next level and reinforce your confidence. You can start training with power on the bike. Running different types of intervals—how about 1 km repeats instead of mile repeats? Challenge yourself in the pool by swimming in a swim meet.

*Hit the gym.* Endurance athletes like to train. A lot. Training takes up an inordinate amount of time, leaving little room for things like strength training, massage, focusing on technique, and eating better. I always tell the athletes I coach that it is better to miss a recovery workout and go to the gym to lift than to skip the gym altogether. Success in endurance sports is predicated on having a healthy body and this can only be achieved by doing things that are not necessarily specific training. A healthy body instills confidence. A body that feels like a jalopy, well, that is just scary.

***Put yourself in a position to succeed.*** If you do poorly in the heat, signing up for Ironman Lanzarote is asking for trouble. Hate the hills? Ironman Lake Placid is not for you. All too often, athletes sign up for races in which they have no chance of doing well, but then after the race they lament their poor performance. It is okay to bypass popular races if they do not fit into your wheelhouse. Stay true to yourself and find races, training routes, and training buddies that will allow you to shine rather than break you down.

*You are not "too old."* Nothing irks me more than people blaming diminished performance on age. I am not naïve enough to believe that one can go on achieving best times forever; however, much of the deterioration that people blame on age is not truly age related. I ran personal bests in the half marathon and marathon at the age of forty-four. Athletes I coach achieved personal bests in the half marathon and half Ironman in their fifties. Dara Torres broke the American record in the 50 meter freestyle at the age of forty. Proper training and recovery will lengthen your athletic life far beyond your imagination. Longer recovery time and slower performances more often come from lack of attention to detail than age itself. Do not let your age diminish your confidence.

*Surround yourself with positivity.* Nothing, and I mean nothing, will shatter your confidence more than people telling you that you aren't good enough. Let the cynics go.

## 10 Tips for a Confidence Mental Makeover

- Confidence perpetuates confidence, so shake off the negativity and anxiety and focus on being relaxed and poised.
- If you are on the wrong side of a confidence cycle, choose a race or a training session that has a high likelihood of providing you with success to swing the pendulum in a better direction.
- Demonstration of ability is the strongest determinant of confidence, so use your training as a mechanism to build your confidence.

- Arrogance is taking confidence too far. Be a humble athlete.
- Before a race, look to your training to figure out realistic pacing and race outcomes.
- Make your weaknesses less of a liability by spending time focusing on them in training.
- Expectations of doing well can create too much pressure and often leads to poor results.
- A detailed training log can help you recall the workouts that will put you in a position to race well.
- Choose races that set you up for success.
- Spend your time with people who are positive. Negativity can shatter your confidence.

# 7

# Racing

I wasn't afraid to fail tonight. I had nothing to lose so I just had to race hard.[1]

—Katie Ledecky, at the 2015 Swimming World Championships in Kazan, after she broke the world record in the 1500 meter freestyle and thirty minutes later came back to swim the 200 meter freestyle semifinals where she qualified for the final (which she won the following evening).

## Understanding the "why" of racing

In my first swim meet, at the age of seven, I swam the 50 meter butterfly. I had very little grasp on how to actually swim that stroke, and a picture I like to show when I give motivational talks exemplifies just how poorly I executed that particular swim. I looked more like a tadpole than a future Olympian; I still cannot figure out how I actually got from one end of the pool to the other. Granted, we all have to start somewhere, and my somewhere left a lot of room for improvement. I don't recall my particular feelings on that day, whether it was enjoyable or odious or just a way to pass some time. Whatever my sentiments were, for one reason or another, I kept going until racing became a part of my being, an endeavor that almost forty years later I still love. I am no longer a tadpole; I don't even participate in pool swimming races anymore. I have undergone an evolution in the types of races I participate in, my goals, and my desires. The one constant, though, has been my passion for racing.

Ask ten different people why they race and you are likely to get ten different answers. No two people share the same motivation, and they needn't. Racing and training fulfill so many roles. Indeed, a person's answer to the query of, "Why do you race?" probably changes over time.

The question of "Why do you race?" has been on my mind a lot lately. First of all, people often ask me how I have been able to maintain such a high level of motivation after so many decades as a competitive athlete. Second, my racing has been on temporary hold during 2015 due to some ongoing health issues from my 2009 bike accident. The absence of racing has made it very clear how integral racing has been to my life.

When I was a youngster, I raced out of spite. Oh, I enjoyed racing, but I was not fast and progressed much slower than my peers. I was the last of my contemporaries to break the thirty-second mark in the 50 yard freestyle, and at one particular swim meet, I was subjected to their ridicule due to my slothfulness. I desperately wanted to improve to demonstrate my mettle. Eventually, as I got older and the swimming events got longer, I made the improvements and my reasons for racing morphed from spite to passion. I set goals that were more and more difficult and I turned myself inside out to achieve them.

As a professional, globe-trotting triathlete, if you asked me, "Why do you race?" my answer would've been, "To win, of course." Oh, I relished the travel, the people, the excitement, and the paychecks, but truth be told, winning was better than all of those things combined. Breaking the tape with my hands in the air was far better than being carried off the course in a golf cart or an ambulance, both of which I unabashedly admit to experiencing more than once.

But beyond winning, each race presented me with the chance to push myself outside the limits I thought possible. The spectacular failures (and there were all too many of them) goaded me to keep racing in an effort to try to perfect the art of racing. I was almost never satisfied with the outcomes, always striving to do better, to correct the mistakes.

In 2010 I raced my last triathlon and at some point I came to realize I wasn't a professional athlete anymore, and sometime beyond that I came to realize I was no longer even a triathlete (I will always be a triathlete at heart, even if I am not competing in them). The day I made the difficult decision to take a prolonged and maybe permanent hiatus from triathlon was a turning point in my life.

I transitioned to running, and new aspirations quickly started piling up. The paychecks are scarce, the travel is less exotic, and the wins far less frequent and of much lower magnitude (most of the time I am solidly mid-pack), but the desire to race and to succeed is no less than it was ten years ago or fifteen years ago or even as a young eighteen-year-old trying to qualify for the Olympic Trials in swimming.

I suppose the best answer I can give to "Why do I race?" is because it is a part of my core and I inherently love it.

When I asked Simon about racing he explained that racing is an important part of self-discovery. He said, "You need to race. Racing is a huge part of learning. Athletes don't realize that every time you go out [and race], whether it is [a] positive experience or a negative experience, you are actually learning subconsciously from the mistakes that you've made. Even if it is a positive, you are just discovering more about yourself as an athlete, who you are, what you are capable of doing. Whether it is a positive or a negative, you can always spin it into a positive and learning from the negatives and next time around try to do things differently."[2]

## The adult-onset racer

Racing may seem like a natural progression once a regular training regimen begins, particularly if you've grown up in the athletic arena. Racing takes courage no matter your background, but adults who begin racing without a history of competitive sports behind them need even more pluck. In the past, racing was often a quiet endeavor; it was easy to blend into the crowd and bury race results. It's hard to imagine, but when I first started racing, nobody knew how I performed until I actually called and told them.

Nowadays, results are generally available in real time or shortly after the race is over. In this era where there is no privacy, racing is not for the meek. Endurance athletes know the dejection of seeing a slow time next to their name, or even worse, a DNF (did not finish). These feelings of post-race melancholy from a less than desirable result can be compounded if you fear that others will look at your results and pass judgment. Since you should be racing for your edification, any negativity from your friends, family, and competitors should not matter.

Having grown up racing with various coaches who cracked the whip and cultivated my competitive spirit, it is always enlightening when I speak with people who did not participate in competitive sports as youngsters but are very active racers as adults. During a recent hike with a friend, we discussed this notion of adult-onset racing. She did not competitively participate in sports as a child. When she began to race triathlon, cycling, and running events as an adult, she had a steep learning curve. One of the biggest obstacles she had to overcome was pushing herself, as that is not something she practiced during her formative and malleable years.

Adults have different reactions to discomfort than children, and many balk when the breathing rate goes up and the muscles start to burn. Adult-onset racers often lack a coach or a mentor to explain that a high heart rate and lactate buildup in the muscles is a natural byproduct of heavy exercise. These feelings can be scary at first, so when your heart rate rises quickly the innate inclination is to slow down and get back into the comfort zone. A coach can help guide an athlete through this phase and explain that the feelings of discomfort are normal.

Everyone has their own set point to how hard they are willing and able to push their bodies. Athletes who raced as children and teenagers have had years to discover and develop their set point. Adult-onset racers will find that, over time, they can raise their set point for discomfort with a proper training plan that methodically builds fitness.

## Nurturing the "when" of racing

Once you've decided to race, the next step is figuring out when to race. Sometimes, planning way ahead is advantageous, particularly if it is a very long event or the race sells out quickly, but sometimes, racing on a whim is also acceptable, such as jumping into a local 5k to test your speed or in lieu of a run workout.

In 1993, I raced my first triathlon. I was riding a borrowed bike that was too big, I did not have any of the proper gear, and I had never even done a run off the bike. My plan was to race a triathlon late in the summer to give myself ample time to transition from being a pure swimmer to a multisport athlete. Plans change, though, and I ended up impulsively making my debut six weeks earlier than scheduled. I was living in Rhode Island, and I competed in a 5k swim on Cape Cod on a Saturday morning in June. After handily winning the event, I decided to rush back to Rhode Island and sign up for a sprint triathlon taking place the following morning. Even with my lack of preparation, I fared well by winning my age group. I ran my first marathon with this same type of spontaneity when I signed up for the Chicago Marathon six weeks before the race, with my previous longest run being a mere thirteen miles.

Despite my history of impromptu decisions regarding racing, most of the time I carefully lay out my race season, choosing races that will ultimately prepare me for my number one race of the year. Your race schedule should take into account not only the bigger picture of your year-end goal, but also what fits into your schedule with work and family commitments. Races should be stepping stones, allowing you to practice pacing, nutrition, and to test your gear—an opportunity to work out the kinks. Since every athlete's racing needs are different, coming up with a yearly schedule is best dealt with on an individual basis conferring with a coach or mentor.

The keys to success of race planning are:

1. Do not schedule your races too close together. You will need time to taper, race, and recover.

2. Add at least one race to your schedule that is half the distance of your primary race. A half-distance race will be long enough to test yourself, but not so long you are imperiling your chances to do well at your A race.

3. Do not race within three weeks of your A race. Racing increases your risk for injury or accident. You do not want to subject yourself to a situation that might hamper your ultimate race.

## Don't fear failure

Bruce Gemmell, coach of swimmer Katie Ledecky, powerfully described why children who were once relaxed swimmers end up with fear of failure: "Sometimes we're not kind to them, the sport's not kind to them, and they sort of become that way." Gemmell added, "It could be classmates, it could be media, it could be teammates, it can be various people who are trying to be very helpful and sort of cast this net of creating failure as something to be afraid of."[3] Fear of failure is often learned from those who are trying to be the most helpful. Once fear of failure becomes ingrained in a child, shedding this fear as an adult is a difficult task.

Fear of failure is a complex, multidimensional construct that can propel an athlete to success, or doom an athlete to oblivion. The reason why fear of failure is difficult to describe and overcome is because of the multitude of causes, including: experiencing shame and embarrassment, devaluation of self-esteem, upsetting important people, uncertainty about the future, and fear that important people will lose interest.[4] Whew, that is a lengthy list of terrible things that will almost never happen, especially if you can accept three things: (1) sometimes things will just go wrong and you will not achieve your goal,

(2) disregard what other people think, and (3) it is never a failure if you tried as hard as you could.

The dichotomy between winning and failing was very clear in 2008. Just a few short weeks after winning the Ironman 70.3 World Championships, I raced Ironman Arizona. By winning the 70.3 World Championships, I automatically qualified for the Hawaii Ironman. I wanted to determine if going back to Kona was wise. I'd had a lot of success at the Hawaii Ironman, with four top-ten finishes, including a fifth place in 2000 a mere five weeks after the Sydney Olympics. The year 2000 was my last successful race in Kona. I followed up that promising performance with a series of DNFs due to a variety of misfortunes, including injuries, dehydration, nutritional problems, and a concussion. Before I embarked on another arduous training cycle for the Hawaii Ironman, I wanted to race Ironman Arizona to determine whether I wanted to even compete in Hawaii and if my body could physiologically handle the rigors of Ironman racing.

The Ironman Arizona race was risky. I had just won a World Championship in world-record time. There was hardly a result that would top the one from five weeks earlier, and with the increased spotlight, I had a lot to lose if my race went poorly.

I swam and biked fast, but comfortably. I noticed toward the end of the bike my stomach was incredibly distended and I was having trouble taking in calories. Despite a fifteen-minute lead coming off the bike, by mile 10 of the run I was relegated to sitting on a wall unable to progress forward due to dizziness and horrendous stomach problems. I was throwing up and using every porta-potty I could find.

Even though I "failed" in a very public manner, rather than feeling embarrassed, I felt like I'd accomplished something: I unequivocally learned that Ironman was no longer physiologically possible for me.

Fear of failure is not something that has ever deterred me from starting races or putting myself on the line in training. Perhaps it is because of dealing with both a chronic condition (asthma) and chronic pain from my bike crash. Both conditions prematurely curtailed workouts (workout failure) and races (race failure). At some point, I decided I would rather try and fail than stay at home wondering "what if." This means I have "failed" in front of family, friends, training buddies, and complete strangers. Early on in my athletic career, I was embarrassed by my inability to complete tasks I embarked upon, stewing that people would think I was weak or a head case. Eventually, I overcame my mortification because I realized that I always tried my best, but sometimes that just wasn't enough for success. In chapter 4, I introduced the notion of losing the E in ego (embarrassment). Over my career, I too, had to make that adjustment and become comfortable with situations that might be construed as embarrassing.

## The joy of risk

That fateful race in Arizona was a risky endeavor; I stepped into the arena with more to lose than to gain. In my mind, though, anything worth having requires a certain amount of risk. My number-one goal for any race is to finish, because finishing is never a given. Anything can happen on the race course, and I have been privy to some crazy occurrences that have caused me not to finish.

I have a laundry list of physical limitations: asthma, a proclivity for dehydration, a gut that hates me, and an incredible aggressiveness that sometimes gets me into trouble. Before I even started a race, I knew that there were any number of things that could prevent me from finishing, and that didn't include race day mishaps such as bike accidents and flat tires. In one triathlon, as I was running into the water, the woman next to me stepped on my foot causing a displaced spiral fracture in my left pinky toe, meaning my toe was at a right angle to the rest of my foot. In another race, I was kicked in the head, resulting in a concussion causing me to pass out. I've had asthma attacks galore. The heat has made me swoon and hit the deck.

It is fair to say that any time I toed the line, there was always some degree of uncertainty. But I relished the opportunity to defy the odds and see how my mind and body could adapt to whatever incident landed my way. With all that can go wrong in any race, it is almost amazing when things actually go right.

Katie Ledecky, whose insightful words are at the start of this chapter, took a big risk on the world stage. Sports pundits can be judgmental and cruel with their words. Even though Katie won the 1500 meter freestyle in world-record time, had she faltered in the 200 free and missed qualifying for the final, the analysts would have certainly expounded on her gluttonous racing schedule and how it was foolhardy for her to think she could defy the odds and race well in two grueling events so close together. Rather than fear failure, Katie embraced the risk and proved that the mind and body can work together to pull off impressive feats. Indeed, the World Championships were a perfect dress rehearsal as Katie withstood the incredible pressure from the media prior to the 2016 Rio Olympics by winning four gold medals and a silver medal.

An athlete needs to decide when to take risks and when to back off. Is the reward of bombing down a hill on a bike during a race worth the risk of crashing? Is the reward of staying with a competitor who just passed you worth the risk of blowing up later? Is the reward of skipping an aid station in order to not slow down worth the risk of bonking? Part of what makes endurance sports exciting is making decisions, especially on the fly, where the outcome is uncertain but could yield prodigious results.

Triathlon in the Olympics is draft-legal on the bike, meaning the athletes are allowed to ride in a pack, sort of like the Tour de France but with less panache. In many of the races, the pack rides together, with as many as forty riders, saving their legs for the run. Breakaways, where a small group of riders tries to split from the main group, occur, but are often unsuccessful. Riders in the breakaway often ride so hard their legs are too tired to run fast enough to stave off the competitors behind them.

At the Athens Olympics in 2004, there was a very tough hill on the bike course. In the men's race, six athletes made a break from the bunch, a very risky move on such a tough course on the world's biggest stage. The risk paid off, though, because all three medalists came from that group.

Contrast that to the Beijing Olympic triathlon where a two-man breakaway occurred on the bike. That risky move did not pan out, as the two bike leaders finished well off the podium (but they did get some excellent TV time).

## Managing performance anxiety

Yes, pre-race anxiety is a normal part of racing. I have always felt that once the pre-race jitters go away completely you aren't truly ready to race; the adrenaline I mentioned above is a pivotal part of your pre-race routine. But there is a distinction between the adrenaline-pumping nerves that get your heart rate up just the right amount and paralyzing nervousness that becomes incapacitating. Indeed, I have seen some of my competitors break down into tears before a race due to the high level of anxiety they experienced. Needless to say, those women did not last long on the pro circuit.

While pre-race anxiety can come from any number of things, I think that the main problem is *self-imposed pressure*. The pressure that we put on ourselves to succeed can become debilitating to the point that it turns into a self-fulfilling prophecy: when you worry so much about failing, failure is often inevitable. The very thing that makes us work hard to reach our goals can also be our downfall.

Luckily there are ways to combat the pressure cooker that we impose upon ourselves. Look, I know that changing an ingrained mindset is no easy task; indeed, that is why I am writing this book!

### Worry less

It doesn't matter how your competition performs or what other people think about how you race or if you miss your PR by a minute or a mile.

Don't waste time on "what ifs." Take care of the things that you can control, such as pacing well, good nutrition, staying healthy, and making sure your equipment works. Ban from your thoughts things that you have no ability to regulate. Most important, don't worry about failing. The greatest triumphs often come on the heels of epic failures.

### Have confidence

A lot of hard work goes into the preparation for a big race. Don't forget about all of the workouts that turned you inside out or made you smile. Go back through your training log and look specifically at the key workouts that have enhanced your fitness. Racing without confidence often leads to race day mistakes. If you are still struggling with confidence, review chapter 6 for a boost.

### Don't be a perfectionist

Things can and will go wrong. It is very hard—in fact, almost impossible—to execute the flawless race. It might be a crappy transition, a swim that was too slow, you might be way behind your competitors, or your pacing could be way off. Any number of things can blemish your race. Don't let a mistake send you into a shame cycle.

One of the reasons I continue to race, year after year, is that I love puzzles. Racing is like a puzzle: the pieces have to fit together just so for a perfect day. Rarely, if ever, do the pieces coincide in such a manner during a race; indeed, chapter 8 covers what I call "racing syzygy," that elusive time when the mind and body cohere perfectly on race day. Since the puzzle never seems to get solved, I am always left with a feeling that things can be better next time, that if I can change $X$ then I can have that elusive perfect day. The problem is that once I think I have learned it all, a new $X$ pops up and throws me for a loop and I am therefore enticed to the starting line to fix that problem. You can see how this cycle repeats itself time and again, continuously beckoning me back to the races.

I have learned, though, that there are certain givens in racing, something I have dubbed the "five tenets of racing." If you learn these, you can at least eliminate some potential problems, which of course leaves room for any number of new problems that will leave your puzzle incomplete.

## The Five Tenets of Racing

1. *What feels easy at the start feels hard at the end.* The first few miles of a marathon or any long endurance event should feel ridiculously easy. In many of the marathons I have run, I amiably chatted and joked with the competitors around me during the early miles. By mile 20, inevitably my demeanor changes from jovial to solemn, not noticing or caring about those in my vicinity. In fact, at a recent marathon, a runner tried to engage me in conversation late in the race and I asked him if we could continue the discussion at the finish line; I just did not have the energy or wherewithal to converse on any topic except maybe about how far we had left. The pace in the first twenty miles of that race felt like jogging, but by the end it was arduous and instead of holding steady my pace was bouncing around like a Ping-Pong ball. Proper pacing is essential: do not be deceived by the relative ease at the beginning, which brings me to point #2.

2. *Don't go out too hard.* The feeling of comfort at the start of a race lures people into a false sense of what they can achieve. An athlete I coach recently competed in an Ironman. He went through the first half of the bike ten minutes faster than any *half Ironman* he had done. The result? A DNF. I asked him why he went so fast in the beginning and he replied that it felt really good. Even with all of the forewarn-

ing, and despite the fact that he had a power meter on his bike giving him real-time feedback that his pace was suicidal, he succumbed to what is perhaps the number one mistake athletes make: he started too hard. Going out too hard is not necessarily a subjective measure—you cannot rely on how you feel, because you should feel good. You need to preset a pace, wattage, or heart rate, all of which are objective measures, to dictate how you will execute the early stages of your races. I always tell my athletes before an Ironman that nobody ever finishes an Ironman and says, "I wish I had gone harder on the first half of the bike."

3. ***It is hard to imagine things going wrong when it feels so right.*** Races often start off spectacularly. The execution is perfect, the weather stunning, the day unfolding according to plan. Then, suddenly, you get a flat tire. Or your stomach starts to rebel. Or your bottle with your nutrition falls off your bike. Or your legs start to cramp. Or you get dizzy. Or you go off course. Or a recurring injury flares up. Or your body just falls apart. Or . . . Any number of things can happen during a race, ending a seemingly ideal day. The most you can do is manage the problem, if possible, or call it a day if your health is at risk.

   At the Vineman 70.3 in 2009, my race started off well, and I came off the bike in second place. It seemed like I might be able to defend my title from the previous year. On the run, I suffered a bout of dizziness that was so overwhelming I laid down on the hood of a car at mile 8 of the run. I was barely coherent, but I do recall my very good friend and training partner, Brandon, running by and asking me for my salt tablets. His comment was, "Well, you were an asphalt pancake, so you didn't need them." The volunteer tending to me was mortified that my friend was so unsympathetic. I know his wry sense of humor well, though, so I laughed, alleviating the tension of my moment of woe.

4. *Nutrition matters.* When I lived in Baltimore, I had a friend who would stop at the 7-Eleven and eat two hot dogs in the middle of a long ride. You know the gross things that "cook" on the rollers all day? Those. He was never able to get his nutrition right in a race, though. He did not eat in training what he ate in a race, causing gastric issues on the run during triathlons. I see this all the time. All too many athletes have no nutritional plan; they are very cavalier with what they eat in training and then wing it on race day. I have done numerous Q&A sessions at races and am constantly bombarded with questions from athletes who want to know what they should eat during their race that is in just a day or two.

I ask my athletes prior to their races to send me their nutritional plan. This allows me to go over it, but also, writing it down helps commit it to memory. I want them to know what they are planning to take and when. On the run, when they come up to an aid station, I want them to be prepared to grab water, Coke, or an electrolyte drink, not ruminate over it once they are there.

Many of the athletes I see on race courses have no clue what they want at the aid station and decide once they are there. How do I know this? Because I have worked at enough aid stations during triathlons of varying distances to make this observation. I can see the indecision on their faces. The few seconds they spend mulling over what they should eat or drink causes a few issues. First, a lot of times they have to go backward to get what they want, which bogs down the flow of aid station traffic. Second, making nutritional decisions on the fly leads to the problem of not knowing how many calories have been ingested or how much liquid has been drunk. I realize that pre-race nutrition plans need to be flexible, but at least there is a starting point with which to work off. If an athlete has no plan and just grabs food and drink willy-nilly, the propensity for gastrointestinal distress increases exponentially.

Plan your nutrition early in the season and enact the plan during training. Our bodies are a sieve, losing electrolytes, water, and calories. It is up to us to keep the sieve just full enough to maintain our energy levels, but not so full it causes gastric issues. The trick is getting to the finish line before the sieve is empty. Every athlete has their own particular needs; it is essential that you figure out yours.

5. *Have fun.* This is the single most important tenet of racing. If it isn't fun you should find another hobby. Success in sport is difficult and requires time, patience, perseverance, and heartache. Ultimately, there must be an element of enjoyment to make it all worth it, to balance out the negatives. I distinctly recall, at mile 16 of the California International Marathon in 2011, thinking to myself, *Wow, I am really enjoying this race.* The crowd support was motivating, my body was cooperating, the course was suited to me, and I had people to run with. I truly took some time to enjoy the moment. Ultimately, fun is the name of the game. Racing is a privilege and we are lucky that we are able to do something that we enjoy so much. And I believe we should adapt the old golf adage of "The worst days golfing are still better than the best days working" to "The worst days racing are still better than not being able to race at all."

## The physiological and psychological components of the wondrous taper

Tapering is a necessary evil. In order to race fast, one must shed the heavy training load and freshen up. I realize this conceptually. In actuality, I detest tapering so much I call it the taper blues. The word *taper* is fraught with so much emotion. It means that a key race is around the corner. Every single workout is carefully dissected into minute detail to determine whether that particular workout has any specific bearing on race day. Workouts are shorter and less intense, which is a bummer when you really enjoy the daily grind. Then you start to question every twinge and ache and wonder if it is a catastrophe in the making. If you hear somebody cough six blocks away there is the fear of contracting Ebola. No question, tapering for an important event sucks.

I have been a competitive athlete since the age of seven. That means I have almost four decades of tapering behind me. It has not gotten any easier! How is that even possible? But it is true. As a swimmer, taper week meant lots of dives off the starting blocks and tons of sprinting. Since I did not like to do either of those things, tapering was a nightmare. Not only did the taper workouts bum me out, but I also had too much energy during taper. Taper time meant that I would be up in the middle of the night pacing in my bedroom, something that really irritated my parents since my room was directly above theirs and to them it sounded like there was an elephant on the loose above them.

When I was old enough to understand the importance of a taper I did learn a very key piece of information—too much taper meant I would be flat for my races and I would underperform. I was envious of the sprinters getting in the pool for fifteen minutes and then spending the rest of the workout in the shower. But I knew I was always better off maintaining decent yardage while cutting back on the hard intervals, a taper method I adhere to even now.

Tapering as a triathlete almost feels like a crapshoot. How on earth is it possible to get three sports to feel good on the same day? For starters, you cannot taper all three sports the same way. You may need more rest for running than swimming and cycling, for example.

I have been known to do some crazy things during a triathlon taper, such that a friend once dubbed my particular mode of tapering "the JZ taper." Here's why. I once did a hundred-mile ride the day before a sprint triathlon (I was second by three seconds and my coach never let me live it down). I rode the entire bike course the day before I won the Buffalo Springs triathlon many years ago. When I was in Sydney preparing for the Olympics, Tim Yount, one of our support staff, would pop his head out his door every single time I left for a run or bike ride. He would say, "Are you resting enough?" and I would answer, "Don't worry, I will be fresh as a daisy on race day." This banter went on every day for two weeks. Sure enough, I was fresh as a daisy on race morning, as I finished fourth. No amount of further rest would have made my legs any faster on race day. It was the right taper for me at that time.

The point of these stories is that taper is individual. I tend to race better off of a higher workload, while others need lots of extra rest and time off of their feet. Since every athlete responds differently to race buildup and to the subsequent rest, there will be some experimenting involved in determining what type of taper works best for you. Do not try something new before your biggest event; use your intermediary races as a time to hone in your taper needs.

Regardless of whether you need a short taper or a long taper, during taper week, maintain some amount of frequency and intensity in your workouts; it is the duration of your workouts that you should decrease. Your body is used to training, so if you cut it back too much, you will certainly feel sluggish. Be sure to include some short, race pace intervals. Do not go out on your regularly scheduled group ride and kill it for two hours, as that will most certainly kill your race. If you feel tired or your legs hurt, shorten your workouts, but do not cut them out entirely unless you are sick.

I am never sure how many days out from the race is the ideal day to start feeling good. Is the Sunday before too early? Is two days before too late? I guess, really, it doesn't matter how you feel before the race as long as you feel good on race day, but as I will mention in chapter 8, you do not even have to feel good during the race to race well. So don't fret about how your body is reacting to the taper until the gun goes off.

## Translating training to racing

On numerous occasions, I have finished a run interval session and wondered how the heck I will be able to maintain that pace for an *entire* marathon. We are talking about 6 to 10 miles' worth of intervals in training compared to 26.2 miles in a race. That is a significant and scary difference in mileage. Somehow, though, on race day, I manage to pull it together and lock into my pace and hold it for the better part of the marathon (I still have yet to nail the final 5 km, but that is more of a nutritional issue than a pacing problem). No matter how many marathons, half marathons, or 10k races I run, I am always astounded when I cross the finish line having managed to hold a pace that is often a struggle in training.

I have done all sorts of race pace intervals, from three minutes to thirty minutes. When the repeat is over and I get to finally slow down and take a few minutes for an easy jog, I am always inordinately relieved to have a small break from the pace. And how about those long runs? I can't tell you how many times I've staggered home from a twenty miler totally wiped out, desperately wondering whether I will be able to cover another 10 km at a pace way faster than I just ran. It's an odd conundrum: the more you train, the more insecure you can become about your ability to race well.

Physiologically, it is not possible to train at race pace every day. How then, is it possible to "fill in the gaps" on race day? Of course, there is the magic of the taper. But a taper only accounts for a portion of why race day allows you to reach new levels generally not seen in training.

*Adrenaline.* You're on the starting line with thousands of other runners. Your heart is pumping. A little sweat is starting to form. Your breathing rate is elevated. Maybe you even feel jittery. All of these symptoms could be the result of too much coffee, but more likely it is the increased adrenaline from the excitement of race morning. Adrenaline is a natural hormone produced by the body in response to stress, fear, or excitement. A surge of adrenaline on race day is certain to make you feel stronger, more energetic, and will heighten your senses. The benefit of a race day flow of adrenaline is that you will be able to go faster than you do in training. Just don't let this natural phenomena take you out at a pace you cannot sustain.

*Pain cave mentality.* On race day, the mind and body should be primed for an epic performance. Why? It is the culmination of all the months of training. We all know training heroes who flounder on race day because they have used up all of their ability to suffer. The best plan is to keep some suffering in reserve so that during the race you can go to the dark place called the pain cave. Every race does not and should not require a special trip to the pain cave (in chapter 5 I discuss going to the well, a parallel theory, and how this type of focus and potential suffering should not be overused). Reserve a trip to this dark cavern for the biggest race of the season and when the going gets tough during the race let your mind and body succumb to the special invitation to the pain cave and see where it leads you. Even if you go to the pain cave and don't achieve the race of your dreams, at least you know you gave it everything on the day.

*Focus.* Racing requires a special focus, an ability to put on your race blinders and shut out distractions. Without race blinders, races become just another training day. My race blinders blocked out so much of the outside "noise" that I often did not even see my family on the sidelines cheering me on; my husband always remarked that if I acknowledged him during a race it meant I was having a bad day. Race blinders are what allows you to push the discomfort to the back of your mind, to disregard poor weather conditions, and to block out the saddle sores and sunburn. Race blinders are what led Eliud Kipchoge to win the 2015 Berlin Marathon in 2:04:00 (that's a breathtaking 4:43 per mile pace) with his insoles flapping against his leg because they slipped out the back of his running shoe.

In 2000, I raced the Chicago Triathlon, a non-drafting Olympic distance stalwart on the pro calendar. The Chicago Triathlon was special to me for many reasons, among them was that in 1998 the race demarcated my first professional win and I lived in Chicago for two years as a graduate student at Northwestern. The 2000 edition of the race was five weeks before the Sydney Olympics, a veritable last attempt to hone fitness and racing skills. Professional rules dictated that during the bike ride, pros were allowed to ride side by side with a certain distance between the bikes. The 2000 race boasted many athletes en route to Sydney for the Olympics. One such athlete was Michellie Jones, who at that time was a two-time ITU World Champion. It so happened, on that day in Chicago, that Michellie and I rode the entire bike portion together. The bike was a two-loop affair along Lake Shore Drive. On the second loop, I turned to Michellie and said, "See that building over there? I used to live there!" She gave me a look of astonishment that I will never forget; she said with her eyes, "Hey, lady, we're in the middle of a race. Focus up!" She beat me that day—we finished first and second—but she also went on to finish as the silver medalist in the Sydney Olympics five weeks later, a race in which I finished fourth.

To this day, I have no idea what compelled me to turn to my competitor and utter such a ridiculous statement. Perhaps, knowing the focus that would be required in five weeks' time made me loosen up the reins and take off my race blinders for just a moment.

*The big picture.* There is a tendency to take each workout as an individual component. Did I nail my long run? Were my intervals fast enough? I skipped a workout; now what? The reality is that no single workout indicates a stellar race or a poor one. But people tend to use a key session as a barometer for how they will perform on race day, which can lead to feelings of insecurity if that workout fails. In reality, it is the conglomeration of all the workouts over the course of a training period that will lead to success. Stepping back and looking at the overall accumulation of workouts leading up to the big race will hopefully give you needed confidence.

*The lead-up to race day.* Are you really ready to race? Have you checked your equipment? Is your nutritional and pacing plan in place? Do you have your transition bag packed? Have you tested your shoes and attire? Success in racing requires more than a proper training plan, it also necessitates attention to detail and establishing a pre-race routine. After you've done enough races, you will have all of the information you need at your disposal as to what works and what does not work. Often, it will take a mitigated disaster to expose the problems, but this is just more information for the future.

Establish a pre-race routine that works and continue to do the same thing every race. Make a list of the equipment you will need and refer to that list before every race so you do not leave something important at home. I had to drop out of the 2005 Ironman Arizona race, while in the lead, due to my inability to change a flat tire because I did not have the right size valve extender; a rookie error that could have been avoided with a proper checklist.

If you are traveling across many time zones to a race, get there early enough to acclimate to the time change, to preview the course, and to ensure your equipment arrives at your destination. Even though airlines insist that you travel with your luggage, I have been separated from my bike dozens of times. It is highly stressful trying to track down your equipment with the race looming. With a little time leeway, you can help reduce this anxiety. It takes one day to acclimate to each time zone you move, so plan your travel accordingly.

The biggest piece of advice: DO NOT DO ANYTHING NEW ON RACE DAY! Did I state that clearly enough? Everything should be tested and approved prior to race day. If you've been eating Snickers bars in training and it worked, race day is not the time to sample the on-course menu; bring the Snickers with you.

Helen Jenkins, two time ITU World Champion and Olympian, had this to say about race day: "Maybe write a little plan for race day, include the time you will get up, eat breakfast, leave the hotel, warm up. Having this set in your mind means less stress on race day. Less stress on race day usually means a better performance!"[5]

*The proper warm-up.* Do you ever wake up in the morning questioning whether to train? Can't even get out of bed? How about standing on the pool deck debating whether to dive in? Your body is tired and your brain is frazzled. What to do? On these days I ask myself: Am I *really* too tired (or sore) to train? If the answer is a resounding yes, then I skip the workout. Usually, however, I prod myself to start the workout with this caveat: if I still don't feel right after twenty minutes, then it is time to pull the pin. I have dubbed this "the twenty-minute rule." It is a highly effective motivator on days when motivation is lacking.

No workout can be judged before it begins or even during the first five minutes, and neither can a race. Just as you need a warm-up prior to a workout, so too do you need one before a race. I have found that twenty minutes is the optimal amount of time to give the mind and body a proper warm-up. After the initial few minutes, the blood starts flowing, loosening up the muscles. The legs start feeling better and the body awakens from its slumber. It is not enough time, though, to do damage to your race. Your pre-race warm-up need not only include the sport in which you are racing—you can also add in some dynamic stretches and drills. Include some easy, aerobic exercise and then increase your heart rate with some very short, faster-paced efforts. Most races require you to line up well in advance of the gun going off. If your heart rate has dropped, you can increase your heart rate easily by doing some jumping jacks if you are on land, or if you are in the water you can bob up and down.

*Race to your strengths.* If you are trying to qualify for a World Championship, place on the podium, or trying to hit a specific time goal, choose races that play to your strengths. For example, if you are not a good hill climber, pick a flatter course. Love the hills? A race like Ironman Lake Placid will be a better choice than Ironman Florida. For the runners trying to qualify for Boston, choose the fastest course possible. Checking race results from previous years will help you to understand which race is best suited to your strengths. For those who race poorly in non-wetsuit swims, try to find races that have traditionally been wetsuit legal.

In 2000, before the Olympics, my coach, Troy Jacobson, said to me, "If you are running neck and neck with someone, start sprinting with a mile to go." This would be ludicrous advice to most people since sprints usually occur over the last one- or two hundred meters of a race. But top end speed was not my forte; my strength was my ability to run hard for a long time. Even though I spent the summer on the track honing my fast twitch muscles with 100 meter repeats, I was still woefully slow. In the Olympics, my fate was decided at four miles; I did not need to engage in a duel to the line. However, the following year at the ITU World Championships in Edmonton, I found myself running neck and neck with a runner I knew could outsprint me. Recalling Troy's advice, I made a surge at four miles until I knew the rubber band had snapped and I secured third place. I knew my strengths (and weaknesses) and raced accordingly.

Olympian Shalane Flanagan recognized that even though she *loves* the Boston Marathon and desperately wants to win there, the course might not be suited to her talents. "It's a hard marathon. I think it's one of the hardest ones out there. Some people are really made for that course and some people aren't. I would put myself in the category of not necessarily made for that course, to be honest, because of my form and my longer legs. The Boston course kind of beats me up a bit more than others."[6] That recognition might help take the pressure off of her deep-rooted desire to conquer the course and cross the line as champion.

*Mix up your distances.* Regardless of whether you are primarily racing long distance or short distance, mixing up your distances will be the most effective way to achieve your goals. A fast 10 km or Olympic distance race will give you some needed speed to run a personal best marathon or Ironman. Running a half marathon or doing a 70.3 will translate into more strength for a 10 km or Olympic distance race. Plus, varying the distances will create a more balanced and fun racing and training schedule.

*Realistic goals.* Nothing can derail a season like setting goals too high. If you are consistently placing twentieth in your age group, it is unlikely that you will qualify for Kona this year. Improvements happen systematically, so allow yourself enough time to make the physiological adaptations. Review chapter 2 for a goal-setting mental makeover.

*Allow enough time to taper.* Cramps, lactate accumulation, and exhaustion come on earlier when we are not rested. Don't skimp on the taper and give in to the "it's never too late to train" conundrum. Panic training does not work the same as cramming for an exam.

*The A race.* Sometimes races serve a purpose beyond setting a personal best or placing high. It is okay to race without specifically training for the race, or using a race as a buildup for another race. Sometimes you will be amazed by how well you can do in a shorter race when all of your preparation has been for a longer race you will do at a later date.

Plan your A workouts for your A race. Think about the training that needs to be done before your key race. If you know that your body responds well to a specific workout four weeks out from your A race, don't plan another race on that weekend. Do not plan your A race of the season close to family vacations, work trips, or other commitments that can potentially take away your focus.

*Run through the line.* At the 2015 Track and Field World Championships in Beijing, American Molly Huddle lifted her arms in celebration of winning a bronze medal in the 10,000 meters. The problem was she hadn't actually crossed the line and her teammate Emily Infield pipped her for the final spot on the podium. Every year, there are instances of athletes raising their arms overhead in triumph at the finishing line only to be overtaken in the final moments. The lesson is that it is not over until it is over. Do not let up until you are over the finish line. Molly was distraught over losing a championship medal, but came back a few weeks later to capture the national title in New Haven, CT, over the 20 km distance, showing her strong mental fortitude. In all, Molly won four national titles in USA Track & Field road championships in five weeks (5 km, 10 km, 10 mile, and 20 km) after her World Championship disappointment. Even though she turned her heartache into victory, the loss of the medal will haunt Molly for a long time. According to her, "I don't think there is an antidote."[7]

*Don't be a "Yeah, but" athlete.* It is very frustrating when I speak to an athlete and I say to them, "You are ready to have an awesome race!" and they say, "Yeah, but what if I get a flat?" or "Yeah, but sometimes there are people in my age group who are faster." Or "Yeah, but what if my shoulders hurt?" There are always circumstances that are beyond our control and we can "yeah, but" all day long with scenarios that will never come to fruition. Certainly, we must be prepared for fiascos, but the "yeah, but" athletes become paralyzed by their fear of the things that can go wrong.

*Proper coping mechanisms.* Maintaining perspective in the face of adversity helps limit the damages of a poor race; this entails creating a positive spin on the situation, not blowing things out of proportion, possessing a sense of humor, staying objective, and reimagining the quandary into something manageable.[8]

## 10 Tips for a Racing Mental Makeover

- Everyone races for different reasons. Explore your rationale for racing at the start of each season, as it can change from year to year.
- If you are an adult-onset racer, seek out advice from a trusted mentor. A knowledgeable athlete is more apt to make progress and experience less anxiety.
- Plan your races carefully and with purpose.
- Failure happens. It is not the end of the world. Trying and failing is better than sitting on the couch wondering, "what if?"
- Take risks. The biggest payoffs come when the stakes are the highest.
- Pre-race jitters are normal and fine. Paralyzing anxiety needs to be managed. Remove the self-imposed pressure.
- Less worry, more confidence, and unlocking the shackles of perfectionism will help lead you to success.
- Allow yourself enough time to shed fatigue with a proper taper.

- Be prepared on race day with a race and nutrition plan, knowing the course, and making sure your equipment is in working order.
- The most important aspect of racing is to have fun.

# 8

# Mind/Body Cohesion

**Performance, I've found,** is usually tied to one thing: subjective feelings of wellness. In other words, competitive athletes generally succeed or fail at an endeavor based upon how they're feeling. I find it curious that the most common things I hear from the athletes I coach after a key training session or race have nothing to do with splits, time results, or whether they were able to properly complete the task at hand, but rather how they *felt*. "I felt tired." "My breathing felt labored." "My legs were heavy." "I felt amazing on the swim, but then I felt horrible on the bike." Too many athletes, I've seen, are convinced that in the heat of battle they need to feel fantastic—and if they don't, they begin to panic and their performance deteriorates. Gwen Jorgensen nailed it when she told a group of junior triathletes: "How many days do you wake up feeling great? Not many. . . . Embrace it. Think about what you want to accomplish tomorrow."[1]

Feeling great during any athletic endeavor is a luxury, and a welcome one at that. But it's certainly not a prerequisite for achieving optimal success. Yes, we've all enjoyed those instances where our exertion level has felt effortless during practice or competition. But those occasions, especially when we're talking about an all-important goal race, are the exception and not the rule. The hope and expectation, of course, is that a solid taper will leave the mind and body feeling superhuman so that come race day all we need to do is settle in for a magic carpet ride filled with euphoria and bliss.

The reality is that I, personally, can count on two fingers when that has actually happened to me. I call this coveted phenomenon "racing syzygy." Syzygy, an astronomy term, is a straight line configuration of three celestial bodies—the sun, the moon, and the earth—during either a solar or lunar eclipse. They're quite rare—as rare, in fact, as those unusual occasions where the endurance athlete's mind, body, and entire race experience perfectly align from start to finish.

When I spoke to Simon Lessing, he, too, articulated that perfect races are incredibly rare. With over twenty years of racing with innumerable wins, he said, "A lot of athletes expect to go on very marginal training and do a race and have the best race of their life every time they go and race. In twenty years of racing pro, and I tell people this all the time and they can't believe that I would say it, *I only had two perfect races.* I didn't realize it at the time; it's only now, ten years after I stopped. And I can kind of look at it a little bit more objectively, I can say that was a pretty damn good race. But, really, in twenty years, two."[2]

On most race days, competitors are encumbered by countless pitfalls such as being improperly trained, fighting through injury or illness, dealing with crappy weather, or coping with GI distress or cramps. Triathletes, in particular, are also prone to having to deal with such unexpected twists as dropped water bottles, flat tires, and bike crashes.

It's a wonder, come to think of it, that any race ever actually goes smoothly. But since the notion of experiencing that syzygetic race is so very tantalizing, we endurance athletes persist in our quest for that wondrous, perfect day.

## Bad feelings can yield a good day (only if you let them)

It's a difficult concept for many competitive athletes to grasp—that fast times and stellar performances can spring forth even on our worst days. But, and it's an important "but," *only* if you open yourself up to the possibility. Let's be realistic. It's called "endurance racing" for a reason. Some of these undertakings can last for several hours and, in the case of ultra-marathons, ultra-swims, or ultra-triathlons, they can last for days. It's inevitable that at some point along the journey the mind or the body will experience a hiccup or two. In the U.K., it's referred to as going through a "bad patch," which I find humorous because the first image that comes to mind is a bibbed runner wandering lost and alone in an endless field of rotting cabbage. As Simon explained, "ninety-nine percent of races, it's a struggle. You go out there and even if you are winning, you're still out there and you're suffering and you're struggling and it has to be that acceptance. You have to go faster, but it's going to hurt." Simon hurt so much in his races that his wife waited for him at the finish line with a towel so he could discreetly throw up.

Champion athletes recognize when their attention or energy level is flagging. What gives them the mental edge, however, is that they refuse to allow the lull to become incapacitating. They understand from experience—experience gained in training or in other races—that there is always a way to work through it. Sometimes, it's simply a matter of being patient while the lull passes. Other times, it's a matter of acknowledging the lull for what it is and having the confidence and wisdom to know that all things, including "bad patches," pass. The key is to refuse to allow the mind to generate negative thoughts based on how the body is feeling at any particular moment. That's the beauty of disassociation.

## Damage-control mode

Things in life rarely go according to plan. Champions, though, are masters of learning how to adapt. When golfing superstars Rory McIlroy or Phil Mickelson hit a poor shot, they don't dwell on their mistake. They're able to immediately put the poor shot behind them and refocus on how to remedy the predicament they've put themselves in. Less-experienced golfers have neither the mental acuity nor the self-confidence to move forward. Their mind focuses on the negative (the immediate past and that disastrous poor shot) instead of on the positive (the immediate future, and an opportunity for atonement with a great shot). Invariably, the less-seasoned golfer will compound the first poor shot with a second poor one. Sometimes, that's even followed by third or fourth ones.

It's the same principle with the mind/body relationship in endurance sports. Those who possess the best damage control are generally the ones who prevail. When Michael Phelps was in the middle of his quest for a perfect eight-for-eight gold medal performance at the Beijing Olympics, he climbed onto the blocks for the final of the 200 meter butterfly. This was the event in which he first made his mark as a sixteen-year-old seven years before when he set his first world record, and he'd pretty much owned it ever since. If any of his races could be considered to be a sure thing over the course of his demanding schedule, this was it.

But something unexpected happened as soon as the horn sounded. When Michael dove into the pool his goggles started to fill with water—every swimmer's nightmare. This was Michael's damage-control moment, and it happened to be unfolding before the eyes of the world. As Michael continued back and forth across the pool, his goggles continued to leak. If anyone had had the power to freeze time to ask Michael how he felt at that moment, he no doubt would have mumbled, "pretty crappy." Other swimmers in his situation would have become unnerved. They may have attempted to either readjust or tear off the faulty goggles at one of the turns. Three-quarters of the way through the race, Michael admitted to reporters afterward, he couldn't see anything. He had no idea whether he was ahead of or behind his competition. Instead of panicking, Michael was able to detach his mind from his predicament. He had confidence that his body knew what to do. He'd raced the 200 meter butterfly dozens of times in topflight competition over the course of his career, so all he had to do was put faith in the fact that his body could perform just as well with or without his vision. Sure enough, when Michael hit the wall at the end of the race, he not only won his fourth gold medal but he beat his own world record.

## The 2000 Hawaii Ironman

Gaining the wisdom and the confidence to turn a negative feeling or situation into a positive outcome usually comes during the course of training. We've all had those workouts where we've started out feeling lethargic, disinterested, unmotivated, and vulnerable. In short, we were convinced that our schedule was calling upon us to do something that seemed humanly impossible. How many of those days, though, have we found ourselves rising to the occasion and how many times have we surprised ourselves by managing to execute the workout far better than we ever could have imagined? Those are the training sessions that champion athletes cling to. They tuck them into their pockets like precious nuggets and keep them there so that whenever self-doubt starts to creep into the picture—and, yes, even the greatest athletes in the world have bouts of self-doubt—they always have them at their disposal to remind them of their abilities.

Some of my best race results have come on days where the mind/body cohesion was all out of whack for me. At the 2000 Hawaii Ironman, for example, nothing, it seemed, was clicking. The race was just a little over a month after the Sydney Olympics and I'd spent the entire summer focusing on getting ready to race for two hours. I did do one long run early on that spring and a few long rides, but that was the extent of my Ironman preparation. I knew I was taking a gamble racing in Kona with such a limited endurance-specific training, but I couldn't pass up the challenge.

As soon as the Olympics were over, I hightailed it over to Hawaii to squeeze in a little more focused long-distance work before race day. Unfortunately, I came down with bronchitis so I still wasn't able to get in those much-needed hours to prep for my bike and run legs. Yes, my lack of endurance training was a recipe for disaster. But since I'd already made the commitment to race and I was all the way there, I decided to go through with it. Sure enough, on race day I felt horrendous from the get-go. By mile 80 on the bike my legs were completely shot and I started having stomach issues. Somehow, I struggled through the last thirty-two miles, helplessly watching as other women sailed past me as if I were a signpost by the side of the road. When I finally got back to the transition area, I was crushed to learn that I had slipped all the way back to fifteenth place.

I knew I was in good running form—probably the best shape of my life up to that point. No, I hadn't done any marathon-specific training to speak of, but my 10 km times and track workouts had been killing it. So even though my stomach hurt and I felt completely drained, I decided to run as hard as I could for as long as I could. Like Michael, I found myself in damage-control mode. Instead of focusing on the training I hadn't done, I began to focus on the training I *had* done. It would have been easy to give in to the feelings of discomfort. I could have cruised during that marathon leg with the goal of simply getting to the finish line. That, when combined with my strong performance at Sydney, would have amounted to an extraordinary double. But I refused to give in to the negative thoughts that had started swirling about my head during the last stages of my bike leg. I shifted my attention to the women ahead of me and, as we made our way out onto the famous

Queen K Highway, I could see that I was gaining ground on some of them. That development became my new positive. The encouragement from my fellow competitors as I passed them, combined with the cheers from the spectators along the road, helped buoy my confidence.

From an outsider's point of view, the shift in my demeanor may have been subtle. Inwardly, though, it was monumental. I just put my body on autopilot and I focused on catching one runner at a time. It wasn't that my change in outlook had made me feel any better out there on the course. I still had an upset stomach and I was still feeling an over-whelming sense of head-to-toe exhaustion because of my lack of quality Ironman training, but I'd managed to relegate those issues to some insignificant corner in the back of my mind. I kept my face stoic, refusing to allow the discomfort of the effort to show.

By the time I exited the Energy Lab at mile 20, I had worked my way all the way up to fifth place. Just as was the case with Michael, my body knew what to do. By disassociating myself from the feelings of negativity, my mind was able to allow my body to perform. I'd come a long way from that day in Mission Viejo all those years ago when my defeatist outlook smothered any chance I had at swimming well. My marathon time that day, 3:06, was one of the fastest ever recorded on the Kona course during that era and it was the second fastest time of the day.

## Why does the body defy the mind?

Physiologically, it's difficult to explain why endurance athletes have good days or bad days in training or in racing. Sometimes it's just a matter of the body needing more time to warm up. Easing into harder efforts, in other words, allows for the all-important psychological shift from feeling bad to feeling good. It could just be that the mind needs a certain amount of time to relax and to allow the shift to occur. Other times, particularly when the bad feelings occur in conjunction with a goal race, the answer may simply be a missed taper. Tapering, as we learned in chapter 7, is tricky business.

And still another explanation may be that our bodies encounter what I like to refer to as "effort anxiety." Effort anxiety crops up when the idea of hitting a certain target during a training session or competition is daunting and the mind's resistance to the task at hand makes the body feel lethargic. In a sense, it's almost like a protective reaction. The body, on high alert, is in self-preservation mode. Once the target has been achieved, however, the mind is essentially liberated so that the next time the body is asked to perform in a similar fashion, the effort anxiety level is greatly diminished or disappears altogether.

## The power of positive self-talk

One of the ways to address the lack of mind/body cohesion during a training session or competition is by engaging in positive self-talk. True, it is difficult to remain upbeat when you feel as if your performance is slipping away. But maintaining a positive outlook is essential to harnessing your mental edge. Nothing, and I mean nothing, can ruin a race like negative thoughts. And feeling bad, in conjunction with *telling* yourself that you feel bad, is the worst of both worlds. A 2013 study showed that motivational self-talk reduced time to exhaustion, reduced perceived effort, and enhanced endurance performance.[3] A study of twenty-one runners about to embark on a sixty-mile race were randomized into two groups: one group received instruction on using motivational self-talk during critical moments while the other group learned to use a concentration grid. The self-talk runners finished an average of twenty-five minutes faster than the concentration group.[4] Those are some wonderful benefits from a few positive words.

I constantly work with the athletes I coach to bolster their confidence levels because I know from experience that even the best-executed training plans will never net good results or PRs without a positive mental approach. I ask each of my athletes to pick a word or phrase that he or she can adopt as their own personal mantra. A solid mantra, I explain, is an invaluable tool that can be used during any time of stress—not just in training or racing, but also in the workplace or at home. One of the phrases I use in the heat of battle is: "Don't give up—just keep going." It's rather mundane and admittedly lacking on the originality scale, but it certainly does the trick for me whenever things are starting to fall apart during a long race. And, as an added bonus, it's really easy to remember when my brain gets a little foggy from the fatigue I'm feeling. Another favorite, especially on those days when things are going particularly poorly, is, "Embrace the suck."

"You suck," "Who do you think you're kidding?" and "You're going to fail" are examples of really bad mantras. That seems pretty obvious, and they're downright comical when read aloud, but those are precisely the types of phrases that far too many people utter to themselves when the going gets tough. Don't allow yourself to become one of them.

Your mantra can be anything. As long as it serves its purpose of chasing away ugly thoughts, it can be silly, funny, or uplifting. It can be a song lyric, a quote, or even a favorite poem. Chrissie Wellington, a World Champion triathlete many times over, used to write Rudyard Kipling's poem, "If" on her water bottle for inspiration. Now that's a surefire way of making sure you never forget your mantra! Deena Kastor's mantra is "Define yourself," meaning she'd ask herself, "How do I wish to define myself in this moment or how do I want to react to this situation, instead of involuntarily throwing myself into it?"[5]

Scott Jurek, seven-time winner of the Western States 100 ultra-marathon, tells himself, "This is what you came for."[6]

Other positive mantras include, "I'm on fire," "I trained hard, this is my reward," "This tough spot will pass soon," "Unleash the fury," and "Nothing can break me." Whatever you come up with for your mantra, rehearse using it during your training sessions so that it comes naturally when you need it most in competition.

## Learning to be an athlete in the moment

Forget the past, ignore the future, and focus on today. Not all the time, but sometimes. Athletes who come from a sporting background love to wax poetic about their accomplishments from "way back when," uttering phrases like, "When I was in high school I could run a sub-five-minute mile" or "I used to be able to swim a sub-five-minute five hundred." We are all products of our pasts and much of what we are trying to do athletically is in the future. Spending too much energy on things that cannot be changed or cannot be predicted creates a problem; we tend to ignore what is occurring *right now*. We become obsessed with chasing goals, hitting our "numbers," and getting ready for the next workout instead of enjoying the moment.

Do you remember the story about Ferdinand the Bull? Rather than participate in bullfights, he liked to lie under a tree and smell the flowers. Endurance athletes need to channel their inner Ferdinand. I recall a run with a friend a few years ago. We were pounding the pavement on a gorgeous Boulder fall day. I pointed out the beauty of the mountains and the crisp, blue sky. She finally looked up and agreed that it was a stunning day, and she admitted that she *never* looked at the scenery during her training. What a shame.

Even though I am known for my focus and drive and dedication to training, I always admire the scenery and never take for granted the beauty that surrounds me. Part of what makes being an endurance athlete so special is our bond with nature and our intimate knowledge of how our bodies work, which allows us to feel things on a regular basis that nonathletes are not privy to, such as: vigor, pain, euphoria, exhaustion, frustration, and the ultimate soreness from a race.

The new buzzword is mindfulness, paying attention to thoughts and feelings in the moment.[7] Mindfulness is often taught through a variety of meditation exercises with sitting meditation the most widely used.[8] The sitting meditation technique represents the core of mindfulness training, which is attentional training, and involves sitting in a relaxed, upright position and directing full attention to breathing; if the mind wanders, attention should return to breathing.[9] This type of training is not for the impatient and should be approached with an open mind.

Practicing mindfulness decreases anxiety and depression, lowers stress levels, increases well-being, affects brain and immune function, and can improve feelings of chronic pain.[10] Mindfulness can be trained, much like many of the other constructs presented in this book. This matters because a 2015 study showed that mindfulness changed neural pathways in elite athletes, resulting in greater adaptation in stressful situations.[11] You can see how this would help with pre-race anxiety, daily stress, muscle soreness, and even finding calm during a race when things are getting tough. Simon Whitfield, Olympic gold and bronze medalist in triathlon explained: "We all meditate. When I first went to an actual meditation class . . . the same feeling that you have when you want to stop in a race, when you think you're going to quit at the end of an interval or whatever, that—to me—that feeling, I recognized when I was sitting trying to stay still and continuously come back to breathing."[12]

## Increase your odds for mind/body cohesion

*Get in a proper warm-up.* The body needs time to loosen up. Whether you're preparing for a hard effort in training or you're getting ready for a race, allow yourself a minimum of twenty minutes of some type of aerobic warm-up (recall the "twenty-minute rule" mentioned earlier in this chapter). Follow that up with three or four sets of fifteen to twenty seconds of short, hard bursts to elevate the heart rate and get the mind and body prepped for something fast. All too often, I've seen athletes try to jump into a hard effort "cold."

Physiologically, the body needs an opportunity to adapt to the higher intensity. It takes patience to properly elevate the heart rate and for the acceleration of $VO_2$ kinetics—the amount of time it takes for oxygen delivery to respond to the demands of exercise.[13] No one in his or her right mind would ever think of vaulting off their couch during a marathon television viewing session to suddenly break into an all-out sprint around the neighborhood. Such a thing would feel terrible! Be kind to your body and it will be kind to you.

*Don't feel compelled to get right on pace.* Even with a proper warm-up, though, sometimes when you tackle your workout or your race your body still doesn't feel quite right. Rather than insisting on forcing yourself immediately into your target pace, give yourself permission to slowly ease into it. It may just be that for whatever reason your warm-up was insufficient and easing into your pace is just the thing to make you start feeling better.

*If you still don't feel good during a long effort, try to troubleshoot the reason.* After a certain amount of time, you might find that you're still not feeling as good as you'd like. This is the time to do a quick assessment as to the reasons why your body is not cooperating. Is it nutritional? Is the pace too hard? Is the weather too hot or cold? Consider all of the things that may be causing your body to rebel against what's being asked of it.

Most often, especially if it is in the early stages of a hard bout of exercise, the effort is simply too hard. Back off in small increments until you find your happy place. Once you've established the effort that your body can tolerate, maintain that pace and give your body an opportunity to get acclimated to the new level. Once your body has made the appropriate adjustment, experiment with gradually raising the pace—with the goal being to eventually work your way back up to your target effort level.

During the later stages of a long, hard bout of exercise, nutrition, dehydration, and overheating can wreak havoc on feelings of wellness. Starting your session or race with a proper nutritional and hydration plan is critical for achieving optimal results. Consult with an expert to obtain a plan that works best for you and your needs and rehearse it in training. Cooling techniques, such as drinking water and icing down, can help alleviate the symptoms of overheating. Keep in mind, though, that your effort level changes when it's hot. Since you will feel like you are working much harder, slow it down.

**For longer efforts or longer races, there is always time to feel better.** In a triathlon, it's difficult to feel great on all three sports on the same day. Don't be surprised if you don't feel good on one thing, such as the swim, but then you feel exceptional on something else. Don't allow bad feelings in one leg color your entire day. In longer swimming or running endurance training sessions or events, you may well find that you will feel better during the second half of the workout or race. The beauty of endurance sports is that there are always plenty of opportunities to turn things around.

**Body language matters.** Natascha Badmann, six-time winner of the Hawaii Ironman, was as famous for her race day smile as she was for her dominance on the Big Island. No matter how hard the conditions were or how much she was suffering inside, she smiled. She always said that smiling gave her "wings." As someone who raced against Natascha way too many times to count, I think that her strategy not only helped her to take flight but it also had a way of unnerving her competitors. It certainly freaked me out when the two of us passed one another on our bikes on the lava fields and I saw her grinning ear to ear when the Kona winds were gusting with so much force that I was having a difficult time staying in my saddle. The other women and I all knew that Natascha must have been feeling the effects of the winds as much as we were, but you'd certainly never know it from her demeanor. You could never tell when her stomach hurt, if her legs burned, or when she was going through a particularly challenging "bad patch," because her broad smile masked whatever it was she was feeling. Contrast that to the image of most Ironman competitors trudging toward the finish line, with shoulders slumped, gazes directed downward, and faces locked in a grimace, and it's easy to see why Natascha stood out not just in her ability but also in her approach. Avoid physical manifestations of pain whenever possible. Change grimaces to smiles, lift the shoulders, and look around rather than down at the ground.

*Make adjustments to your goals on the fly.* Sometimes, no matter how many positive mantras you recite, how much you back off your effort, or how many changes you make to your race day nutrition, the day just isn't going to turn around. It's important to know when to give the extra effort and when to back off and save yourself for another day. Even days that fall short of a particular goal can still prove to be beneficial. Every experience, and especially every race, is an opportunity to learn. Redefine success and failure. Look at what aspects of the race were successful and build on those. Perhaps you nailed your nutrition. Or maybe you were able to maintain your positive mental energy even in the face of your most difficult adversity.

## 10 Tips for a Mind/Body Cohesion Mental Makeover

- Understand from the outset that sometimes you will not feel good during training or racing, but you can still perform well.
- Racing syzygy (i.e., a perfect race) occurs only very rarely. Appreciate those races when they happen.
- It is possible to turn a bad day into a good day with an open mind and a positive attitude.
- If you are not feeling your best, allow some time to troubleshoot to determine the cause of the poor sensations.
- Use mantras to get through bad patches.
- Focus on the now and not what happened in the past and what might happen in the future.

- Mindfulness can help decrease stress, anxiety, and depression, which in turn can help your performance.
- Increase your chances of feeling good by warming up properly and working into your pace.
- If your mantra is not working, change your body language. Smile rather than grimace, lift your shoulders higher, and exude strength and confidence.
- Sometimes, no matter how hard you try to turn things around, the day just stinks. Amend your end goal to stave off utter disappointment.

# 9

# Overcoming Obstacles

Funny enough, even though it's been a tough year, I am not
discouraged. If anything, I'm hungrier than ever.[1]

—Mel Hauschildt, two-time Ironman 70.3 World Champion
after withdrawing from the 2015 Hawaii Ironman due to a
sacral stress fracture. She also withdrew from the 2014 Hawaii Ironman
due to a torn pectoral muscle.

**Where do I** even begin with setbacks? Three Hawaii Ironman dropouts
in a row after four top-ten finishes in a row? Missing out on qualifying
for the 2004 Olympics due to a back injury? Dropping out of the 2008
Ironman Arizona with a fifteen-minute lead during the marathon due
to stomach problems and incapacitating dizziness? Crashing at the 2009
Ironman 70.3 World Championships, causing a career-ending injury
and a six-year battle with chronic chest wall pain? Asthma attacks at
innumerable races? My athletic life is littered with setbacks, chronic
conditions, injuries, and disappointment. I have been to the medical
tent at so many races, I have thought about doing Yelp reviews to alert
other athletes to those they should try to avoid or plan to visit.

The champion mindset is what helped me cope with and overcome the obstacles. To this day, I never wallow too long, I always analyze
ways to improve my performances, and I delve into methods to prevent
future recurrences. And I approach each disappointment with the eye
of an optimist determining what went right coupled with my ability to

look forward and not backward. Ultimately, though, what keeps me chugging along year after year is my unconditional passion for sport.

I thought writing this chapter would come easily given my abundance of experience in managing setbacks, injuries, and chronic conditions. On the contrary, it was a challenging task to recall the obstacles since it is deeply embedded in my nature to let the past be and focus on whatever the future may bring—I do not believe in regret, and I do not rue the past. My recollections of the adversity I experienced throughout my athletic career are more matter of fact than laden with emotion. I do submit, though, that the past shapes our present and our future and the manner in which we handle athletic adversity will dictate the ability to succeed in all of life's endeavors.

In the end, writing this chapter became educational, leading me to fascinating journal articles, impressive athlete stories, instructive Web sites, and disarming blog posts. And, most important, I learned that my two favorite defense mechanisms, crying and swearing, are actually beneficial to mood improvement and pain reduction. It boils down to this: every athlete has their cross to bear and there is no such thing as success in sport without a hurdle thrown in the way, so you better learn how to jump.

## The race that went wrong

Normann Stadler, 2004 Ironman World Champion, on the Queen K Highway in Kona at the 2005 Ironman World Championships having a temper tantrum due to a flat tire. Deena Kastor, 2004 Olympic marathon bronze medalist, dropping out of the 2008 Olympic marathon with a broken foot. World record holder in the marathon, Paula Radcliffe, crying on the side of the road during the late stages of the marathon at the 2004 Athens Olympics. These athletes and hundreds of other high-profile sportsmen and sportswomen have experienced the racing roller coaster of stellar performances followed by crushing defeat;

the main difference between these standouts and the everyday athlete is that they suffered their misfortune in front of the public.

For most endurance athletes, races are the culmination of all their hard work, so it is appropriate to begin this chapter with dealing with race disappointment. A key race comes with a lot of emotional and physical investment. The hours spent training and mentally preparing are too numerous to count. Anticipating the event can cause moments of excitement nestled in an anxiety-ridden wrapper. Thoughts of well-executed training sessions are intermingled with memories of horrendous workouts. All of this momentum culminates in The Day—the months of hard work all come down to a few hours of racing. What happens if the race turns out like crap?

Races can come in all manner of disappointment: time standards missed, horrible weather conditions that cause a poor performance, equipment failure, falling, a drafting penalty, and a "did not finish" (DNF) next to your name in the results. One of the athletes I coach had a whole litany of race disappointments over the span of just a few months, varying from flat tires, illness, a car accident on the way to the race, and a heart-wrenching Ironman DNF. I thought the Ironman DNF was going to break her spirit, but she explained all of the positives that occurred during that race. She told me she was most certainly not done racing and she was highly motivated to race again.

Oftentimes, a mishap occurs during a race; maintaining a positive outlook can often override the potential damage. Susie Cheetham, a British long course athlete, placed seventh at the 2015 70.3 World Championships. A penalty on the bike cost her five minutes. She started the run in eighteenth place, but she didn't let the setback deter her from running fast and making up a lot of time. She said about overcoming a setback: "I think it's a really important lesson in long distance racing. Very rarely do people have perfect races. If you're having a bad day, it's more than likely someone else is having a worse day and if you push to the end, more than likely you'll be positively surprised with the outcome."[2]

No matter what caused a race to fall short of expectations, though, there are certain ways to handle the unhappiness to improve the chances of having a banner day the next time.

**It is okay to shout out a few expletives.** A 2009 study showed that swearing can actually relieve pain.[3] Seriously, somebody truly studied the association between swearing and pain tolerance (my favorite part of the article is when they defined swearing: "the use of offensive or obscene language").[4] I felt thoroughly vindicated when I read that because throwing around an F-bomb or two in the middle of a race going wrong or later in the day when remembering the race that went wrong goes a long way in making me feeling better. When I ran the Shamrock Marathon in March 2014, the wind was blowing relentlessly. You know what I did? I cursed at the wind. The wind gave me the middle finger and kept on blowing, but my expletives to the wind definitely made me feel less frustrated.

**Stick to a twenty-four-hour grieving period.** After a bad race I used to walk around in a dark haze for days, debilitated by the poor race. Now, I give myself twenty-four hours to cry or curse or be sullen. Nobody wants to hang around with a morose person who raced poorly. I know this because my husband said to me once, "Nobody wants to hang around with a morose person who raced poorly." And he's right. One day of temper tantrums, anger, and tears is plenty. And about those tears. They really do work. Crying is beneficial to improving mood, so if you cannot find another outlet for your post-race melancholia, do not be afraid to shed some heartfelt tears.[5] Even if "there's no crying in baseball," there is certainly crying in endurance sports, and apparently boxing.[6]

Jajaira Gonzalez is an Olympic hopeful in boxing. She has the support of her entire family, particularly her father, who is her coach. Speaking about her family, Jajaira said, "They don't care if something is wrong one day; I've got to work. My dad is always saying, 'I'd rather have you cry in the gym than cry in a fight.'"[7]

Once you embrace the tears, you might find they come frequently and last longer than you expected.

*Learn from your mistakes.* Usually a race goes wrong for a reason. After my twenty-four hours of tears and tantrums, I put on my detective hat and hunt for answers. I always aim to learn from my mistakes. I ask Dr. Google: Why did I race poorly? Dr. Google usually asks for more information, which I gladly insert into the search. I then reach out to experts in an effort to fine-tune my training or race day plan so I can prevent a poor race in the future. Most of the answers are out there; it is a matter of taking the time to find them. There is a wealth of knowledge in the endurance sports universe and most people are more than happy to share it with you.

*Do not chase races.* A disappointing performance can affect your recovery or the way you prepare for your next race. By that, I mean, do not try to hurry up and recover and get back to training too hard or too quickly in an effort to do better next time. The hurry up and recover method can lead to haphazard training, which will spoil your next race before you even toe the line. Generally, it just isn't a good idea to "make up" a race. I offer up this analogy: chasing races trying to find that perfect day is akin to a gambler playing one more hand of blackjack to win back the lost money. Chasing races is a game of chance that most often will not work in your favor.

Several years ago, I dropped out of the Twin Cities marathon. I wanted to chase a race, so I was thinking about running another marathon six weeks later. It was in the back of my head for a few weeks, and I started to train hard but my body was clearly not ready, because I got bronchitis and laryngitis and had to take some time off. The body knows better than the brain!

*Focus on the positives of the lead-up to the race.* Whether it is gains in running speed, improved swim technique, or increased power on the bike, there is always something positive to glean from a training block.

*Pick a new goal.* Unquestionably, finding a new focus is imperative. Having a concrete goal helps ease the frustration that comes with a race that does not live up to expectations. This does not undermine point #4, though. You want to choose a goal quickly, but not necessarily enact it immediately.

*Make your training fun.* Here is the crux of it all: training HAS to be fun. You spend way more hours training than racing. If the training is fun, then a poor race is less upsetting.

## The psychology of long-term injuries

*Flowers for Algernon* is the story of a man with an IQ below 70 who undergoes an operation which triples his IQ. Over time, though, his IQ starts to drop and eventually returns to its original level. I read the book way back in junior high, but I still vividly recall feeling so much compassion for this man who suffered so much. I cannot help but think about this story with regards to my six-year battle with rib injuries. I had six operations to correct a myriad of problems. After my first surgery, I experienced a few months of lessened pain, giving me feelings of hope. Pain returned, though, because not all of the issues were addressed at that time. Each surgery left me with renewed hope that was dashed within weeks or months.

My fifth surgery was very successful, and within a few weeks I felt like a new and improved model of myself, a JZ 2.0. But. There was still dread and apprehension. How long would the good feelings last before I reverted back to a shell of myself? I worried that I was Algernon and my immediate relief would relapse back to pain after an undisclosed amount of time. I expressed my concerns to the surgeon, and he was optimistic that he had fixed the problem, and even if he hadn't he would remain an ally and work with me in the future. I had heard those empty words from doctors in the past who ultimately abandoned me due to the complexity of my case, but in this situation, I had no reason to believe that he would not follow through.

He stayed true to his word. I needed a sixth surgery in May 2016, which he obligingly performed.

Despite reaching milestone after milestone, the little voice in my head still wonders if I will have the same fate as the man in *Flowers for Algernon*. I am not sure how much time has to pass before those thoughts dwindle into thin air.

Long-term injuries undoubtedly change a person; I know, at the very least, it changed me. While the rib injuries were not psychological, there assuredly was a psychological component because injuries inevitably wreak havoc on the mind as well as the body. Chronic pain, a failing body, and an inability to complete normal tasks of daily living took a toll, leaving me depressed and angry.

Anyone who has faced a long-term injury or has overcome chronic pain knows what I am talking about. The injury can be in your foot, but if you have a hangnail all of a sudden you are petrified the foot injury is back. The irrational thought process is this: at any moment, without warning, the injury will rear its ugly head. The problem is that athletes are controlling. We like to feel that we can regulate our bodies, our workouts, and our destiny. In the end, though, injuries and pain end up controlling us, a terrible turn of events that is hard to cope with. In fact, if the injury is serious enough or lasts long enough, an athlete can go through the five stages of grief: (1) denial, (2) anger, (3) bargaining, (4) depression, and (5) acceptance.[8] I went through all five of those stages, sometimes all in one day.

Collegiate athletes with short-term injuries scored better on mood state profiles than their noninjured counterparts, indicating that there were no significant psychological issues.[9] Long-term injuries show a much different pattern, though, where a total mood disturbance is high early in the injury, dips for a period of time, and then increases again.[10] However, it turns out that even those mood changes are not usually severe, and clinical levels of depression is the exception, not the norm, when dealing with long-term injuries.[11]

No doubt, our happiness is directly related to our level of pain from an injury, because pain makes a person grumpy, frustrated, depressed, anxious, and angry, particularly if the pain becomes chronic (i.e., pain lasting more than six months).[12] An athlete who had a serious knee injury wrote to me: "One thing I realized with this setback is that my mood is directly correlated to my pain level. I was at my lowest when I had pain with every step. Even the kicking in swimming was painful. Now that I can at least walk, swim, and bike without pain, I am much 'happier.' Pain is so powerful. We all try to 'control' it, especially as an athlete. It's a constant battle with it [the pain] during training, racing, and everyday living. We win or the pain wins."[13] I know from personal experience that when the pain is bad enough, it wins.

A survey of eight hundred medical practitioners who work with athletes, including orthopedic surgeons, physiatrists, and family physicians, showed that more than 90 percent of them discussed with their athlete-patients fears about reinjury, fear about surgery, and impatience with rehabilitation.[14] Do you know what was rarely or never discussed by the physicians with the injured patient? Difficulty with dealing with pain, addiction to painkillers, feeling isolated, an inability to engage in rehab tasks, and difficulty letting go of the injury.[15] The psychological impact of an injury and the related pain from the injury are topics not broached with the patient by their physician. It is easy to see, then, why athletes retain their fear about their injury.

## Overtraining syndrome/chronic fatigue

Ryan Hall dealt with an enduring slump after the 2012 Olympic Trials marathon. He described his issues thusly: "It's been the most frustrating challenge I've faced in my running career because I haven't been able to figure out exactly why it's happening. Running is very tough on the body in many ways but I think one of the biggest ways is hormonally. Every time I've had blood work done, I've had clinically low testosterone levels, which affects everything. It has been really frustrating to put together months of really good training only to lose it all due to sudden fatigue that requires complete rest. This has kind of been the trend for me over the last couple of years, which is why my results have been so up and down and why sometimes I am so hopeful about my running and other times not so much."[16] Eventually, Ryan succumbed to the fatigue and officially retired from professional running a few weeks before the 2016 Marathon Olympic Trials.

Over the last many years, there has been a proliferation of extreme exhaustion in endurance athletes. Some have overtraining syndrome, a condition "associated with frequent infections and depression which occurs following hard training and competition. The symptoms do not resolve despite two weeks of adequate rest and there is no other identifiable cause."[17] A diagnosis of chronic fatigue syndrome, often confused with overtraining syndrome, requires a six-month minimum duration of fatigue and encompasses symptoms of fever, sore throat, debilitating fatigue, headaches, muscle soreness, sleep disturbance, neurological symptoms, and general weakness.[18]

This section is not a treatise on detecting overtraining syndrome or chronic fatigue. Rather, the purpose is to inform you about their existence and how to heed the warning signs to possibly prevent an occurrence of long-term fatigue that will compromise your ability to train and race. The propagation of overtraining in endurance athletes precipitated an article in *Outside* magazine detailing the stories of ultra-runners who suffered from overwhelming fatigue that caused in extreme cases a complete withdrawal from the sport.[19] The article points out the lack of studies on overtraining in endurance athletes, with no clear-cut markers or physiological determinants for diagnosis. Perhaps it is an immune response, as Professor David Neiman stated: "Eighty-five percent of people I've worked with who have this syndrome trained or raced while they were sick."[20] This sentiment was backed by the director of the Etixx-Quick-Step cycling team, Brian Holm. One of his top sprinters, Marcel Kittel, spent much of 2015 ill. "Kittel should not have raced when he was ill and it destroyed him," Holm said. "If he comes back after his virus, it will be exciting."[21]

I've encountered dozens of athletes who suffered from overtraining syndrome or chronic fatigue syndrome. They all had a single commonality: there were warning signs before their fatigue became all-encompassing. They didn't just wake up one day and say to themselves, "Self, I am too tired to get out of bed." Instead, each and every athlete had a check-engine-light go off, alerting them to a potential problem in the system. They pushed though low levels of energy for weeks or months. Many did not replenish with adequate carbohydrates after training sessions. They trained or raced sick. Simply, they pushed too hard and for too long without a respite.

One friend, Mark, a former professional triathlete, asked me how he could be so irresponsible to allow himself to keep pushing day after day, knowing he was training beyond his limits but still convinced he was not doing enough. I assured him that his self-flagellation was not uncommon. I, myself, fall victim to thoughts that I am not doing enough or going hard enough. And I have constant talks with my athletes about overtraining and how to moderate their efforts during workouts (it is much easier to dole out advice than actually listen to it).

It is a difficult predicament. The very attributes for success—the drive, the will to work hard, never being satisfied—are the same qualities that can lead to a demise. Most endurance athletes do not seem to have an "off" button. There is a very tenuous relationship between fitness and success and fitness and overtraining.

When training is going well, it is easy to push yourself over the limit by turning easy workouts into hard ones and making the hard workouts even harder. Bobby McGee, running coach to multiple Olympians, once told me, "If you are at the track and you are nailing your times or going faster than prescribed and it feels super easy, go home. That is the day you will hurt yourself." Lisa Bentley, winner of eleven Ironman races, once said, "We are all just one good workout away from an injury."

How true. The time you are most likely to get sick is after a series of hard sessions or a race. Your body is more tired and your immune system low.[22] Without recognizing the warning signs or taking a break, the body will eventually fail. Ignore the signs long enough and suddenly only months of rest will undo the damage; some unlucky athletes never return to sport.

When you are on a hot streak, nailing workouts and always ready for more, it is hard to imagine a day that you will wake up unable to complete an easy run. But just ask Mark, who I mentioned above; he knows that beyond high wattage and fast runs lies exhaustion, loss of appetite, and lack of motivation.

Part of the problem is the notion that everyone else is doing more. The Internet is replete with descriptions of the training regimens of athletes held in high esteem. Training partners boast about their latest training endeavors. Certainly, living in Boulder provides a warped perspective on normality; no matter the time of day you are sure to find someone training somewhere and doing more than you.

As athletes (and coaches) we have to be tightrope walkers. Move a little to the right and off the high wire you go—overtrained. Move a little to the left and you fall off—injured or sick. Making it across, from one platform to the other, requires extreme focus, balance, and nerves of steel. Luckily, you can monitor your fatigue without any fancy tests. Subjective measures of mood disturbance, impaired well-being, and perceived stress all increase with a chronic training load, meaning if you see changes in your mood and well-being over time, you need to back off your training because you are in danger of overtraining syndrome.[23]

Balance. That is the elusive answer. It is imperative to find the right combination of training hard, but not too hard, backing off when things are not right, and resting. Knowing your limits. The theory looks good on paper but are we smart enough to execute?

## Chronic illness

Endurance sports have slowly been flooded with athletes dealing with chronic conditions such as diabetes, exercise-induced asthma, cancer, and heart disease. Endurance sports are an incredible opportunity for those with a chronic illness to forget about the demands of their disease and experience a semblance of normality, because anyone with a chronic condition will tell you how difficult it is to manage their illness in their regular life. Certainly, exercising enhances the complexity, but the benefits of an athletic lifestyle mostly outweigh the negatives. A caveat, though: it is imperative that when you are dealing with a chronic illness you formulate a plan with your medical team before embarking on an exercise program.

I asked Lisa Bentley to share her story about competing as a top-level professional triathlete while managing Cystic Fibrosis (CF). Her fortitude and attitude are a wonderful lesson, not only for anyone trying to juggle their chronic illness with a sporting life, but for anyone looking for inspiration. I am including Lisa's story, in her words.[24]

I am susceptible to chronic chest infections so I am usually on antibiotics at least three times each year and the drug of choice during my career was Ciprofloxacin (Cipro). A chest infection would take about six weeks to clear so I raced many races while sick—which again was my choice so nothing to feel sorry about. I just accepted my limitations and did the best that I could.

My susceptibility to chest infections (every cold and sniffle becomes a chest infection and a course of antibiotics) and sweating out a higher concentration of sodium than other athletes (sodium is key for fluid absorption and muscle functioning)—those two things made it tough.

And Cipro, the drug of choice for killing pseudomonas, can lead to Achilles tendon rupture. Ironically, I have had Achilles injuries from 2003 to 2015.

Mental visualization and preparation was the key to overcoming some of the setbacks with CF. I came up with some pretty "mission statements" that helped get me to the start and finish lines with a hundred percent mental focus and maybe just eighty percent health: (1) Attitude is more important than fact. The fact is that I have CF. My attitude is that I will be the best that I can be with CF. (2) What I might lack in health, I will make up for in determination and positive thinking and heart. (3) I will control what I can control and leave the rest in God's hands. (4) I will do the best I can with my deck of cards and if a chest infection is in my deck, then I will play it the best I can. (5) Anyone can do good when the going is good but a true champion does good when the going gets tough. I will be that champion. (6) I can do all things through Christ who strengthens me.

Here is a story about the power of positive thinking I used in Kona 2004:

I had met an incredible woman named Tracy Richardson in New Zealand in 2003. She has two children, Makena and Cameron, with very serious CF. I had met them to chat about CF and how I dealt with it. They struggled with the daily routine of CF—the inhaled therapies and antibiotics.

After that meeting, Tracy decided to race IM NZ 2004 to raise money so that kids with CF could do sport. The antibiotics are very expensive so it is hard for moms and dads to afford to put their kids in sport after they pay for all of the medicine. But sport and play and exercise and movement is so important for kids with CF since it moves the chest and lungs and lets them clear the dangerous mucous out of their lungs. So rather than raise funds for research she wanted to get kids exercising and playing sport.

So Tracy did IM NZ 2004.

Then NBC caught wind of this story and invited Tracy to race the Ironman World Champs and use that race to continue to raise money for her campaign. They would highlight Tracy, the mother racing for her kids with CF, and myself, a professional athlete trying to win the race with CF.

On Monday, five days prior to the Saturday race day, I woke up with a cough and sore throat. By noon, it had the makings of a full-blown chest infection. By three p.m., I had a prescription for Ciprofloxacin from the St. Mike's Adult CF Clinic. I was so sad. I was about to race in the World Championships and now I had limited lung capacity and a chest infection. I tried everything to clear my lungs—diving deep in the salt water to provoke cough fits, massage, and of course rest.

On Wednesday, I went to a press conference with Tracy Richardson to highlight her campaign, "Use your Breath for CF." I had been feeling a bit sorry for myself but the moment I saw her face, I had a huge awakening. I was so upset that I might not win the Ironman World Championships because of my CF; meanwhile she has two children who might die because of CF. I was so ashamed of myself. And in that instant, I realized my gift. I was so fortunate that I got to race. I was so lucky that I, a person with CF, even got to race in the World Championships, never mind the fact that I got to race with the best professional women in the world in the World Championships. Shame on me.

And it was then that I made it my mission to be the best person on that start line with CF. I would be the best person on that start line with a chest infection. I would be the best that I could be with my deck of cards. That mental attitude allowed me to rise above the illness and have the race of my life.

I was happy and grateful all day. I didn't cough once. I don't remember feeling hot. I don't remember the wind. I was racing so in the moment and loving every minute and just so happy to be able to race, that I embraced every minute of the opportunity to race at the World Championships. I finished fourth place on that day—fourth in the World Championships despite being on strong antibiotics with decreased lung function.

The power of the mind and attitude was never more clear to me and I was so pleased to have been able to start the race, finish the race, and place so well on a day when I likely should not have even started. That was a race on mental power.

Did you get chills from reading Lisa's story? I know that my eyes tear up every time I reread her narrative. Lisa's mechanisms for managing CF while racing as a top professional in one of the world's most grueling sports required so many of the concepts introduced in this book.

## It's not all in your head

In the summer of 2015, Olympic hopeful middle distance runner Sarah Brown was struggling. After setting personal bests in her events early in the year, she traveled to Europe to compete in the esteemed Diamond League race in Monaco where she finished last in the 1500 meters. Her husband, who also is her coach, had this to say: "When I look back at some of those workouts that went so terribly wrong, I thought she was just being stressed out and mental. I'm telling you, it's the worst feeling as a husband and a training partner."[25] Even Sarah thought she had to "woman up." How wrong they were. Sarah was pregnant.

It comes down to this simple fact: if a workout is cut short, a race uncompleted, time taken off, or a slump occurs, it is not for psychological reasons. A deeper look will reveal that *something* is wrong. We, as athletes, thrive on our sports. Do we really want to sit on the sidelines, come home early, miss those last two intervals, or finish a race far off our goal?

Every time an issue has emerged threatening to disrupt my training, my answer has always been the same. Go harder. Work through it. Gut it out. When I was struggling with rib pain, I wrestled with my inner voice, telling myself that maybe the pain wasn't truly there, that it was a figment of my imagination. I would go to the track and run workouts that I could nail when I was healthy. In my mind, if I could achieve that workout, then I wasn't really injured.

The rationale for these irrational thoughts is complex. Is it denial? Refuse to believe there is a problem and it might go away. Is it fear of ridicule from others? Perhaps it is easier to accept a psychological reason for poor performance than yet *another* physical issue. Is it stubbornness? Deny there is a physical problem, then training can continue. Is it a sense of infallibility? Our bodies cannot break down, but our minds can.

And here is the real difficulty. Once you finally admit there is a physical problem during the search for answers, you are confronted with medical professionals, coaches, friends, coworkers, and family, who may tell you that what you are experiencing is a psychological problem, not a physical one. I myself had this predicament when investigating my multiple rib injuries. One doctor who could not figure out the source of my pain insinuated that there wasn't really a problem and actually said to me, "I'd like you to schedule an appointment with my friend who is a psychiatrist." I felt demeaned, frustrated, and misunderstood.

I work with athletes that have had doctors tell them their fatigue was due to psychological issues, only to find out upon further investigation they were severely anemic. Another "fatigued" athlete was diagnosed with celiac disease. And yet another had a hormonal imbalance. I refer you back to this statement: Do we really want to sit on the sidelines or come home early, or miss those last two intervals? The answer is unequivocally NO. Because, if the answer was yes, we would just retire and not bother searching for answers.

And therein lies the problem. When a doctor cannot diagnose a problem, stress and anxiety are viewed as the root cause. An astute physician, Alex Lickerman, explained: "Unfortunately, doctors frequently reach for a psychosomatic explanation for a patient's symptoms when testing fails to reveal a physical explanation, thinking if they can't find a physical cause, then no physical cause exists. But this reasoning is as sloppy as it is common."[26] A survey of twenty-four hundred women suffering from chronic pain showed that 75 percent heard from physicians that they just have to learn to live with their pain, 57 percent were told that doctors didn't know what was wrong, and perhaps most disturbingly, 45 percent were told that the pain was all in their head.[27]

If doctors are perpetuating the "it's all in your head" myth, how are we, as athletes, supposed to believe that it's not? The answer is simple: it's the athlete mindset. The outlook that propels us to finish endurance events when our bodies are failing, to train in the harshest conditions, to train beyond our imaginable limits, is the very same mindset that will trigger the dismissal of the cynics who infer that it is all in your head.

If you search hard enough, you will find that diamond in the rough, the one who believes you. My salvation came when I had my fourth rib surgery in the fall of 2015. I thanked the surgeon for his compassion and for not telling me my problem was psychological, as so many others before him had. His words were: "It is not a psychological problem when you have accomplished what you have athletically and intellectually." I would take that a step further and declare that any athlete willing to do what needs to be done to succeed in endurance sports does not manufacture their injuries in their head.

## Mental healing

After the 2009 bike crash, I experienced the expected anger and disappointment. Those emotions were quickly supplanted by pain and the desire to diminish the pain. I focused on my recovery, getting back to training, and starting to work again. However, nightmares about the crash often jolted me awake in the wee hours of the morning, reminding me that there were issues that needed reflection and resolution. I knew there would be catharsis at some point, I just did not know when. Unfortunately, this moment of letting out the pent-up emotions occurred on Thanksgiving evening, a few weeks after the accident. I erupted, completely decompensating, crying uncontrollably and feeling depressed. The timing could not have been worse. After this episode, I presumed the worst was over and my mental healing was accomplished.

How wrong I was. I was shocked to realize that my mental healing was not complete, not even close. It all came to pass during a bike ride, three months after the accident. One of my favorite workouts of the week was the long ride—not a long ride on the trainer, but a long ride outside enjoying a beautiful day in the company of good friends. After many weeks of trainer workouts due to cold and snow, Boulder was treated to a spate of warm days, enabling me to enjoy the great outdoors. The prospect of a fifty-five-degree weekend day was thrilling and the haggling with riding buddies began on Thursday for a Saturday ride, to determine a time and place to commence what would be our first "long" ride of the year.

As the cast of characters on the ride grew so did my level of anxiety. When we set off in a group of nine I felt unsettled. As the pace quickened and we started passing riders on the road and even picked up a pack, my body tensed and my brain was overwhelmed with thoughts of falling. I could not relax. I wanted to turn back. I wanted to scream. I wanted to crawl off my bike. I couldn't breathe. At some point, a rider passed me on the left and skimmed my shoulder, still fresh from collarbone surgery. I had a full-blown anxiety attack and had to pull over to the side of the road and engage in deep-breathing exercises. Immersion therapy seemed like the best plan to overcome the fears quickly; apparently, I was not ready.

There it is. Physical wounds tend to heal more quickly than the deeper wounds, the ones that cannot be seen and cannot be fixed by medicine. Those mend with continued patience and time and the process cannot be rushed.

## The comeback

Americans love comeback stories. Tales of cranky, washed-up, fallen-from-grace athletes have been Hollywood fodder for years. (My favorite is *The Champ,* the first movie that made me cry. And how cute was little Ricky Schroder?) What constitutes a comeback? Athletes suffer injuries regularly. I think it must be written in the preamble of the Athlete's Constitution: if you train you will pay the consequences with some type of bodily harm. Since injuries and time off are implicit in the world of endurance sports, returning to the field after something mundane, such as a muscle tear or stress fracture, does not comprise a comeback.

A true comeback requires premature retirement, prolonged absence due to illness, a slump followed by success, the return after childbirth, overcoming a potentially career ending injury, or in the case of Tiger Woods, overcoming humiliation. Michael Jordan's comeback was closely followed in the 1990s and Brett Favre only retired for a few months before coming back at the young old age of forty. The most decorated Olympian of all time, Michael Phelps, wasn't satisfied with his collection of gold medals and returned to the pool after "retiring" to train for the 2016 Olympics. His comeback netted him five golds and a silver, a fancy collection that brings his total medal count to a mind-boggling twenty-eight. The bottom line: athletes hate being on the sidelines, regardless of their past successes.

Comebacks are difficult and necessitate more than putting down the donuts and announcing to the world that you are back. Or in the case of endurance sports, announcing it to your inner circle, because really, endurance sports just reside in the shadow of all other sports (even professional bowling garners more TV time). Returning to action after an absence entails months of hard work, patience, setbacks, self-doubt, and naysayers. Most important, a comeback depends on a strong, committed team, which you can learn how to assemble in chapter 3.

Ultimately, a successful comeback depends on the athlete's perseverance. It is no easy task returning to previous form after a break or long-term injury. The work is harder than ever, the pain is worse, and the potential for failure high. People inquire why anyone would put themselves through such a regimen. In the case of endurance sports, we are not making comebacks for fame and fortune. But I imagine that athletes in mainstream sports are not coming back for those reasons either. The allure of the comeback is broad, but the single most important reason is the love of the sport. Unquestionably, disappointments and unachieved goals exist, but athletes who persist for long periods of time in their sport focus on the highs, the friendships, the games won, and challenging their bodies to achieve more. If you see a crotchety old athlete with a beer belly at the bar, do not be surprised if they are throwing touchdowns, winning races, or dunking baskets on national TV in the near future.

## Injuries suck

Do a search for "athletes and toughness" and hundreds of sites pop up offering a plethora of information. There are sites that can teach you how to bring your A game, steps to improve mental toughness, the secrets of elites, ways to develop focus, and how to build the mind as well as the body. Mental toughness and the ability to succeed as an athlete are synonymous.

Certainly, without mental toughness, as athletes we cannot achieve our potential and reach the goals we set out for ourselves. The daily grind of training is hard, while the mental and physical strain during a race can test even the most elite athletes. With so much emphasis on toughing it out, we have been programed to ignore pain. This can be an asset, but it can also be a detriment.

In December of 2014 I spent five days at the Steadman Clinic in Vail, Colorado, assisting my sister who had hip surgery to repair a torn labrum. During my stay, I encountered numerous athletes of all ages who play all sorts of sports, gimping around on crutches or with their arm in a sling. Each athlete had their own unique story about how they got injured, but many of them had something in common—they were in pain for quite some time before they needed a surgical repair of their injured body part.

Being surrounded by injured athletes, who rehabbed like crazy with the hope they would be healthy enough to one day resume their sport of choice, made one thing very clear: there has to be a differentiation between good pain and injury pain. It does happen that repeated bouts of intense exercise increases pain tolerance, meaning athletes will endure a lot of pain for a long time.[28] Enduring pain changes how one perceives pain, indicating that the mind is trained as well as the body when it comes to bearing pain.[29]

An athlete's ability to withstand high amounts of pain begs the question: Where does mental toughness end, acknowledging that harmful pain has begun? Certainly, we have all experienced pain of some type; running a marathon or doing an Ironman is painful. But sometimes pain goes bad, and it becomes more than just gutting out a workout or a race. That distinction is not always easy. Nobody wants to admit that there is something wrong, and sometimes it is even difficult to get the proper care or medical imaging needed to figure out the problem.

My sister, for example, first started having pain related to her injury eighteen months before she had surgery. But the pain moved around and it was not debilitating. She was able to train, albeit it with varying degrees of pain. She sought out the expertise of medical professionals, and none of them indicated that there was something terribly wrong that couldn't be addressed by physical therapy, massage, and strength training. After she ran the Chicago Marathon in October before her surgery, the injury became so bad it was impossible to ignore that the problem was serious. On her own volition, she got an X-ray and MRI and discovered that there were some bony protrusions on her hip, which caused a tear in the labrum and an impingement. Surgical repair was needed.

During my years as an athlete, I have had a multitude of injuries. I learned a lot during my tenure on the disabled list. There is so much that can be done to make an injury less malevolent and allow you to take back some control.

*It's an injury when* . . . something hurts for more than a few days, if pain comes on acutely, you've had a trauma or accident, or if the pain gets worse with exercise.

*It's imperative to get a proper diagnosis.* This step cannot be ignored and can take a very long time. Until there is a diagnosis, it is difficult to treat the injury or know the long-term prognosis. Don't give up on this step, even if it means seeing or talking to multiple doctors. You have to be your own advocate and don't take no for an answer.

*Make an action plan.* Determine how long recovery should take. Read up on the injury until you are an expert. You need to understand how it happened, how to make it better, and how to prevent it in the future.

*Find good rehab therapists.* Massages, acupuncture, and PT all play an important role in recovery. I have used all of those modalities with a lot of success.

*Be diligent with rehab exercises.* I work on rehab and prehab exercises every single day. I hate it. It works. Discuss with your therapist how to distinguish rehab pain from the injury pain. Pain is an inevitable part of the rehab process. After all of my surgeries, the doctors told me, "Let pain be your guide" in reference to my return to sports. That is a lot of (too much?) latitude for most athletes, especially those who are not familiar with injury rehab. As athletes, we are used to pushing the limits and managing pain, so it is important to obtain clear-cut guidelines to differentiate good pain from bad pain.

*Find other ways to get your exercise fix.* One of the biggest problems with an injury is the inability to get the endorphins we love so much. Be creative and find other activities that you enjoy or somewhat enjoy and embrace them. Doing something is better than doing nothing. I despise walking, but I made it a huge part of my daily activities when I could not do anything else. Chapter 1 has an endorphin calculator that may help you achieve your fix during your recovery.

*Don't ever give up.* It is easy to become disheartened and lose faith that there will be a conclusion to your injury woes. If you are not satisfied with the care you are receiving, look elsewhere. In the course of solving my six-year battle with rib injuries, I met with over a dozen doctors, many of whom told me that nothing could be done. I kept searching until I found doctors who were not only willing to believe that something was wrong, but also had the ability to fix my problems.

As I mentioned in the beginning of this chapter, I have a proclivity for optimism, even during the most trying times. My usual hopefulness was tested repeatedly during the summer of 2015, with chronic pain permeating every facet of my life. There were days where I could not imagine living the rest of my life so compromised. Twice during that summer—indeed, the only two times in my life—I verbalized my desire to throw in the towel and just give up. Give up on sports, which always kept me grounded in even the worst circumstances. Give up trying to find a solution. Give up on life. My hope was gone. Fortunately, I overcame this negativity with the support of my family, but not everyone is lucky enough to have such a caring and equipped network. Do not be afraid to seek out professional help if your feelings of giving up become overwhelming and turn into something potentially nefarious.

*Trust your instincts.* I encountered a lot of medical professionals who told me: (1) I was crazy, (2) nothing was wrong because no abnormalities showed up on imaging such as X-ray, MRI, or CT scans, (3) my pain was psychological, and (4) I needed to go on long-term pain meds or neuropathic medications, both of which have terrible side effects, so I took the bare minimum amount of narcotics and avoided the neuropathic medicine completely. Athletes know their bodies, and I knew that things were wrong, and each surgery discovered anatomical but fixable abnormalities. Part of not giving up is trusting your instincts when you are certain that something is not right. If your injury has not resolved within a reasonable amount of time, ask for further testing or obtain another opinion.

*A positive attitude goes a long way in recovery.* Believing in yourself, even when others do not believe in you, is probably the most pivotal step in the process. If you know you will get better, eventually you will. It is easy to feel contempt toward your training buddies who are able to put in the workouts and race while you are on the sidelines. Part of maintaining a good attitude is cheering them on rather than seething with envy.

*Don't dwell on would've, could've, should've.* For six years, I spent month after month doing strength exercises. I tried every modality of physical therapy. I perfected my biomechanics. I danced around the totem pole. Nothing restored my functionality or completely reduced my pain because nothing nonsurgical could. Rather than lament the time I'd lost, I focused on all that I was able to accomplish with the limitations I had. Indeed, the countless hours of rehab exercises allowed me to train and race despite my constraints and subverted any compensation injuries.

Champion runner Lauren Fleshman dealt with a two-year Achilles injury. Traditional therapy and diagnostic modalities did not reveal the extent of her injury. Her travail led her to Sweden where a comprehensive workup and ultimately a surgery put her on the path to pain-free running. In her blog she wrote: "I got pissed. Really pissed. Thinking about all the things I tried that were doomed from the get-go is a thought I only allow myself to think for an instant before pushing it away, because all you can do is the best you can with the information you have at the time. That goes for me and everyone who has gone above and beyond to try to get me well . . . I wasn't really getting steamy about the lost time. It was never lost."[30]

## 10 Tips for a Mental Makeover to Overcome Obstacles

- If you've missed your race goal, you can shout, cry, or pout, but only for twenty-four hours.
- Use your mistakes as a springboard to educate yourself and create a new plan for the future.
- Long-term injuries tend to create psychological consequences such as anger, anxiety, and depression. Fend these off by focusing on the activities that are possible and reaching out to your support network for comfort.
- Chronic pain can become all-consuming. Distraction by engaging in activities can provide some relief.
- Overtraining syndrome and chronic fatigue are affecting endurance athletes in ever-increasing numbers. Pay attention to the early warning signs of fatigue lasting several days, a sore throat that won't go away, and/or consistent drops in performance.
- A proper balance of training and rest/recovery will decrease the chances of injury and fatigue.
- Learn to manage a chronic illness by working with medical personnel familiar with the demands of an endurance sports life. Personal experience will also inform you of what works and what makes things worse.

- An inability to properly diagnose an illness or injury does not mean it is a psychological problem. Keep looking until you find answers.
- After a long-term injury or a traumatic event, allow your mental wounds to heal just as you would your physical ones.
- Try to smile, even in the most desperate times. Maintaining a modicum of positivity provides real benefits.

# 10

# Finding Meaning

## The gratitude approach

I never appreciated my health more than when I didn't have it. It usually goes that way, though, doesn't it? You don't miss something until it is gone. In the summer of 2015, I hit a low point with respect to my rib issues. The pain was bad enough that I had to take an extended break from swimming and many of my runs were canceled or cut short. My ability to exercise on a given day was a mystery. The uncertainty was galling, but the experience also gave me a new perspective on health and wellness and how that duo is finicky, unpredictable, and absolutely necessary. Mostly, though, I was able to change my perception about what I could or should expect from myself on any given day and the ability to do *anything*, whether it was an easy jog, a walk, or a run, was a reward for patience and tenacity. Since I am an optimist, I also viewed the reduced laundry due to the diminished exercise with immense gratitude.

Lisa Bentley's outlook on living with Cystic Fibrosis (CF) is an important lesson in gratitude. Rather than wallow in defeatism, she handles her illness, and the associated limitations, with aplomb. Her positive outlook comes across in this sentiment: "I literally believed that CF was a gift. It gave me an opportunity to bring hope to families with kids with CF. They might see how healthy I was and then they could hope for the same for their young child and then let them 'live and play.' I believed that by racing with CF, I was showing the benefit of sport with chronic respiratory disease. I am as healthy as I am because of sport."[1]

The gratitude approach implies maintaining optimism by focusing on the positives and appreciating the impressive functions that we demand from our mind and body, even if it falls short of our ultimate aspirations.

## Refining or redefining

I have had quite a bit of experience "reinventing" my athletic self. I started out my athletic career as a swimmer, at the age of seven. It was my identity for so many years that chlorine became my scent of choice over any fancy perfume. Indeed, the extended swimming hiatus I spoke about in the summer of 2015 made me miss the scent terribly. When I graduated from college, I muddled around without any athletic goals and I felt aimless. I turned to triathlon and I obtained a new identity. I even had an ID card from USA Triathlon to prove it. Again, my life was wrapped up in my new sport and I embraced it wholeheartedly. I never imagined a day when I wouldn't be a triathlete anymore.

A freak accident in 2009 ended my triathlon days; the injuries I sustained made riding a bike impossible (and to this day, I still am not able to ride). I mourned for a little while and wondered what the heck I was going to do to sustain my competitive spirit. I parlayed my love for running into yet another new identity, I became a competitive masters runner; I even got an ID card from USA Track & Field to prove it.

Many athletes go through a period of time where they are confronted with a crossroads and must decide whether to stay the course or make a change. Olympian Colleen De Reuck reached such a crossroads in 2013 at the age of forty-nine. She explained that the inevitable slowing down that comes with age was initially difficult to handle; the training intensity was the same, but the times did not reflect the effort. It took her some time to accept the fact that she could no longer race at the level at which she became accustomed. In terms of running, to keep things fresh she said, "with no more PRs (personal records) available, I will race events that are favorites and on my bucket list. Enough years have now passed, I just look back and can't believe what I used to do. As they say, time heals."[2]

Rather than fight the slowdown, Colleen started doing triathlons. After two years in the sport, and conquering her immense fear of open-water swimming, she turned her age group upside down with standout performances. I asked why she decided to make the switch. She told me, "I was at the end of my running career and needed a new, fresh incentive to keep motivated, so why not?" Even though she has shown tremendous success as a triathlete, with wins in her age group at the 2014 Ironman 70.3 World Championships and at the 2015 Ironman World Championships, she said, "deep down I think of myself as a runner. Maybe after a few years of doing triathlons I might change my mind."

This conflict of the mind was evidenced in Colleen's training, where she initially lamented the necessary decrease in run mileage to accommodate bike and swim sessions. I witnessed the evolution in her acceptance of bringing the new sports into her training regimen, and the more adept she became in triathlon, the more she embraced the different training program. Colleen's ambivalence about her transition from one sport to another exemplifies the importance of inching higher on the confidence meter and instilling a positive confidence cycle. As she

208 The Champion Mindset

has become more confident in biking and swimming through deliberate practice and success, her view of herself as a multisport athlete has begun to change. Part of redefining yourself is building confidence in your new challenge through repetition, achievement, and/or enjoyment.

Simon Lessing discussed with me the difficulty of moving from a professional athlete back to the "real world." His thought was that making the transition is "the toughest decision for any pro athlete who has been at it for a lengthy period of time." I agree! I had a solid backup plan in place, and I still mourned the loss of my professional career for months. Simon explained that the struggle comes from several angles. Athletes fear dealing with reality, there is a lack of acceptance that the athletic career is over, and there is also the issue of figuring out what to do next. He compared the challenge to a midlife crisis.

Every time I moved from one situation to the next, there was a period of frustration, sadness, and readjustment. But ultimately, I found satisfaction, opportunities to accomplish new tasks, and fun. The process of reinventing oneself is not an easy undertaking, but it can potentially lead to new avenues that are even more fulfilling than previous endeavors. Having gone through several iterations myself, I can offer up some advice:

- *Take action quickly.* When a situation occurs that is prompting a reinvention, allow yourself a fixed amount of time to be depressed, angry, irritable, or bitchy. Then figure out your next step and execute a plan.
- *Figure out your talents.* Then think about how to apply them in a new way.
- *Talk to anyone and everyone.* You never know who has a life-changing idea or fantastic connections.
- *Don't be afraid of change.* Yes, change can be scary. Kick its ass.

+ *Opportunities abound.* View these novel prospects as a chance to meet new people, do innovative things, and have more fun.
+ *Get involved in a different capacity.* No longer a triathlon competitor, I continue a very active involvement in the sport as a coach, writer, and educator. I avidly peruse results, stay up to date on technology, learn about new races, and keep informed about rules changes.

## Become a joyful athlete

The first time I went for a run, I loathed it. I was a lifelong swimmer, and swimmers generally don't thrive doing land sports, dying outside the water like a fish. At the outset, there was no way of predicting how my body would react, what the new sport would evoke, or if there was potential to excel. My initial rocky relationship with running evolved over time into one of respect, then joy, and now running is an integral part of my life, first through my time as a triathlete, and now as a masters runner. I learned how to take an activity that I disdained and turn it into one that I value. If I had not made that transition, assuredly I would have ceased my running career immediately, and what a shame that would have been considering how running effectively changed my life by unlocking years of opportunity and delight.

After knowing the joy that a sport can bestow through my years as a swimmer, I could not have borne participating in an activity that brought me misery. That is the crux of everything: if you do not enjoy what you are doing as an athlete, nothing else matters; if your passion for endurance sports is nil or waning or in flux, your results are inconsequential.

Endurance sports have been a stable entity in my life since the age of seven. Endurance sports ground me during times of disarray and uncertainty, provide an incomparable social network, generate prospects for travel, and create an opportunity to test my physical and mental limits on a regular basis. I have seen the world on foot and by bike, a most invigorating way to sightsee. Many of the ideas for this book occurred during periods of exercise; seemingly, sweating has always had a miraculous way of freeing my mind of nonsense, making room for productive thoughts. A good bout of exercise has often turned around even the most challenging days.

The reason I initially disliked running was because it was difficult. It made me sore; my waterlogged body was not prepared for a sport that required coordination, gravity, and a different type of heavy breathing. I imagined, though, beyond the initial discomfort and disharmonious nature of the sport, something special was on the horizon, so I pressed on, albeit five years later. It wasn't until I understood the fundamentals of running that I was able to really embrace this new sport; I finally became a joyful runner.

Going back to my running origins is an allegory about the evolution from loathing an activity to making a complete about-face and learning to relish it. My first run turned out to be quite eventful, as I jumped in too quickly, something that is somewhat of a theme in my life and unfortunately quite common for type A athletes. I tend to do things with gusto and suffer the ramifications later.

It was August of 1988 in Austin, TX, a few months after I graduated from high school. The previous day I'd finished my last event at the swimming Olympic Trials and a teammate who had run cross-country in addition to swimming (what an overachiever) had a lofty idea. She suggested that we run from our hotel to the pool to watch the afternoon events.

"How hard can that be?" I mused. I was obviously fit; I had just swum in the Olympic Trials. "Bring it on," I replied. I rued those words thirty minutes later.

As a sidebar, I should mention that I was a breaststroker. This is an important distinction from excelling at the other strokes. Breaststrokers spend a lot of time in external rotation, meaning we walk like ducks.

This translated into running with my feet pointing out and giving me a very distinct running style such that people a mile away could see that I was coming. I had thought I abolished my crazy style of running until I heard the announcer at a race call out "There's Joanna Zeiger coming down the stretch. I would know that running style anywhere!"

Back to the run: we set off in the blazing Texas heat with humidity so high my curly hair grew to three times its original size. Of course, we had no water, no gels (they didn't even exist back then), and just an inkling of how to actually get to the pool without running down the middle of the highway.

I donned my fancy white Reebok aerobic shoes—they were a must-have in those days, and painfully wrong attire. (Who knew about sports bras?) I was huffing after five minutes and my teammate was out of sight within ten. When I eventually dragged my sweat-soaked self to the pool ninety minutes later, exhausted from the heat and hobbled by muscle spasms, I vowed to never run again. My promise to reject running forever was only solidified the next day. I was so sore I could hardly walk, and going down stairs required the use of a handrail. I had no idea my fit body could hurt like that and how so many muscles could be underutilized as a swimmer.

Five years later I began to run in earnest. My life changed, I was a retired competitive swimmer, and I needed a new challenge. I was lured into running with an eye on someday competing in a triathlon.

I was still struggling with the transition to a new sport, but I began to enjoy it more because I'd acquired knowledge about the nuances of running. I learned that running with joy required a keen understanding of the sport. Even though running is considered one of the most basic sports, its simplicity can be deceiving. Running joyfully seemingly necessitates little more than a well-fitting pair of shoes and an open road, but the catch is—and I learned this the hard way—obtaining those perfect shoes can be almost a lifelong project.

It is not a coincidence that as I learned more about running I enjoyed it even more, and eventually my desire to succeed increased and I became faster. At the root of these successes was a basic enjoyment in the process of running. I never took for granted the beauty of my surroundings or that my body had the ability to do what I asked it to do.

Becoming a joyful runner is knowing that a pair of running shoes does not last forever. I learned that with a stress fracture in my left leg. I thought one bought new running shoes when the old ones were dirty, not when they were worn out from logging hundreds of miles. I certainly did not enjoy being injured. A joyful runner knows that choice of attire can impact an entire run. Chafe, blisters, shoes that are too stiff or soft or tight, or an ill-fitting sports bra can ruin the most glorious of runs. Running joyfully requires honing the mental game as much as the physical one. Running joyfully is understanding how running too fast or too many miles will impact your body over time, or having the knowledge that better biomechanics can help prevent dreaded injuries. Running joyfully is having reliable and compatible running companions, very often the family dog. A joyful masters runner (over forty) knows that they can go fast even when everyone believes otherwise.

Mary Cain, a running phenom, learned the lesson that without joy athletics is moot. As a teenager, Mary broke high school, national, and world junior records in events from 800 meters up to 5,000 meters, culminating in a gold medal in the 3,000 meters at the IAAF World Junior Championships in 2014. Mary moved to Oregon from her home in New York to train with her coach, the renowned Alberto Salazar. Mary's results in 2015 were less than stellar, a step backward after years of astounding feats. She simply wasn't happy. Mary moved back to New York and within a few months her bubbly persona reemerged. After a cross-country race in the fall of 2015, Mary explained to the press, "I'm not the down Mary Cain in interviews anymore! I'm super happy! I think one of the biggest things for me is just having fun again. . . . When

I was out in Portland there was a lot of really great things about it. But being home, I'm a New Yorker and I think I've really enjoyed being back out here."[3]

Colleen De Reuck is still kicking butt at fifty-one. She told me, "enjoyment was always important. When I found I was not enjoying running from too much pressure, I would always step back from it and take a break."

Remember Christian Taylor from chapter 1? He elucidated on the topic of finding joy: "I realized in order to improve I needed to have fun again. The college system was very team-oriented and had been a lot of fun, yet I'd found life as a professional athlete was at times very lonely. You were an individual, very much on your own. You can find yourself often in the middle of a random city, eating foods you have never tried before. What I realized after Moscow [site of the 2013 World Championships] is I needed to find the sport fun again. So in 2014 I decided I wanted to run the 4 x 400 meters at World Relays—what better fun can you have than a trip to the Bahamas? That year was a game changer for me. It was rare for me not to be smiling. I was having fun again and it reminded me why I loved the sport."[4] His newfound love for the sport catapulted him to a gold-medal performance at the 2015 World Championships in Beijing, which he backed up with a gold medal at the 2016 Rio Olympics.

Lisa Bentley told me, "The mental game was my strength as an athlete. I could turn a negative into a positive very quickly. I could find joy and happiness in nothing. I knew that my fellow competitors were far more talented than I was, but I knew that I had more passion for the sport than most. I loved what I did and that would elevate my game."

My lesson about joy can be applied to any sporting activity because the tenets are the same. Joy in sport comes from knowledge, a proper environment, understanding your potential, social experiences, believing in oneself, sticking to a plan, and honing the mental game. Find joy first, and success will come after.

## Don't lose hope

Endurance sports are predicated on hope; indeed, it is practically the cornerstone of the mental aspects of sport. Hope that you can train. Hope that you stay injury-free. Hope that the weather cooperates. Hope that you can balance training with the rest of your responsibilities. Hope that you don't get sick. Hope to overcome adversity. Phew, that is A LOT of hope.

There is limited research about hope and athletics, possibly due to the focus of sport psychology on "deficits and problems" within the athlete. C. R. Snyder, a preeminent researcher in the field of hope, defined hope within the context of goal-oriented behavior as having two parts: agency (goal-directed determination) and pathways (planning to meet goals).[5] In this framework, pathways refers to the perceptions of being able to create "workable routes to the goal" and agency as the will to begin and continue along the pathway to the goal.[6]

Clearly, the components of hope are complex, because they are comprised of a duo of interacting factors *and* individuals can differ in their hope across domains, such as family, relationships, work, leisure activities, and academia—meaning, for example, there can be high athletic hope, but low academic hope.[7] Adding to the intricacy is the fact that individuals can fluctuate in their level of hope over time according to life's circumstances (state hope), although people do fall into a general range from which they do not substantially vary (dispositional hope).[8]

Hope is not an insignificant paradigm. It is important because "hope not only facilitates attaining a goal when that goal is unimpeded, it also helps individuals better cope when negative events or feelings arise."[9] Indeed, hope has been associated with higher proficiency in life, superior coping mechanisms, increased positive thoughts, less depression, and a better outlook during stressful events.[10]

I think of hope as the grains of sand in an hourglass, not in the soap opera kind of way (you know, from *The Days of Our Lives*), but in a more existential way. At some point your hourglass is full of hope sand. But the sand is always filtering down because hope is volatile, waiting to escape, attempting to shake your resolve, and eventually causing low hope or a total lack of hope.

Luckily, even though there is always leakage of the hope sand, there is a certain amount of hope tolerance. Hope sand will spill down after a bad workout, but a single dreadful workout is usually shaken off with the hope that the next one will be better, so the top level of the hourglass is refilled with hope sand. How about when you are sick? Your hope sand will spill down quickly until you feel better and you can resume your training. Once you are well, flip the hourglass over and you have lots of hope again. Suffering from an injury makes the hope sand disappear quickly into the low hope level. But once you get ahold of the problem, the process will slow down and eventually, when you recover, you can move your hope sand away from the low hope level and you will have lots of hope once again.

What happens when *all* of the sand filters out of the top of the hourglass and fills the bottom of the hourglass?

In the summer of 2015, for the first time in my life, I had no hope sand left in the top of my hourglass. My pain became ruthless, my life utterly altered, and to compound the issue, there was no sign of a solution. I lacked hope.

The lowest point, the time when all of the sand seeped to the bottom of the hourglass, was in early August of 2015. I had a consultation with the surgeon who had removed the titanium plates from my ribs that May to determine whether he could or would perform another surgery to help alleviate continued abdominal wall and neuropathic pain. The problem was that the MRI he ordered did not show any abnormalities. He did not examine me. He based his decision solely on the MRI imaging that had a very low likelihood anyway of turning up anything irregular. He was unwilling to do an exploratory surgery. I reminded him of two comments that he'd made in May: (1) he would address the neuropathy after surgery, and (2) I was now his patient, in his care, and he would follow through to help me. He did not do either.

I left his office in tears, the top level of my hope hourglass completely devoid of hope sand. I was confused and seemingly out of options. My mental state was shattered and my thoughts went to some very dark places.

On a whim, I called my physical medicine doctor who was always an ally, and scheduled a nerve block to help alleviate the pain until a more permanent solution was found. Luckily, the doc fit me in two days later. The relief I felt from the nerve block allowed some hope sand to find its way back into the upper end of the hourglass. The pain dissipated enough that I could think more clearly.

My father did some research and found the surgeon who performed my surgery in September 2015. The moment I met this surgeon, my hope was renewed, and my hourglass refilled immediately. I instinctively knew that this doctor would be able to help me.

Five weeks after surgery, I noticed some major improvements in my health and overall well-being. However, there was still some sand on the bottom of the hourglass, though, as I managed some lingering issues, namely a persistent and uncomfortable abdominal muscle spasm , sternum pain, and shortness of breath (eventually I needed two more surgeries in 2016 to remedy these problems).

## Measuring hope

The Adult State Hope Scale is a tool to determine your level of hope.[11] It can be used to measure hope for just about anything, but in the context of this book, you can use it to examine your level of hope with respect to endurance sports. If you recall from the above discussion about hope, there are two dimensions within the construct of hope: agency (will to begin) and pathways (routes to the goal). The Adult State Hope Scale measures the two dimensions, as well as overall hope. Take the test and establish your level of hope. An objective measure can alert you to an impending hope disaster before it even registers, or it can solidify that there is a hope problem that needs to be addressed.

### The Adult State Hope Scale (Snyder et al., 1996)

Read each item carefully. Using the scale shown on the next page, please select the number that best describes how you think about yourself right now and put that number in the blank before each sentence. Please take a few moments to focus on yourself and what is going on in your life at this moment. Once you have this "here and now" set, go ahead and answer each item according to the following scale:

| **1** | **2** | **3** | **4** | **5** | **6** | **7** | **8** |
|---|---|---|---|---|---|---|---|
| Definitely False | Mostly False | Somewhat False | Slightly False | Slightly True | Somewhat True | Mostly True | Definitely True |

_____ 1. If I should find myself in a jam, I could think of many ways to get out of it.

_____ 2. At the present time, I am energetically pursuing my goals.

_____ 3. There are lots of ways around any problem that I am facing now.

_____ 4. Right now, I see myself as being pretty successful.

_____ 5. I can think of many ways to reach my current goals.

_____ 6. At this time, I am meeting the goals that I have set for myself.

**Scoring information**

**Pathways subscale score**: Add items 1, 3, and 5. Scores on this subscale can range from 3 to 24, with higher scores indicating higher levels of pathways thinking.

**Agency subscale score**: Add items 2, 4, and 6. Scores on this subscale can range from 3 to 24, with higher scores indicating higher levels of agency thinking.

**Total hope score**: Add the pathways and agency subscales together. Scores can range from 6 to 48, with higher scores representing higher hope levels.

When my hourglass was overflowing with sand in the less-hope level, I was fortunate to be able to bide my time while I refilled the more-hope level. Restoring hope when it seems there is none to be had is imperative to break the lack-of-hope cycle. Because without hope, truly, endurance sports are meaningless. Reestablish hope with my suggestions, below.

*Family and social support.* My family and friends offered more support than I could have imagined. I was very open and honest with my feelings, and being able to express my lack of hope allowed them to give me the proper consolation and help.

Lisa Bentley expressed her hope in dealing with impending foot surgery in 2015, after many years of nagging pain, during a phone conversation with me: "In dealing with chronic disease or injury, you look for hope and others in similar situations. I have done a lot of mental preparation for the surgery and some of that involved speaking to other people like yourself. Hearing the stories of other elite athletes helps to 'frame' the situation and turn the negative into a positive. Just knowing that those alliances are out there makes me feel supported. So I surround myself with good people—getting advice and a variety of perspectives. We do the same with disease—you just want to find one person with the disease that is healthy and you have hope."

*Do your research.* I knew from my reading of journal articles exactly what was wrong and what needed to be done even though MRI, CT, and X-ray imaging did not reveal the problems. Once the surgery was performed, my hunches were confirmed. Education is a powerful tool.

*Focus on what you can do and not on what you can't do.* Ugh, this was really hard. I took a lot of walks and hikes with my husband (and the ever-faithful dog, of course) where all I did was complain about how I would rather have been running. My grousing was not at all productive. Eventually, I embraced the walking/hiking because it was much better than sitting on my couch.

Lisa Bentley's approach is both mature and pragmatic: "Both injury and disease have unknown long-term effects. I don't know if I will need a lung transplant one day. I don't know if after foot surgery I will run again. I believe I will be fine in both cases but I don't really know. So I position myself to do the best I can do with the capabilities I have. I used to be able to run every single day. This injury meant I have only been able to run three days a week since 2007. I kept on racing. I just had to get smarter with training. With illness, I just keep on going the best I can—maybe I can't run as fast or as long but I keep on moving the best that I can."

*Find purpose.* When you are feeling hopeless, often purposelessness creeps into the picture. We all have some kind of purpose, it is just a matter of exposing it and cultivating it. My purpose was to not annoy my husband too much, accommodate the athletes I coach, write this book, and work hard for my consulting clients.

The triad of hope, sports, and purpose did not go unnoticed by the International Olympic Committee (IOC). The IOC created the Olympic Solidarity Program, an initiative which extends financial assistance to National Olympic Committees to develop Olympic programs for refugees. Countries such as Austria, Belgium, Bulgaria, Denmark, and Slovenia have already received funds. The IOC told *Outside* magazine, "We are hopeful, however, that this initiative will bring hope to the refugee athletes who long to go back to training and compete at the Olympic Games."[12]

*Dream big, but stay within reason.* When hope disappears, so do the dreams. Do not let your dreams slip away, they are important and propel you forward. As each day passes, the probability of my qualifying for the 2016 Olympic Trials marathon diminishes, but one can still dream, and it serves a dual function because it also gives me purpose in my training.

## Longevity

Simon Lessing raced as a professional triathlete for nearly twenty years. He now competes in rowing to quench his competitive thirst. How about Colleen De Reuck? She raced in four Olympics and continues to wreak havoc on her competition in triathlon in her fifties. Lisa Bentley's professional career spanned twenty years and now, in her forties, she races marathons and half marathons as a masters runner. The common thread? These athletes have been in the endurance sports game for a very long time. If I add myself to that list, I can say that I swam competitively for fifteen years, raced triathlon for fifteen years—twelve of them as a professional—and now I am in my sixth year as a competitive masters runner.

Endurance sports offer so many benefits that participation should be viewed as a long-term undertaking. First, mastering the art of endurance sports requires a lot of time and practice, and this mastery is a lifelong pursuit in and of itself. Second, endurance sports is an *existence* just as it is a means to an end, with the end assuredly being goal attainment. Participate in endurance sports long enough and it implants itself into your very being, its essence coursing through your veins like blood.

Simon Lessing extolled the virtues of triathlon when he said, "Multisport is a lifestyle sport. It is a healthy way for middle-agers to exercise without the repetitiveness of a single element sport. This offers some very good cross-training possibilities. It's a nice way to balance things out. The goal is to keep involved in years of sport."

Ironman has become a bucket list event, with many participants competing only once and then moving on to another endeavor. This group is missing out and missing the point.

Endurance sports, apart from the health benefits, offer so many tangible rewards. There are lasting friendships and opportunities to travel. Athletes possess the ability to truly test the mind and body and really learn the meaning of walking the fine line between ultimate fitness and ultimate disaster and how to stay on the right side of that line. And, of course, there are the famous endorphins. Who doesn't want a lifetime of those?

## 10 Tips for Finding Meaning in a Mental Makeover

- Appreciate your ability to move your body and endeavor to achieve your goals.
- When you are at a crossroads in your athletic life, do not be afraid to try something new.
- Redefining your athletic self comes from determining your talents and desire and creating new opportunities for yourself.
- A joyful athlete will find more appreciation in sport and will tend to have a longer athletic life.
- Joy can stem from a multitude of factors, which will differ between athletes and can even change within an athlete over time. Define what provides joy in your athletic life and ensure that you get a good dosage of it.
- Athletes of all levels, novice to professional, have expressed that, without joy, their results were not stellar.
- Hope is necessary for athletic success, as it tends to create positive thoughts, lower levels of depression, and increased ability to cope in the face of adversity.
- Hope can be measured and it can fluctuate over time.
- Arm yourself with knowledge to increase your hope and joy in endurance sports.
- When you find that your hope is waning, look to your social network for support, and define a tangible purpose. Purpose can restore hope.

# Epilogue

My quest for the Olympic Trials standard in the marathon effectively ended when I had surgery in September 2015. The qualifying window would close on January 17, 2016, not leaving me enough time to prepare for a marathon at the speed required to run 2:43:00. I tried self-handicapping by telling myself I wasn't ready to run a marathon anyway and that the Olympic Trials course was not one suited to my strengths. The excuses didn't lift my spirits, though, because no matter how I framed the situation, missing qualifying by fifty-nine seconds in 2014 was a devastating blow. I was dismayed to end the exciting pursuit.

My first foray back into racing was a half marathon in San Diego on November 21, 2015. I was not ready to perform anywhere near my best. My runs (and daily living) were impeded by sternum pain and an irritating and persistent abdominal muscle spasm that had started seven months prior. It was only a few short weeks preceding the race that I started stringing together consistent interval sessions, a necessity to run fast in a race.

In spite of those shortcomings, I still decided to race. Most athletes would choose to forgo racing in such a tenuous condition, where the probability of underperforming was a given. I put my pride aside and swapped it for something better: the chance to do the very activity that would make me feel normal again.

I chose this particular race because it was in my hometown, and I thought the familiar sights and being surrounded by my family would be comforting. I ran one of my slowest half marathons in a decade (I stopped the clock at 1:23:30, which put me atop the masters podium), but I particularly relished the race environment. The start line and finish area were a festival of fitness and strength, a pleasant diversion from the tumultuous months of frustration and poor health leading up to the race.

As a competitor, it was hard not to place judgment on that performance. My initial reaction was one of disappointment, which, in hindsight, I realize is ridiculous. The mere fact that eight short weeks after major surgery I even had the ability to race a half marathon was a victory, rendering the time I finished secondary. Training doesn't lie, and certainly, my training really did let me know that I was not ready to run any faster.

I considered my options for racing in 2016. My San Diego performance informed me that a marathon would be something for further in the future, maybe the following spring or fall.

Imagine, then, my absolute and utter surprise when USA Track & Field announced on December 11, 2015, that they amended the Olympic Trials standard to 2:45:00 in accordance with a change made by the governing body of track and field to the Olympic standard itself. All of a sudden, I qualified for the Olympic Trials in the marathon for the third time. My emotions ranged from exuberance, to disbelief, to concern. Would I be ready? Could my body even handle running 26.2 miles?

Upon reflection, I understood that none of my apprehensions mattered. What mattered was that I maintained hope. I never gave up pursuing my goal. I assembled a team that helped me physically and emotionally. I never feared failure. I took chances. I raced well when my body felt terrible. I raced with integrity. I did not take no for an answer. I cried. A lot. I cursed when needed. I shook off despair and desperation. Most important, I trained and raced with joy, in full appreciation that being able to do anything physical with all of my limitations was a gift.

Despite my persistent sternum pain and the horrible abdominal spasm, I decided to continue with my training for the Olympic Trials, albeit altered to accommodate my impediments. I delved into a test race 4 weeks out from the Olympic Trials, a half marathon in Houston. It was disastrous; by mile 8 of the race I vomiting profusely and I had to walk much of the remaining 5 miles.

The information gained in Houston was invaluable, though. It gave me four weeks to practice what I preach and put to use all of the concepts I wrote about in *The Champion Mindset*. I altered my goal, from attaining a stellar time to just finishing. I amassed my team of experts to help me devise a plan for pacing, pain management, and most important for moral support. Copious amounts of desire, perseverance, and a positive attitude propelled me through my final weeks of training and throughout the race itself. Even though I had an excuse at the ready to not start or not finish, I did not allow this to self-handicap my performance. I knew that the race would not *feel* good, but I would make myself as comfortably uncomfortable as possible. Most important, I had to push aside my ego and not focus on any potential ridicule at the notion I would probably finish last, if I even finished at all.

Five days before the Olympic trials, an abnormality was spotted on a CT scan. It was determined I would require yet another surgery to remove some bony tissue from behind my sternum. I pushed aside my feelings of disappointment and fear to keep my mind clear for the looming marathon.

When race day dawned, I was ready for my assault on the hardest 26.2 miles I had ever run. My only parameters for dropping out were if the pain was intolerable or if I was risking further damage. Barring those situations, I planned to run and walk to the finish. The whole notion of running the marathon, under conditions that were so far from ideal, was scary. But, when the gun went off, I was ready for whatever unfolded on that day, including the pain from my injury, the excessive heat, and the uninspiring course. I was at the back of the field from the moment the gun sounded, and of the 149 women who finished (out of 201 starters, there was a high dropout rate due to the abnormally warm temperature) I finished 149th. I was elated.

Six days after the race, I had my fifth chest wall operation. The surgeon removed a 3.1 cm xiphoid process that grew abnormally behind my sternum (it was pressing on my abdominal muscle and diaphragm), a veritable medical marvel, since I had my xiphoid process surgically excised in 2014 (we have yet to uncover the mystery of the origin of this "new" xiphoid).

The mindset that I took with me on my journey from a chronic pain patient to Olympic Trials finisher may seem unusual, but it is not. During a hike with a longtime friend, I explained in great detail the contents of this book and the countless hours of research I embarked upon to familiarize myself with the thought processes of champion athletes, trying to determine if there was such a thing as a champion mindset. In particular, I relayed to him the podcasts I listened to and the many interviews I read, and how I was inspired by the words of so many great champions. He intuitively asked me, "Whose words were the most inspirational?"

I thought about his question for a moment before I responded. My answer was that I was most intrigued by the similarity in the words of all the extraordinary athletes and that beyond their obvious physical prowess that there was indeed a champion mindset that propelled them to victory. The traits of the athletes whose stories I conveyed, along with the many other champions whose accounts I could not incorporate into the book but were equally compelling, fit into a mold that can be emulated by any athlete of any ability.

What, then, comprises the mindset of a champion athlete? I hypothesize that if a composite mindset was created to encapsulate the qualities of the great champions in endurance sports, it might look something like the Champion Athlete Mindset Profile diagram shown below, the mindset gold standard, if you will. An athlete can possess anywhere from zero to 100 percent of any given trait. Generally, I would imagine, most people do not meet either extreme, but they fall somewhere on the continuum.

In this hypothetical situation, a champion athlete possesses high levels of positive and productive traits: hope, taking ownership, having balance, extrinsic motivation, joyfulness, and confidence. The negative and unproductive traits of self-handicapping and amotivation are low, while intrinsic motivation is somewhere in the middle. It is this mindset that kept me afloat during my prolonged bout of chronic pain and ultimately led me to my improbable goal of qualifying for and finishing the 2016 Marathon Olympic Trials.

## Champion Athlete Mindset Profile

|  |  |
|-------|-------|
| Hope | 90% |
| Ownership | 90% |
| Balance | 75% |
| Self-handicapping | 10% |
| Intrinsic motivation | 80% |
| Extrinsic motivation | 15% |
| Amotivation | 5% |
| Joyfulness | 95% |
| Confidence | 90% |

A novice endurance athlete, a seasoned veteran, or even a professional athlete waiting for the big breakthrough might have an Athlete Mindset Profile quite different from the one of a champion athlete. I speculate that a fledgling athlete will show lower levels of the positive traits and higher levels of the negative traits, but theoretically, by reading this book, the Fledgling Athlete Mindset Profile can shift over time to more closely mimic the Champion Athlete Mindset Profile.

**Fledgling Athlete Mindset Profile**

|  |  |
|---|---|
| Hope | 65% |
| Ownership | 70% |
| Balance | 45% |
| Self-handicapping | 80% |
| Intrinsic motivation | 35% |
| Extrinsic motivation | 50% |
| Amotivation | 15% |
| Joyfulness | 95% |
| Confidence | 60% |

Every athlete has a ceiling when it comes to physical ability and therefore their athletic improvement is finite. On the other hand, the mind is malleable and open to infinite possibilities for development. A mental makeover can bridge that gap between physical limitations and endless opportunity.

The chapters in this book are meant to set the stage for you to take control of your mindset and add a newfound mental-self to your physical prowess. The concepts introduced in this book were carefully chosen and researched based off my own personal journey from an inexperienced swimmer to Olympian and World Champion. I understand, and hope that now you do, too, that success is never guaranteed, but the manner in which we handle failure will dictate future success or failure. A mental makeover can help you manage your mistakes and missed goals and set you up to realize your potential in the future. Mastering the champion mindset is a lifelong pursuit, not unlike the mastery of golf or chess. The only way to achieve that mastery is to practice often, challenge yourself, and be prepared for anything. Remember the Sisu Survey mentioned in Chapter 1? Here is the link again: sisu.racereadycoaching.com. Retest yourself to learn whether you have improved upon your mental toughness skills or if there are traits of mental toughness that still need development.

# Acknowledgments

*The Champion Mindset* uses sports as an illustration of how a change in the mental game can revolutionize your pursuit of any goal, whether it is related to business, family, or even writing a book. The ideas I put forth in this book not only propelled me to reach my athletic potential, but also came in handy during the process of preparing the book itself. In chapter 3, I expound upon how to build your team to achieve success. Without a proper team in place, over a number of decades, this project would not have come to fruition.

My athletic gifts and unyielding mindset were nurtured over the years by coaches in swimming, triathlon, and running: Chuck Hay, Doug Russel, John Weckler, Mark Johnston, Troy Jacobson, Dave Scott, Phil Skiba, and Darren De Reuck. From each of these coaches I learned the important lessons of how to work hard without working too hard, and the power of communication.

Oftentimes, a writer can distinguish the turning point when writing morphs from an onerous task forced by school into a passion. My moment was a tenth-grade assignment that initially caused so much angst I was utterly paralyzed with an inability to even start. This breakthrough assignment was the brainchild of a teacher, Mr. Bob Litchfield, who forever changed the way I looked at sentence structure, punctuation, and storytelling.

My health, a subject which is prominently covered in this book, was compromised in the more than six years since my bike accident in 2009 until the present. A number of physicians and health care professionals helped me salvage my decrepit body. Drs. John Tobey, Mark Saxton, Daniel Saltzman, and Jeffrey Cross provided relief when none seemed possible. Robin Galaskewicz spent countless hours on Skype helping me with strength and conditioning. Kim McCormack (massage therapist) and Bob Cranny (physical therapist) used their incredible skills to keep my ailing body working the best it could under the circumstances.

A big thanks to Tito Morales whose mentorship allowed me to write my proposal when I was stymied by the Herculean task. His vigilant tutelage gave me the confidence I lacked and our discussions helped formulate the chapters and topics covered in the book. Coleen O'Shea, my agent, read through some pretty awful initial proposals, but she stuck with me by seeing the forest through the trees. My editor at St. Martin's Press, Daniela Rapp, provided insightful comments and her editing skills overcame my lack of perfectionism (see chapter 4).

I cannot thank Colleen De Reuck, Simon Lessing, and Lisa Bentley enough for their time and candor. Top athletes are asked to be interviewed constantly, and I fully appreciate that they not only agreed to work with me, but also that they were so incredibly thorough and thoughtful with their answers. I also want to express my gratitude to the other athletes whose quotes and stories I included in the book; I found their words through podcasts, magazines, and blogs. Researching these athletes and delving into their mindset only compounded my respect for their achievements.

My family was my lifeline and without them this book never would have happened. My father, Bob, read every page of every chapter as I wrote them. His keen eye, objectivity, and willingness to discuss the theories and concepts presented in the book pushed me to be a better writer, researcher, and thinker. Mark, my husband, was always available for a pep talk, a cup of tea, and a hug. He also created the images found throughout the book. It is a good thing that long-distance calls are free these days, because I spent many hours on the phone with my mom, Karen, who provided much-needed support and was an excellent "filler" when I needed some time away from my computer.

# Notes

## 1. The Mental Game Exposed

1. http://spikes.iaaf.org/post/christian-taylors-words-of-wisdom
2. Ibid.
3. http://www.witsup.com/the-selfless-triathlete-a-paradigm-shift-could-be-the-secret-to-increasing-participation/#.VgIofldHOv4.twitter
4. https://www.supermoney.com/2014/05/endurance-athletes-wealthy/
5. http://www.forbes.com/sites/entrepreneursorganization/2015/07/14/why-ironmen-and-ironwomen-make-great-ceos/
6. Sprouse-Blum, A. S., et al. (2010). "Understanding endorphins and their importance in pain management." *Hawaii Medical Journal, 69(3):* 70–71.
7. Fernandes, M. F. A., et al. (2015) "Leptin suppresses the rewarding effects of running vis STAT3 signaling in dopamine neurons." *Cell Metabolism.* In press, available online.
8. Fuss, J., et al. (2015). "A runner's high depends on cannabinoid receptors in mice." *Proceedings of the National Academy of Sciences.*
9. Personal communication.
10. Ericsson, K. A., Krampe, R. T., & Tesch-Römer, C. (1993). "The role of deliberate practice in the acquisition of expert performance." *Psychological Review, 100(3):* 363.
11. Tsianos, G., et al. (2004). "The ACE gene insertion/deletion polymorphism and elite endurance swimming." *European Journal of Applied Physiology, 92(3):* 360–362.

12. Epstein, D. (2013). *The Sports Gene*. New York: Penguin Group. Chapter 5.
13. Ross, R., de Lannoy, L., & Stotz, P. J. (2015). "Separate effects of intensity and amount of exercise on interindividual cardiorespiratory fitness response." In *Mayo Clinic Proceedings*, 90(11): 1506–1514. Elsevier.
14. http://www.runnersworld.com/elite-runners/kim-smith-perseveres-through-medical-trauma
15. Epstein, D. (2013). *The Sports Gene*. New York: Penguin Group. Chapter 14.
16. http://well.blogs.nytimes.com/2010/05/19/phys-ed-do-our-genes-influence-our-desire-to-exercise/
17. From Twitter: @Triathletemag, 10/10/15 10:11PM
18. Burzynska, A. Z., et al. (2015). "Physical activity is linked to greater moment-to-moment variability in spontaneous brain activity in older adults." *PLOS ONE*, 10(8): e0134819.
19. Cho, J., et al. (2015). "Treadmill running reverses cognitive declines due to Alzheimer's disease." *Medicine & Science in Sports & Exercise*, 47(9): 1814–24.

## 2. Proper Goal Setting

1. @jfriel 10/24/15, 2:39 PM
2. Arvinen-Barrow, M., et al. (2015). "Athletes' use of mental skills during sport injury rehabilitation." *Journal of Sport Rehabilitation*, 24(2): 189–197.
3. Personal communication.
4. http://www.runnersworld.com/newswire/shalane-flanagan-on-her-boston-marathon-a-bad-day-at-the-office
5. http://www.slowtwitch.com/Interview/Joe_Maloy_-_king_for_a_day_5458.html
6. http://www.scienceofrunning.com/2015/07/why-we-are-bad-at-predicting-our-own.html?m=1
7. Schmuck, P., Kasser, T., & Ryan, R. (2000). "Intrinsic and extrinsic goals: their structure and relationship to well-being in German and U.S. college students." *Social Indicator Research*, 50: 225–241.
8. Arvinen-Barrow, M., et al. (2015). "Athletes' use of mental skills during sport injury rehabilitation." *Journal of Sport Rehabilitation*, 24(2): 189–197.
9. http://triathlete-europe.competitor.com/2012/10/22/pro-tips-visualization-and-training-your-brain-to-perform#CQXHxDfptEj30I8L.99
10. http://www.pontoontri.com/entrevista-delly-carr/2015/7/13/brett-sutton

## 3. Building Your Team

1. https://www.yahoo.com/beauty/soccer-star-ali-krieger-on-the-power-of-being-a-121027616478.html
2. Fredericson, M., & Misra, A. K. (2007). "Epidemiology and aetiology of marathon running injuries." *Sports Medicine*, 37(4–5): 437–439.

3. Personal communication.

4. Baxter-Jones, A.D.G., & Maffulli, N. (2003). "Parental influence on sport participation in elite young athletes." *The Journal of Sports Medicine & Physical Fitness*, 43: 250–55.

5. http://triathlon.competitor.com/2015/12/news/ryf-makes-history-with-1 -million-win_126565#KRPfRdoYJlzqjDhA.99

6. Carron, A.V., Hausenblas, H.A., & Mack, D. (1996). "Social influence and exercise: a meta-analysis." *Journal of Sport and Exercise Psychology*, 18: 1–16.

7. http://www.slowtwitch.com/Interview/Gwen_How_far_can_she_go__4447 .html

8. Personal communication.

9. Pyne, D. B., et al. (2000). "Training strategies to maintain immunocompetence in athletes." *International Journal of Sports Medicine*, 21(1): S51.

10. Nabhan, D. C., et al. (2015). "Laboratory tests ordered by a chiropractic sports physician on elite athletes over a 1-year period." *Journal of Chiropractic Medicine*, 14(2): 68–76.

11. http://running.competitor.com/2015/07/interviews/qa-with-lauren-fleshman _131929#LT5OG1yCbUyuImWD.99

12. Dixon, M. A., Warner, S. M., & Bruening, J. E. (2008). "More than just letting them play: parental influence on women's lifetime sports involvement." *Sociology of Sport Journal*, 25: 538–559.

## 4. Taking Ownership

1. http://www.cbc.ca/sports/trackandfield/lanni-marchant-sends-strong -message-by-crushing-olympic-marathon-standard-1.3278463

2. Vlachopoulos, S. P., Karageorghis, C. I., & Terry, P. C. (2000). "Motivation profiles in sport: a self-determination theory perspective." *Research Quarterly for Exercise and Sport*, 71(4): 387–397.

3. Ntoumanis, N. (2001) "Empirical links between achievement goal theory and self-determination theory in sport." *Journal of Sports Sciences*, 19(6): 397–409.

4. See Vlachopoulos, cited in 42.

5. See Vlachopoulos, cited in 42.

6. Edmunds, J., Ntoumanis, N., & Duda, J. L. (2006). "A test of self-determination theory in the exercise domain." *Journal of Applied Social Psychology*, 36(9): 2240–2265; see also Gillison, F. B., Standage, M., & Skevington, S. M. (2006). "Relationships among adolescents' weight perceptions, exercise goals, exercise motivation, quality of life and leisure-time exercise behaviour: a self-determination theory approach." *Health Education Research*, 21(6): 836–847.

7. Personal communication.

8. Personal communication.

9. Personal communication.

10. Zuckerman, M., Kieffer, S. C., & Knee, C. R. (1998). "Consequences of self-handicapping: effects on coping, academic performance, and adjustment." *Journal of Personality and Social Psychology, 74*(6): 1619.

11. Zuckerman, cited in 46 above; see also Hausenblas, H. A., & Carron, A. V. (1996). "Group cohesion and self-handicapping in female and male athletes." *Journal of Sport and Exercise Psychology, 18*: 132–43; see also Finez, L., & Sherman, D. K. (2012). "Train in vain: the role of the self in claimed self-handicapping strategies." *Journal of Sport and Exercise Psychology, 34*(5): 600.

12. See Zuckerman, cited in 51.

13. Ibid.

14. See Finez, cited in 51.

15. Ibid.

16. Ibid.

17. Kuczka, K. K., & Treasure, D. C. (2005). "Self-handicapping in competitive sport: influence of the motivational climate, self-efficacy, and perceived importance." *Psychology of Sport and Exercise, 6*(5): 539–550.

18. Strube, M. J. (1986). "An analysis of the self-handicapping scale." *Basic and Applied Social Psychology, 7*(3): 211–224.

19. See Finez, cited in 51.

20. Ibid.

21. Stoeber, J., Uphill, M. A., & Hotham, S. (2009). "Predicting race performance in triathlon: the role of perfectionism, achievement goals, and personal goal setting." *Journal of Sport & Exercise Psychology, 31*(2): 211.

22. Ibid.

23. Ibid.

24. Ibid.

25. Ibid.

26. Reprinted with permission from Gotwals, J. K., & Dunn, J. G. H. (2009). "A multi-method multi-analytic approach to establishing internal construct validity evidence: the sport multidimensional perfectionism scale 2." *Measurement in Physical Education and Exercise Science, 13*, 71–92. DOI: 0.1080/10913670902812663.

27. http://www.runnersworld.com/new-york-city-marathon/how-meb-keflezighi -balances-his-status-as-elite-and-celebrity

28. Ibid.

29. Ibid.

30. http://www.runnersworld.com/runners-stories/cheaters-beware-this-guy-is-on -to-you?cid=soc_Runner%27s%20World%20-%20RunnersWorld_FBPAGE _Runner%E2%80%99s%20World_News

31. http://www.runnersworld.com/newswire/what-drives-people-who-cheat-in -road-races

32. http://www.theguardian.com/sport/2015/mar/09/doping-cycling-uci
-commission-epo-worldtour

33. http://www.usnews.com/news/sports/articles/2014/07/23/survey-finds-sharp
-increase-in-teen-use-of-hgh

34. Dietz, P., et al. (2013). "Associations between physical and cognitive doping: a cross-sectional study in 2,997 triathletes." *PLOS ONE*, *8(11)*. e78702. DOI:10.1371/journal.pone.0078702.

35. http://www.theguardian.com/sport/2015/aug/02/athletics-facing-new
-doping-crisis

36. https://gfny.com/gfny15-winner-was-doping/ & http://www.stickybottle.com
/latest-news/gran-fondo-winner-stripped-of-victory-after-testing-positive-for
-drugs/

37. http://www.si.com/more-sports/2015/11/09/wada-russia-doping
-investigation-alysia-montano-mariya-savinova-olympics-medals

38. http://www.iol.co.za/sport/athletics/caster-cheated-out-of-gold-1.1943024#
.VkJPNuITDOu

39. http://espn.go.com/sports/endurance/story/_/id/12016066/endurance-sports
-meb-keflezighi-explains-how-won-boston-marathon

40. Shepperd, J., Malone, W., & Sweeny, K. (2008). "Exploring causes of the self-serving bias." *Social and Personality Psychology Compass*, *2(2)*: 895–908.

41. Santamaria, V. L., & Furst, D. M. (1994). "Distance runners' causal attributions for most successful and least successful races." *Journal of Sport Behavior*, *17(1)*: 43.

42. Ibid.

43. See Shepperd, cited in 80 & Santamaria, cited in 40.

44. Personal communication.

45. http://www.babbittville.com/videos/breakfast-with-bob-day-2/

## 5. Intention

1. Norman, P., & Conner, M. (2005). "The theory of planned behavior and exercise: evidence for the mediating and moderating roles of planning on intention-behavior relationships." *Journal of Sport and Exercise Psychology*, *27(4)*: 488.

2. Ibid.

3. De Bruijn, G. J., & R. E. Rhodes. (2011). "Exploring exercise behavior, intention and habit strength relationships." *Scandinavian Journal of Medicine & Science in Sports 21(3)*: 482–491.

4. From Twitter, @usatriathlon 0:48 AM; Oct. 25, 2015.

5. See Norman, cited in 81.

6. See Norman, cited in 81.

7. http://triathlon.competitor.com/2015/09/news/true-to-form-racing-lessons
-from-top-american-sarah-true_122655

8. http://www.topendsports.com/testing/records/vo2max.htm

9. Bernard, T., et al. (2010). "Age related decline in Olympic triathlon performance: effect of locomotion mode." *Experimental Aging Research*, 36: 64–78.

10. Tanaka, H., & Seals, D. R. (2008) "Endurance exercise performance in masters athletes: age-associated changes and underlying physiological mechanisms." *The Journal of Physiology*, 586(1): 55–63.

11. Marcell, T. J., et al. (2003). "Longitudinal analysis of lactate threshold in male and female master athletes." *Medicine & Science in Sports & Exercise*, 35(5): 810–817.

12. Vidoni, E. D., et al. (2015). "Dose-response of aerobic exercise on cognition: a community-based, pilot randomized controlled trial."

13. See Tanaka, cited in 10.

14. Bishop, P. A., et al. (2008). "Recovery from training: a brief review: brief review." *The Journal of Strength & Conditioning Research*, 22(3): 1015–1024.

15. Sherman, W. M. (1992). "Recovery from endurance exercise." *Medicine & Science in Sports & Exercise*, S336–S339.

16. See Bishop, cited in 14.

17. Barnett, A. (2006). "Using recovery modalities between training sessions in elite athletes." *Sports medicine*, 36(9): 781–796.

18. Ibid.

19. Ibid.

20. http://www.outsideonline.com/1971446/recovery-ice-bath-isnt-always-such-good-idea

21. See Barnett, cited in 17.

22. See Barnett, cited in 21.

## 6. Developing Confidence

1. Bandura, A. (1997). *Self-efficacy: the exercise of control*. New York: W.H. Freeman.

2. Vealey, R.S. (1986). "Conceptualization of sport-confidence and competitive orientation: preliminary investigation and instrument development." *Journal of Sport Psychology*, 8: 221–246.

3. Machida, M., et al. (2012). "Predictors of sources of self-confidence in collegiate athletes." *International Journal of Sport and Exercise Psychology*, 10(3): 172–185.

4. Kingston, K., et al. (2010). "A temporal examination of elite performers sources of sport-confidence."

5. Austin, M. W. (2014). "Is Humility a Virtue in the Context of Sport?" *Journal of Applied Philosophy*, 31(2): 203–214.

6. Brymer, E., et al. (2008). "Extreme sports: A positive transformation in courage and humility." *Journal of Humanistic Psychology*.

7. Ibid.

8. See Austin, cited in 5.

9.  See Austin, cited in 5.

10. See Kingston, cited in 4.

11. http://www.letsrun.com/news/2015/10/wisdom-from-meb-keflezighi-and -bob-larsen-how-meb-is-approaching-his-first-marathon-as-a-master/

12. Personal communication.

13. Johnson, M. A., et al. (2015). "Locomotor muscle fatigue is not critically regulated after prior upper body exercise." *Journal of Applied Physiology*, 119(7): 840–50.

14. Ibid.

15. From ironman online coverage of the 2015 Hawaii Ironman.

16. From @ironmantri 10/8/15, 11:47 AM

17. http://www.babbittville.com/videos/breakfast-with-bob-day-3/

18. From @ironmantri 10/9/15, 5:22 AM

19. From @ironmantri 10/8/15, 1:40 AM

20. Borkovec, T. D., et al. (1998). "Worry: A cognitive phenomenon intimately linked to affective, physiological, and interpersonal behavioral processes." *Cognitive Therapy and Research*, 22(6): 561–576. DOI: 10.1023/A:1018790003416

21. During interview on NBC 2012 Ironman World Championship coverage ~00:04:15 in the video

22. From @ironmantri 10/8/15, 6:25 AM

23. http://competitorradio.competitor.com/2013/09/frederik-van-lierde/

24. From @ironmantri 10/8/15, 5:37 PM

25. From @ironmantri 10/9/15, 10:04 AM

26. From @ironmantri 10/8/15, 3:48 AM

27. http://www.runnersworld.com/chicago-marathon/deena-kastor-targets-us -masters-record-at-chicago-marathon

28. https://www.youtube.com/watch?v=nV-c2mFktMo

## 7. Racing

1.  http://www.nytimes.com/2015/08/05/sports/katie-ledecky-again-sets-record -in-1500-but-isnt-done-for-the-night.html?emc=edit_th_20150805&nl =todaysheadlines&nlid=40388035&_r=1

2.  Personal communication.

3.  See link cited in 1.

4.  Conroy, D. E., et al. (2002). "Multidimensional fear of failure measurement: the performance failure appraisal inventory." *Journal of Applied Sport Psychology*, 14(2): 76–100.

5.  http://pedalcover.co.uk/our-news/gb-athlete-advice-for-itu-chicago-world -championships/

6.  http://www.runnersworld.com/newswire/shalane-flanagan-on-her-boston -marathon-a-bad-day-at-the-office

7. http://www.runnersworld.com/elite-runners/how-is-molly-huddle-winning -so-many-road-races

8. Crust, Lee. (2008). "Mental toughness and coping in an ultra-endurance event." *British Psychological Society.*

## 8. Mind/Body Cohesion

1. from Twitter, @usatriathlon 10/25/15, 10:52 AM.

2. Personal communication.

3. Blanchfield, Anthony W., et al. (2013). "Talking yourself out of exhaustion: the effects of self-talk on endurance performance." *Medicine & Science in Sports & Exercise.*

4. ttp://www.runnersworld.com/sweat-science/self-talk-for-ultramarathoners

5. http://www.huffingtonpost.com/michael-sandler-and-jessica-lee/10-ways -runner-olympian-d_b_7649238.html

6. http://www.runnersworld.com/race-training/the-magic-of-running-mantras

7. Brown, K. W., & Ryan, R. M. (2003). "The benefits of being present: mindfulness and its role in psychological well-being." *Journal of personality and social psychology, 84(4):* 822.

8. Jha, A. P., et al. (2007). "Mindfulness training modifies subsystems of attention." *Cognitive, Affective, & Behavioral Neuroscience, 7(2):* 109–119.

9. Ibid.

10. Morgan, D. (2003) "Mindfulness-based cognitive therapy for depression: a new approach to preventing relapse." *Psychotherapy Research, 13(1):* 123–125; see also Jha, cited in 150; see also Brown, cited in 149; see also Davidson, R. J., et al. (2003). "Alterations in brain and immune function produced by mindfulness meditation. *Psychosomatic medicine, 65(4):* 564–570; see also Kabat-Zinn, J. (1982). "An outpatient program in behavioral medicine for chronic pain patients based on the practice of mindfulness meditation: theoretical considerations and preliminary results." *General Hospital Psychiatry, 4(1):* 33–47.

11. Haase, L., et al. (2015). "A pilot study investigating changes in neural processing after mindfulness training in elite athletes." *Frontiers in behavioral neuroscience, 9.*

12. http://trstriathlon.com/why-do-so-many-high-performance-athletes -meditate/

13. Hajoglou, A., et al. (2005). "Effect of warm up on cycle time trial performance. *Medicine & Science in Sports & Exercise, 37(9):* 1608.

## 9. Overcoming Obstacles

1. http://firstoffthebike.com/news/breaking-news-fractured-sacrum-forces -hauschildt-to-withdraw-from-kona/

2. http://www.slowtwitch.com/Interview/A_chat_with_Susie_Cheetham _5442.html

3. Stephens, R., et al. (2009). "Swearing as a response to pain." *Neuroreport, 20(12):* 1056–1060.

4. Ibid.

5. Rottenberg, J., et al. (2008). "Is crying beneficial?" *Current Directions in Psychological Science, 17(6):* 400–04.

6. Quote from the movie, *A League of Their Own.* The entire quote: "Are you crying? Are you crying? Are you crying?! There's no crying! **There's no crying in baseball!"**

7. http://www.nytimes.com/2015/10/25/sports/olympics/sister-fights-older-brothers-while-preparing-for-shot-at-olympics.html?mabReward=CTM&_r=0

8. http://grief.com/the-five-stages-of-grief/

9. Wiese-Bjornstal, D. M., et al. (1998). "An integrated model of response to sport injury: psychological and sociological dynamics." *Journal of Applied Sport Psychology, 10(1):* 46–69.

10. Ibid.

11. Ibid.

12. Linton, S. J., & Shaw, W. S. (2011). "Impact of psychological factors in the experience of pain." *Physical therapy, 91(5):* 700–711.

13. Maggie Fournier, direct communication.

14. Mann, B. J., et al. (2007). "A survey of sports medicine physicians regarding psychological issues in patient-athletes." *The American Journal of Sports Medicine, 35(12):* 2140–2147.

15. Ibid.

16. http://running.competitor.com/2015/10/features/qa-ryan-hall-on-his-recent-struggles-his-running-future-and-his-growing-family_136951#sob2bvmiqRkqvgL4.99

17. Budgett, R. (1998). "Fatigue and underperformance in athletes: the overtraining syndrome." *British Journal of Sports Medicine, 32(2)* 107–110.

18. Derman, W., et al. (1997). "The 'worn-out athlete': a clinical approach to chronic fatigue in athletes." *Journal of Sports Sciences, 15(3):* 341–51.

19. http://www.outsideonline.com/1986361/running-empty

20. Ibid.

21. http://www.cyclingnews.com/news/holm-says-racing-while-ill-destroyed-kittel/

22. See Derman, cited in 18.

23. Saw, A. E., Main, L. C., & Gastin, P. B. (2015). "Monitoring the athlete training response: subjective self-reported measures trump commonly used objective measures: a systematic review." *British Journal of Sports Medicine.*

24. Personal communication.

25. https://sports.vice.com/en_us/article/what-to-expect-when-youre-expecting-while-training-for-the-olympics

26. https://www.psychologytoday.com/blog/happiness-in-world/200910/when-doctors-dont-know-whats-wrong

27. http://nationalpainreport.com/your-pain-is-your-fault-what-women-were-told-by-their-doctors-8824787.html

28. http://www.theglobeandmail.com/life/health-and-fitness/health/pain-during-exercise-trains-your-mind-as-well-as-your-muscles/article26951185/

29. Ibid.

30. http://asklaurenfleshman.com/2015/09/an-unexpected-victory/

## 10. Finding Meaning

1. Personal communication.

2. Personal communication.

3. http://www.letsrun.com/news/2015/10/back-to-the-future-re-energized-mary-cain-explains-move-east/

4. http://spikes.iaaf.org/post/christian-taylors-words-of-wisdom

5. Snyder, C. R., et al. (1991). "The will and the ways: development and validation of an individual-differences measure of hope." *Journal of Personality and Social Psychology*, 60(4): 570.

6. Da Costa Rolo, C. M. R., & Gould, D. (2004). *An intervention for fostering hope, athletic and academic performance in university student-athletes.*

7. Ibid.

8. http://positivepsychology.org.uk/pp-theory/hope/100-what-is-hope-and-how-can-we-measure-it.html

9. Roesch, S. C., et al. (2010). "Dispositional hope and the propensity to cope: a daily diary assessment of minority adolescents." *Cultural Diversity and Ethnic Minority Psychology*, 16(2): 191.

10. Ibid.

11. Snyder, C. R., et al. (1996). "Development and validation of the state hope scale." *Journal of Personality and Social Psychology*, 70: 321–335.

12. http://www.outsideonline.com/2030746/international-olympic-committees-search-refugee-athletes?utm_source=twitter&utm_medium=social&utm_campaign=tweet

# Bibliography

Arvinen-Barrow, M., Clement, D., Hamson-Utley, J. J., Zakrajsek, R. A., Lee, S. M., Kamphoff, C., & Martin, S. B. (2015). "Athletes' use of mental skills during sport injury rehabilitation." *Journal of Sport Rehabilitation*, 24(2): 189–197.

Austin, M. W. (2014). "Is humility a virtue in the context of sport?" *Journal of Applied Philosophy*, 31(2): 203–214.

Bandura, A. (1997). *Self-efficacy: the exercise of control*. New York: W.H. Freeman.

Barnett, A. (2006). "Using recovery modalities between training sessions in elite athletes." *Sports Medicine*, 36(9): 781–796.

Baxter-Jones, A.D.G., & Maffulli, N. (2003). "Parental influence on sport participation in elite young athletes." *The Journal of Sports Medicine and Physical Fitness*, 43: 250–55.

Bernard, T., Sultana, F., Lepers, R., Hausswirth, C., & Brisswalter, J. (2010). "Age related decline in Olympic triathlon performance: effect of locomotion mode." *Experimental Aging Research*, 36: 64–78.

Bishop, P. A., Jones, E., & Woods, A. K. (2008). "Recovery from training: a brief review." *The Journal of Strength & Conditioning Research*, 22(3): 1015–1024.

Blanchfield, A. W., Hardy, J., de Morree, H. M., Staiano, W., & Marcora, S. M. (2013). "Talking yourself out of exhaustion: the effects of self-talk on endurance performance." *Medicine & Science in Sports & Exercise*.

Borkovec, T. D., Ray, W. J., & Stöber, J. (1998). "Worry: a cognitive phenomenon intimately linked to affective, physiological, and interpersonal behavioral processes." *Cognitive Therapy and Research*, 22(6): 561–576. DOI: 10.1023/A:1018790003416.

Brown, K. W., & Ryan, R. M. (2003). "The benefits of being present: mindfulness and its role in psychological well-being." *Journal of Personality and Social Psychology*, 84(4): 822.

Brymer, E., & Oades, L. G. (2008). "Extreme sports: A positive transformation in courage and humility." *Journal of Humanistic Psychology*.

Budgett, R. (1998). "Fatigue and underperformance in athletes: the overtraining syndrome." *British Journal of Sports Medicine*, 32(2): 107–110.

Burzynska, A. Z., Wong, C. N., Voss, M. W., Cooke, G. E., Gothe, N. P., Fanning, J., & Kramer, A. F. (2015). "Physical activity is linked to greater moment-to-moment variability in spontaneous brain activity in older adults." *PLOS ONE*, 10(8): e0134819.

Carron, A.V., Hausenblas, H.A., & Mack, D. (1996). "Social influence and exercise: a meta-analysis." *Journal of Sport and Exercise Psychology*, 18: 1–16.

Cho, J., Shin, M. K., Kim, D., Lee, I., Kim, S., & Kang, H. (2015). "Treadmill running reverses cognitive declines due to Alzheimer's disease." *Medicine & Science in Sports & Exercise*. 47(9): 1814–1824.

Conroy, D. E., Willow, J. P., & Metzler, J. N. (2002). "Multidimensional fear of failure measurement: the performance failure appraisal inventory." *Journal of Applied Sport Psychology*, 14(2): 76–90.

Crust, L. (2008). "Mental toughness and coping in an ultra-endurance event." British Psychological Society.

Da Costa Rolo, C. M. R., & Gould, D. (2004). "An intervention for fostering hope, athletic and academic performance in university student-athletes."

Davidson, R. J., Kabat-Zinn, J., Schumacher, J., Rosenkranz, M., Muller, D., Santorelli, S. F., & Sheridan, J. F. (2003). "Alterations in brain and immune function produced by mindfulness meditation." *Psychosomatic medicine*, 65(4): 564–570.

De Bruijn, G. J., & Rhodes, R. E. (2011). "Exploring exercise behavior, intention and habit strength relationships." *Scandinavian Journal of Medicine & Science in Sports*, 21(3): 482–491.

Derman, W., Schwellnus, M. P., Lambert, M. I., Emms, M., Sinclair-

Smith, C., Kirby, P., & Noakes, T. D. (1997). "The 'worn-out athlete': a clinical approach to chronic fatigue in athletes." *Journal of Sports Sciences,* 15(3): 341–351.

Dietz, P., Ulrich, R., Dalaker, R., Striegel, H., Franke, A. G., Lieb, K., & Simon, P. (2013). "Associations between physical and cognitive doping: a cross-sectional study in 2,997 triathletes." *PLOS ONE, 8(11):* e78702. DOI:10.1371/journal.pone.0078702.

Dixon, M. A., Warner S. M., & Bruening, J. E. (2008). "More than just letting them play: parental influence on women's lifetime sports involvement." *Sociology of Sport Journal, 25:* 538–559.

Edmunds, J., Ntoumanis, N. & Duda, J. L. (2006). "A test of self-determination theory in the exercise domain." *Journal of Applied Social Psychology, 36(9):* 2240–2265.

Epstein, D. (2013) *The Sports Gene.* New York: Penguin Group. Chapters 5 & 14.

Ericsson, K. A., Krampe, R. T., & Tesch-Römer, C. (1993). "The role of deliberate practice in the acquisition of expert performance." *Psychological review, 100(3):* 363.

Fernandes, M. F. A., Matthys, D., Hryhoczuk, C., Sharma, S., Mogra, A., Alquier, T., & Fulton, S. (2015). "Leptin suppresses the rewarding effects of running vis STAT3 signaling in dopamine neurons." *Cell Metabolism.* In press, available online.

Finez, L., & Sherman, D. K. (2012). "Train in vain: the role of the self in claimed self-handicapping strategies." *Journal of Sport and Exercise Psychology, 34(5):* 600.

Fredericson, M., & Misra, A. K. (2007). "Epidemiology and aetiology of marathon running injuries." *Sports Medicine, 37(4–5):* 437–439.

Fuss, J., Steinle, J., Bindila, L., Auer, M., Kirchherr, H., Lutz, B., & Gass, P. (2015). "A runner's high depends on cannabinoid receptors in mice." *Proceedings of the National Academy of Sciences.*

Gillison, F. B., Standage, M. & Skevington, S. M. (2006). "Relationships among adolescents' weight perceptions, exercise goals, exercise motivation, quality of life and leisure-time exercise behaviour: a self-determination theory approach." *Health Education Research 21(6):* 836–847.

Gotwals, J. K., & Dunn, J. G. H. (2009). "A multi-method multi-analytic approach to establishing internal construct validity evidence: the sport multidimensional perfectionism scale 2." *Measurement in Physical Education and Exercise Science, 13(2):* 71–92. DOI: 0.1080/10913670902812663

Haase, L., May, A. C., Falahpour, M., Isakovic, S., Simmons, A. N., Hickman, S. D., & Paulus, M. P. (2015). "A pilot study investigating changes in neural processing after mindfulness training in elite athletes." *Frontiers in Behavioral Neuroscience, 9.*

Hajoglou, A., Foster, C., De Koning, J. J., Lucia, A., Kernozek, T. W., & Porcari, J. P. (2005). "Effect of warm up on cycle time trial performance." *Medicine & Science in Sports & Exercise. 37(9), 1608.*

Hausenblas, H.A., & Carron, A.V. (1996). "Group cohesion and self-handicapping in female and male athletes." *Journal of Sport and Exercise Psychology, 18:* 132–143.

Jha, A. P., Krompinger, J., & Baime, M. J. (2007). "Mindfulness training modifies subsystems of attention." *Cognitive, Affective, & Behavioral Neuroscience, 7(2):* 109–119.

Johnson, M. A., Sharpe, G. R., Williams, N. C., & Hannah, R. (2015). "Locomotor muscle fatigue is not critically regulated after prior upper body exercise." *Journal of Applied Physiology, 119(7):* 840–850.

Kabat-Zinn, J. (1982). "An outpatient program in behavioral medicine for chronic pain patients based on the practice of mindfulness meditation: theoretical considerations and preliminary results." *General Hospital Psychiatry, 4(1):* 33–47.

Kingston, K., Lane, A., & Thomas, O. (2010). "A temporal examination of elite performers sources of sport-confidence."

Kuczka, K. K., & Treasure, D. C. (2005). "Self-handicapping in competitive sport: influence of the motivational climate, self-efficacy, and perceived importance." *Psychology of Sport and Exercise, 6(5):* 539–550.

Linton, S. J., & Shaw, W. S. (2011). "Impact of psychological factors in the experience of pain." *Physical Therapy, 91(5):* 700–711.

Machida, M., Marie Ward, R., & Vealey, R. S. (2012). "Predictors of sources of self-confidence in collegiate athletes." *International Journal of Sport and Exercise Psychology, 10(3):* 172–185.

Mann, B. J., Grana, W. A., Indelicato, P. A., O'Neill, D. F., & George, S. Z. (2007). "A survey of sports medicine physicians regarding psychological issues in patient-athletes." *The American Journal of Sports Medicine, 35(12):* 2140–2147.

Marcell, T. J., Hawkins, S. A., Tarpenning, K. M., Hyslop, D. M., & Wiswell, R. A. (2003). "Longitudinal analysis of lactate threshold in male and female master athletes". *Medicine & Science in Sports & Exercise, 35(5):* 810–817.

Morgan, D. (2003) "Mindfulness-based cognitive therapy for depression: a new approach to preventing relapse." *Psychotherapy Research,* 13(1): 123–125.

Nabhan, D. C., Moreau, W. J., & Barylski, C. (2015). "Laboratory tests ordered by a chiropractic sports physician on elite athletes over a 1-year period." *Journal of Chiropractic Medicine, 14(2):* 68–76.

Norman, P., & Conner, M. (2005). "The theory of planned behavior and exercise: evidence for the mediating and moderating roles of planning on intention-behavior relationships." *Journal of Sport and Exercise Psychology, 27(4):* 488.

Ntoumanis, N. (2001) "Empirical links between achievement goal theory and self-determination theory in sport." *Journal of Sports Sciences, 19(6):* 397–409.

Pyne, D. B., Gleeson, M., McDonald, W. A., Clancy, R. L., Perry, C., & Fricker, P. A. (2000). "Training strategies to maintain immunocompetence in athletes." *International Journal of Sports Medicine, 21(1):* S51.

Roesch, S. C., Duangado, K. M., Vaughn, A. A., Aldridge, A. A., & Villodas, F. (2010). "Dispositional hope and the propensity to cope: a daily diary assessment of minority adolescents." *Cultural Diversity and Ethnic Minority Psychology, 16(2):* 191.

Ross, R., de Lannoy, L., & Stotz, P. J. (2015). "Separate effects of intensity and amount of exercise on interindividual cardiorespiratory fitness response." In *Mayo Clinic Proceedings, 90(11):* 1506–1514.

Rottenberg, J., Bylsma, L. M., & Vingerhoets, A. J. (2008). "Is crying beneficial?" *Current Directions in Psychological Science, 17(6):* 400–404.

Santamaria, V. L., & Furst, D. M. (1994). "Distance runners' causal attributions for most successful and least successful races." *Journal of Sport Behavior, 17(1):* 43.

Saw, A. E., Main, L. C., & Gastin, P. B. (2015). "Monitoring the athlete training response: subjective self-reported measures trump commonly used objective measures: a systematic review." *British Journal of Sports Medicine.*

Schmuck, P., Kasser, T., & Ryan, R. (2000) "Intrinsic and extrinsic goals: their structure and relationship to well-being in German and U.S. college students." *Social Indicator Research, 50:* 225–241.

Shepperd, J., Malone, W., & Sweeny, K. (2008). "Exploring causes of the self-serving bias." *Social and Personality Psychology Compass, 2(2):* 895–908.

Sherman, W. M. (1992). "Recovery from endurance exercise." *Medicine & Science in Sports & Exercise,* S336–S339.

Snyder, C. R., Harris, C., Anderson, J. R., Holleran, S. A., Irving, L. M.,

Sigmon, S. T., & Harney, P. (1991). "The will and the ways: development and validation of an individual-differences measure of hope." *Journal of personality and social psychology, 60(4):* 570.

Snyder, C. R., Sympson, S. C., Ybasco, F. C., Borders, T. F., Babyak, M. A., & Higgins, R. L. (1996). "Development and validation of the state hope scale." *Journal of Personality and Social Psychology, 70:* 321–335.

Sprouse-Blum, A. S., Smith, G., Sugai, D., & Parsa, F. D. (2010). "Understanding endorphins and their importance in pain management." *Hawaii Medical Journal, 69(3):* 70–71.

Stephens, R., Atkins, J., & Kingston, A. (2009). "Swearing as a response to pain." *Neuroreport, 20(12):* 1056–1060.

Stoeber, J., Uphill, M. A., & Hotham, S. (2009). "Predicting race performance in triathlon: the role of perfectionism, achievement goals, and personal goal setting." *Journal of Sport & Exercise Psychology, 31(2):* 211.

Strube, M. J. (1986). "An analysis of the self-handicapping scale." *Basic and Applied Social Psychology, 7(3):* 211–224.

Tanaka, H., & Seals, D. R. (2008) "Endurance exercise performance in masters athletes: age-associated changes and underlying physiological mechanisms." *The Journal of Physiology, 586(1):* 55–63.

Tsianos, G., Sanders, J., Dhamrait, S., Humphries, S., Grant, S., & Montgomery, H. (2004). "The ACE gene insertion/deletion polymorphism and elite endurance swimming." *European Journal of Applied Physiology, 92(3):* 360–362.

Vealey, R. S. (1986). "Conceptualization of sport-confidence and competitive orientation: preliminary investigation and instrument development." *Journal of Sport Psychology, 8:* 221–246.

Vidoni, E. D., Johnson, D. K., Morris, J. K., Van Sciver, A., Greer, C. S., Billinger, S. A., & Burns, J. M. (2015). "Dose-response of aerobic exercise on cognition: a community-based, pilot randomized controlled trial."

Vlachopoulos, S. P., Karageorghis, C. I., & Terry, P. C. (2000). "Motivation profiles in sport: a self-determination theory perspective." *Research Quarterly for Exercise and Sport, 71(4):* 387–397.

Wiese-Bjornstal, D. M., Smith, A. M., Shaffer, S. M., & Morrey, M. A. (1998). "An integrated model of response to sport injury: psychological and sociological dynamics." *Journal of Applied Sport Psychology, 10(1):* 46–69.

Zuckerman, M., Kieffer, S. C., & Knee, C. R. (1998). "Consequences of self-handicapping: effects on coping, academic performance, and adjustment." *Journal of personality and social psychology, 74(6):* 1619.

# Index